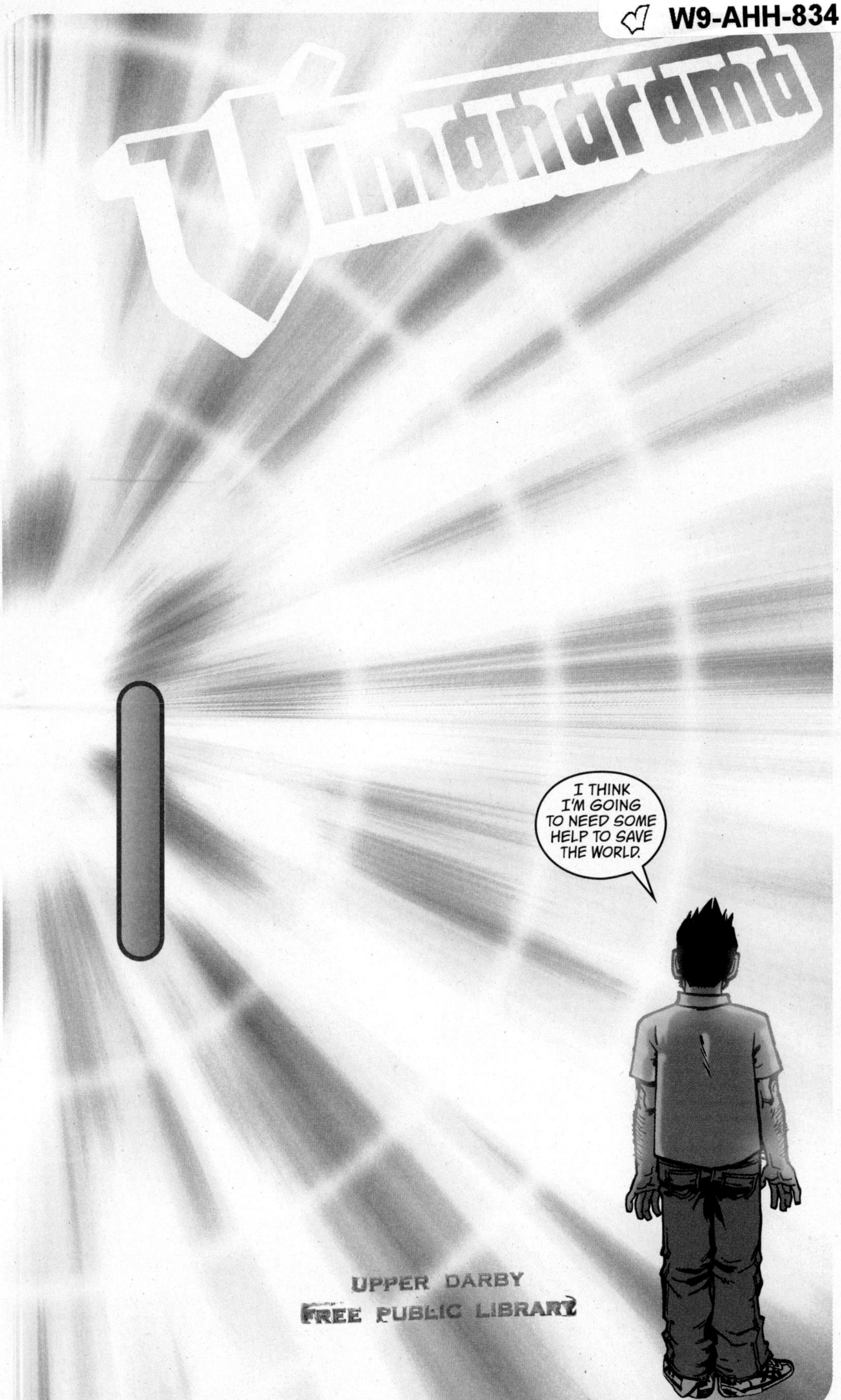
Vimanarama
I THINK I'M GOING TO NEED SOME HELP TO SAVE THE WORLD.

GRANT MORRISON WRITER PHILIP BOND ARTIST BRIAN MILLER COLORIST TODD KLEIN LETTERER VIMANARAMA CREATED BY GRANT MORRISON AND PHILIP BOND

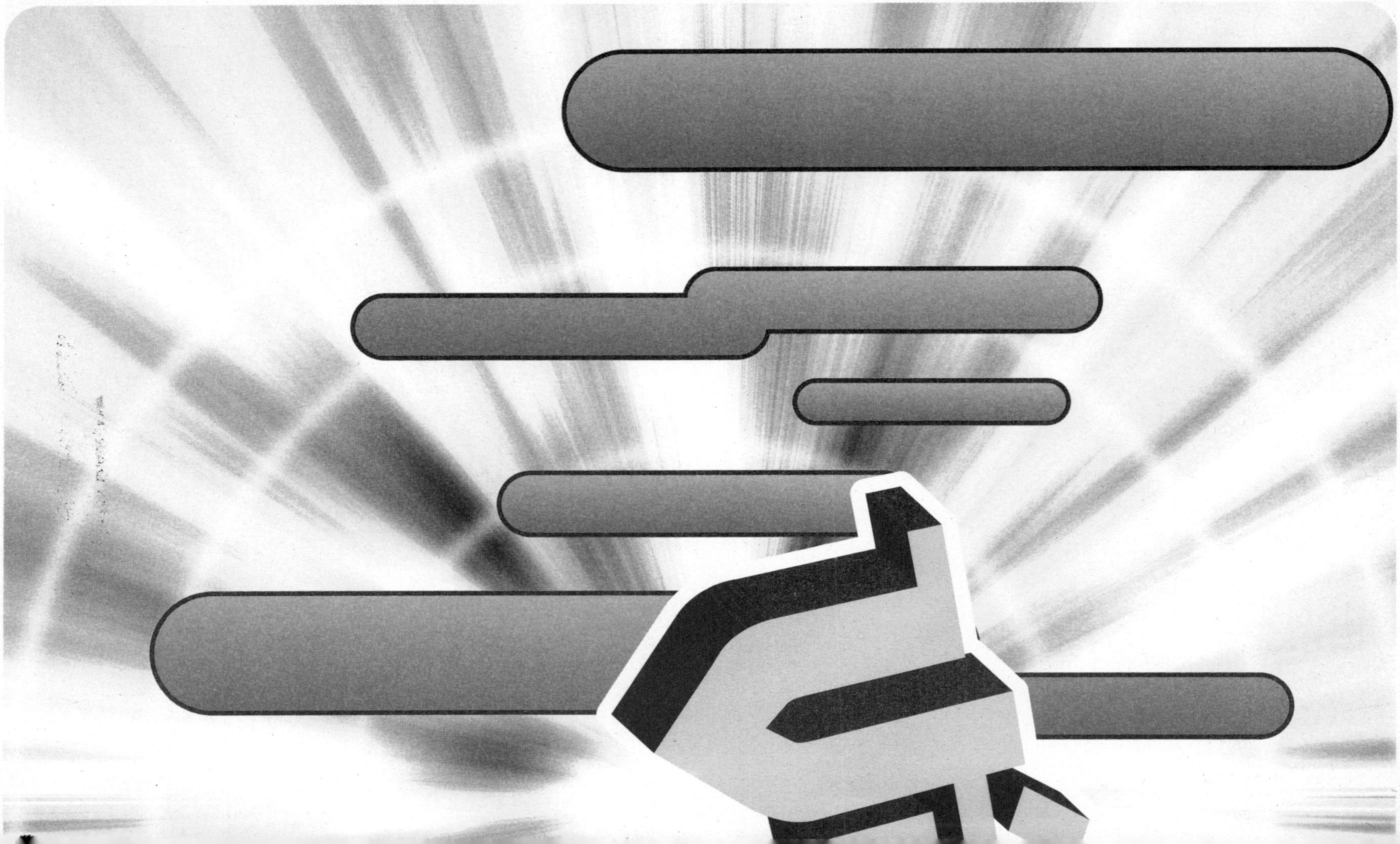

Karen Berger VP-Executive Editor & Editor-original series Pornsak Pichetshote Assistant Editor-original series Scott Nybakken Editor-collected edition Robin Brosterman Senior Art Director Paul Levitz President & Publisher Georg Brewer VP-Design & DC Direct Creative Richard Bruning Senior VP-Creative Director

Patrick Caldon Senior VP-Finance & Operations Chris Caramalis VP-Finance Terri Cunningham VP-Managing Editor Stephanie Fierman Senior VP-Sales & Marketing Alison Gill VP-Manufacturing Rich Johnson VP-Book Trade Sales Hank Kanalz VP-General Manager, WildStorm Lillian Laserson Senior VP & General Counsel

Jim Lee Editorial Director-WildStorm Paula Lowitt Senior VP-Business & Legal Affairs David McKillips VP-Advertising & Custom Publishing John Nee VP-Business Development Gregory Noveck Senior VP-Creative Affairs Cheryl Rubin Senior VP-Brand Management Jeff Trojan VP-Business Development, DC Direct Bob Wayne VP-Sales

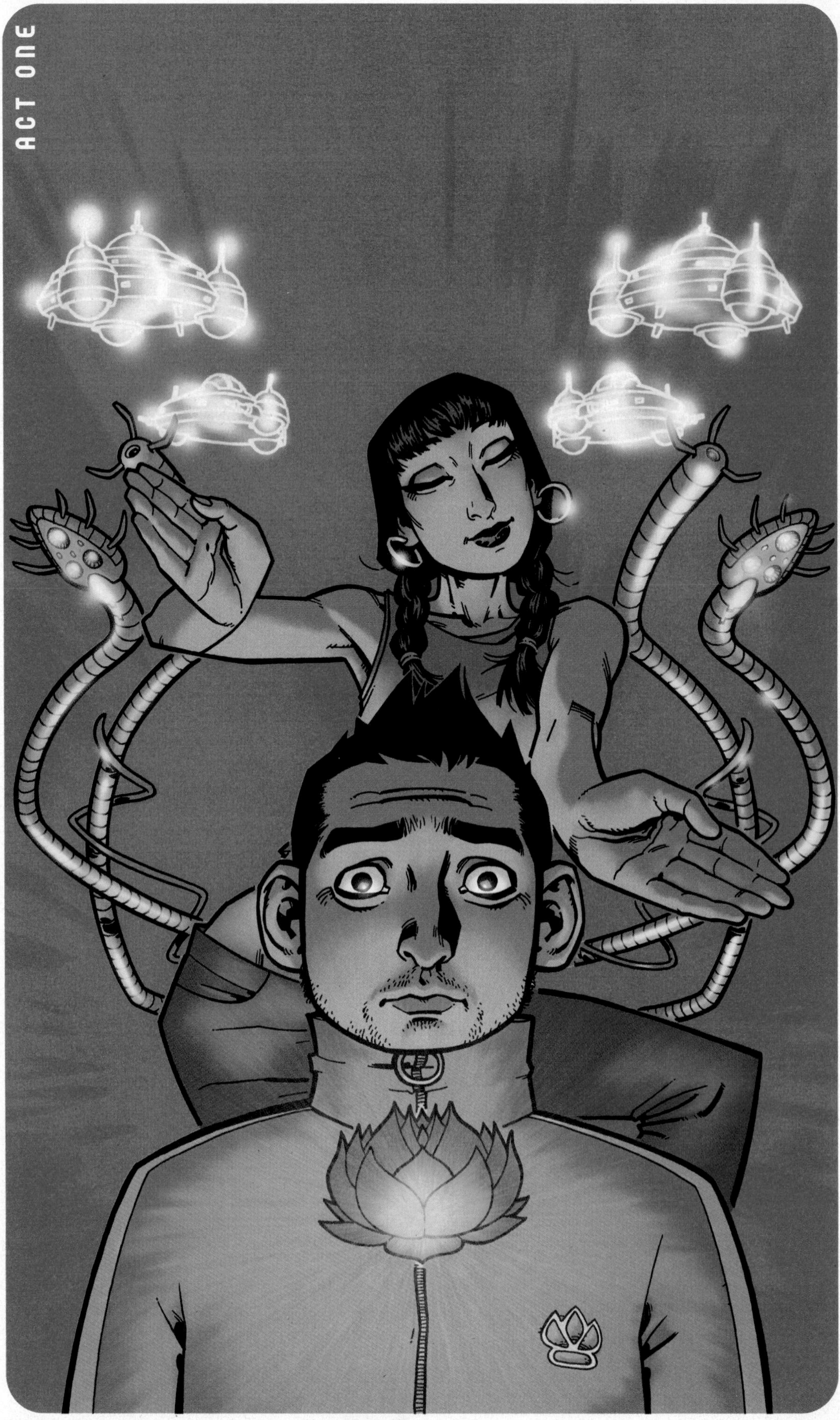
ACT ONE

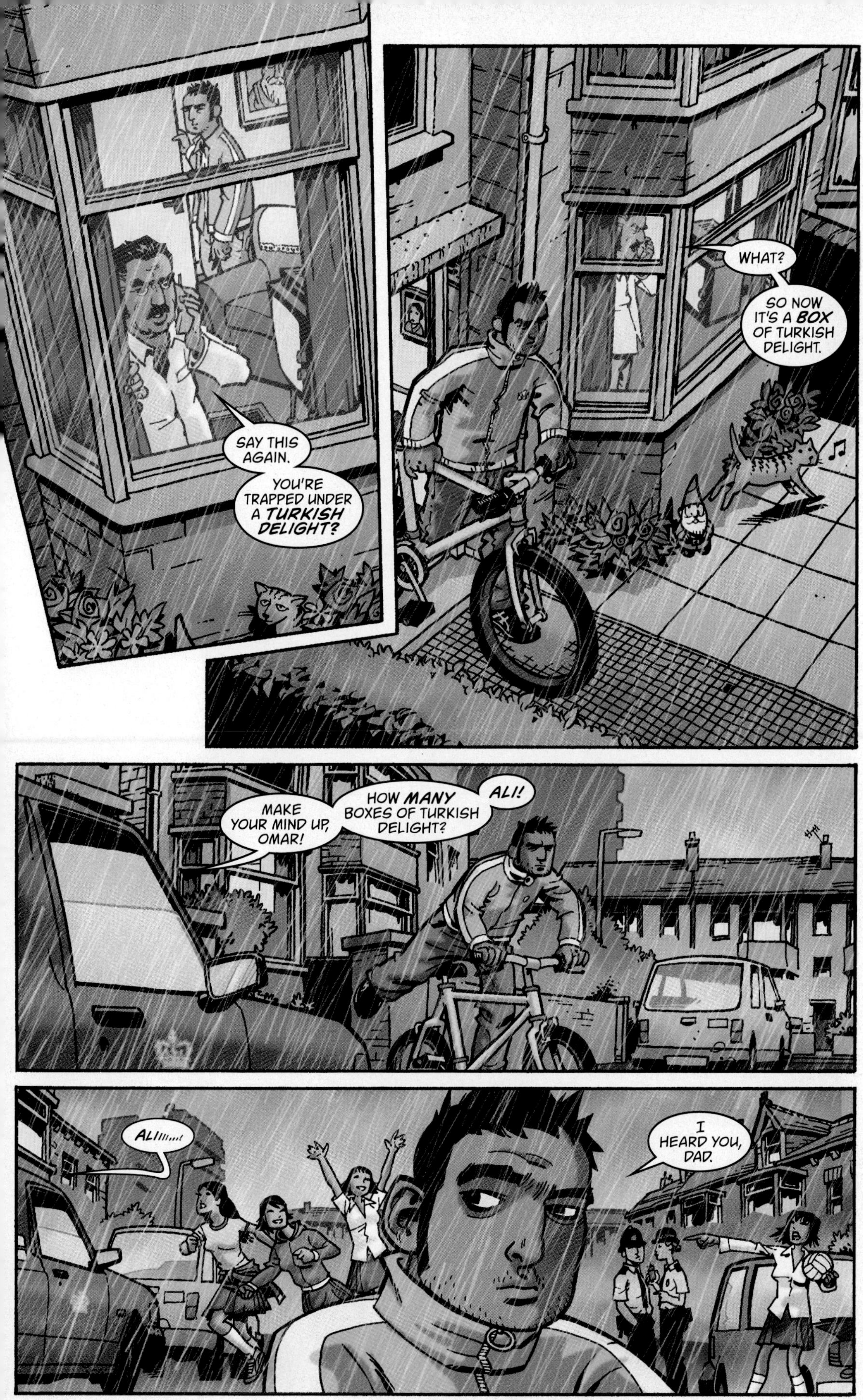
SAY THIS AGAIN.
YOU'RE TRAPPED UNDER A TURKISH DELIGHT?
WHAT?
SO NOW IT'S A BOX OF TURKISH DELIGHT.
MAKE YOUR MIND UP, OMAR!
HOW MANY BOXES OF TURKISH DELIGHT?
ALI!
ALI!!!!...!
I HEARD YOU, DAD.

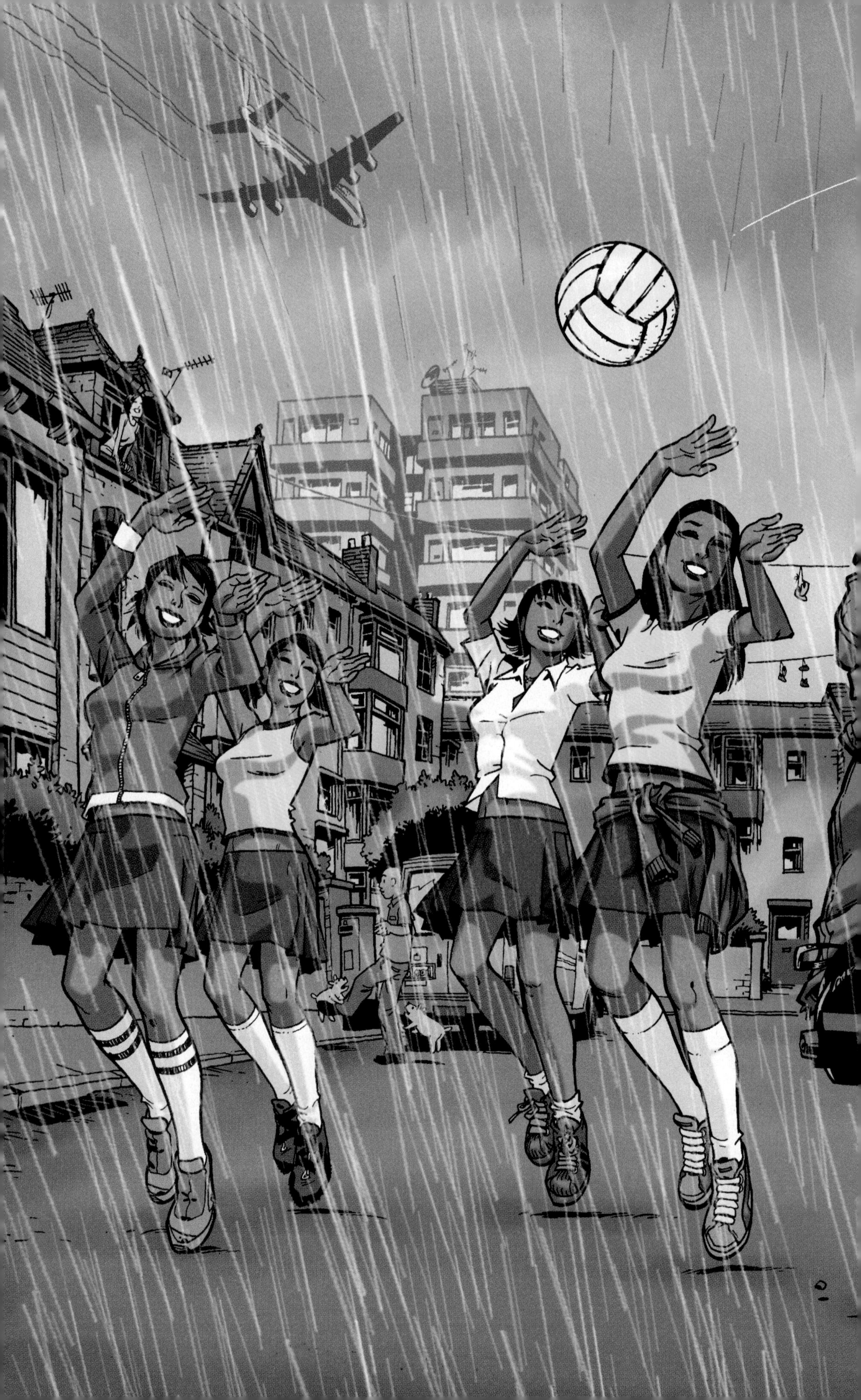

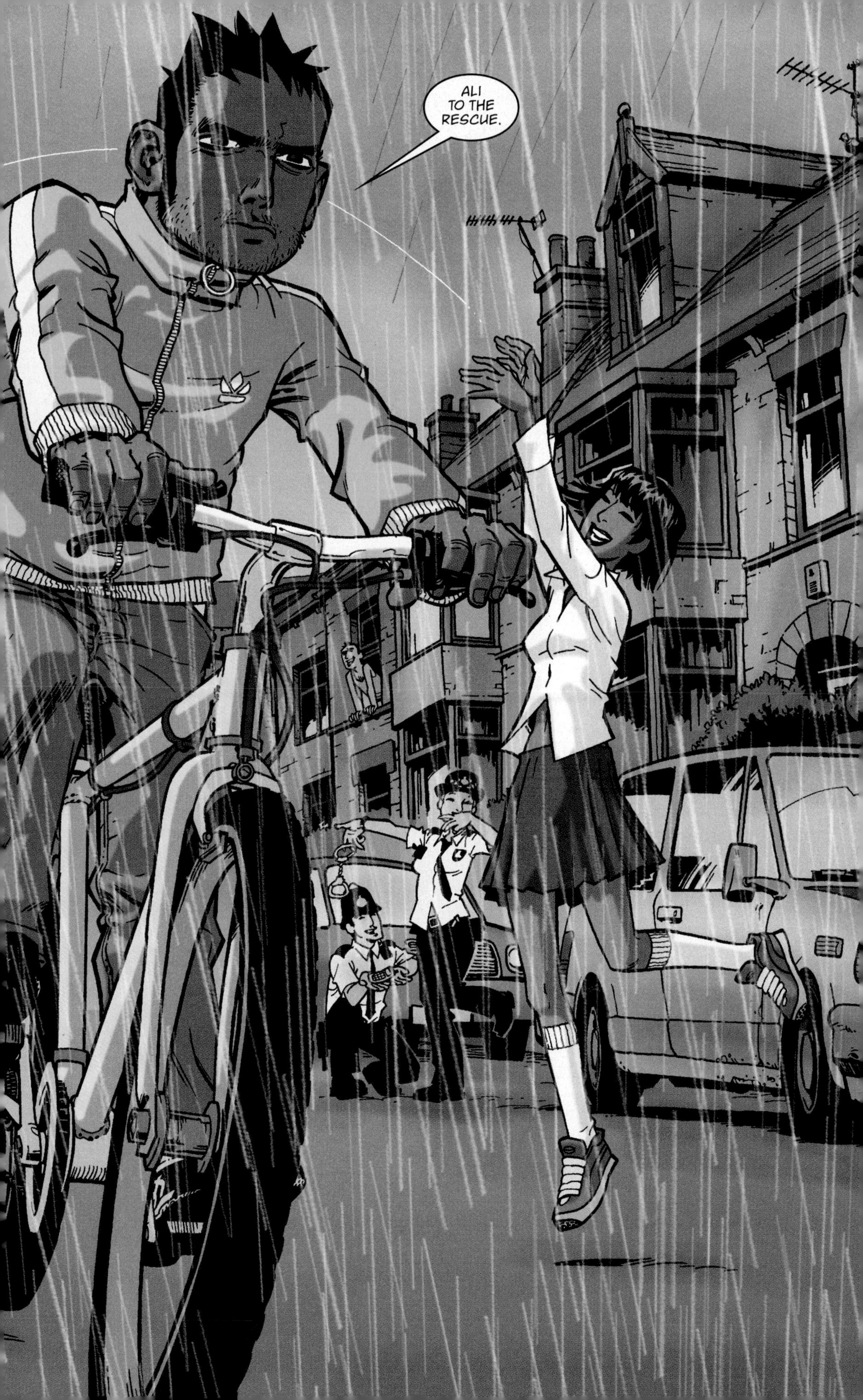
ALI TO THE RESCUE.

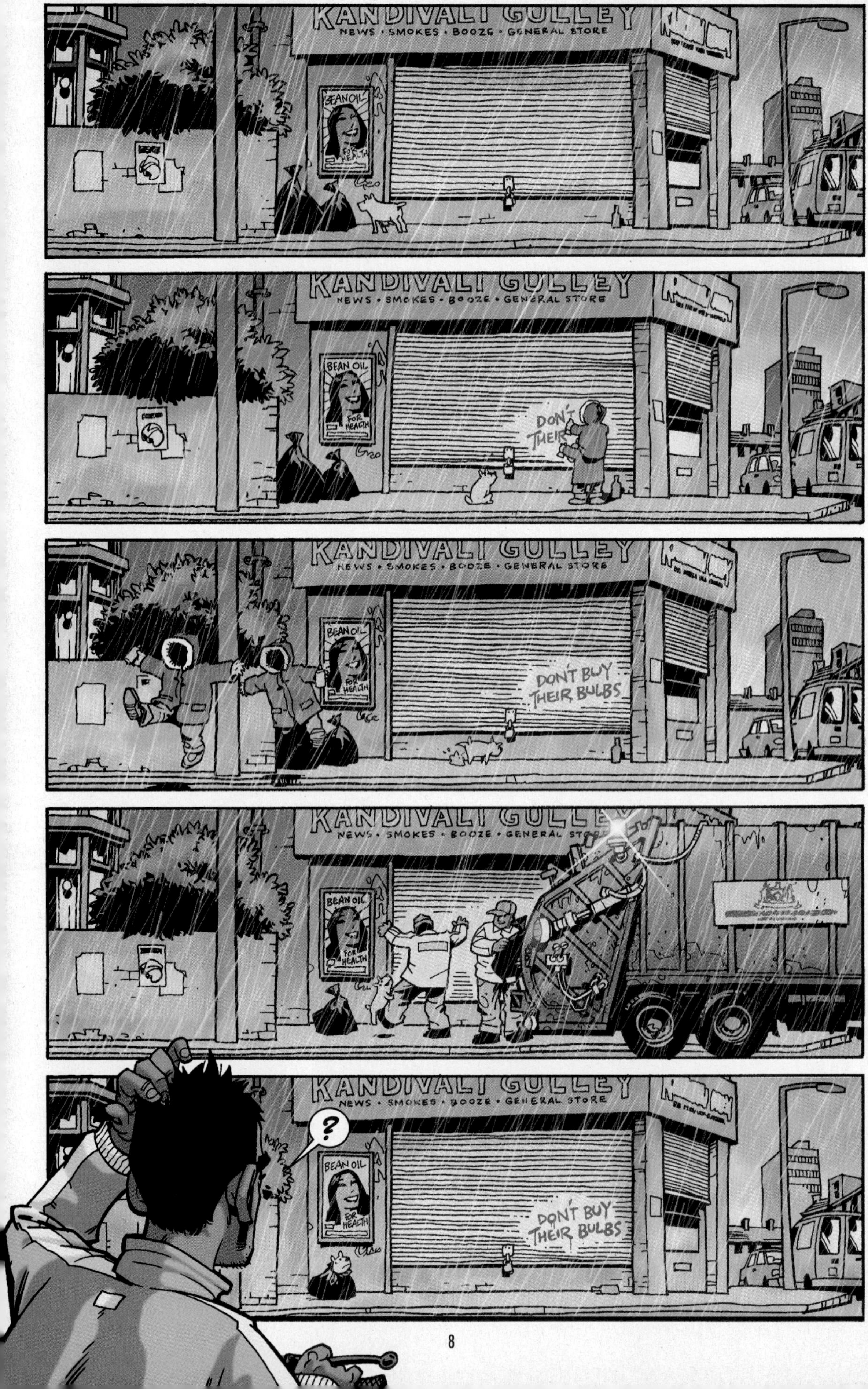
KANDIVALI GULLEY
NEWS • SMOKES • BOOZE • GENERAL STORE
BEAN OIL
FOR HEALTH
KANDIVALI GULLEY
NEWS • SMOKES • BOOZE • GENERAL STORE
BEAN OIL
FOR HEALTH
DON'T
THEIR
KANDIVALI GULLEY
NEWS • SMOKES • BOOZE • GENERAL STORE
BEAN OIL
FOR HEALTH
DON'T BUY
THEIR BULBS
KANDIVALI GULLEY
NEWS • SMOKES • BOOZE • GENERAL STORE
BEAN OIL
FOR HEALTH
KANDIVALI GULLEY
NEWS • SMOKES • BOOZE • GENERAL STORE
?
BEAN OIL
FOR HEALTH
DON'T BUY
THEIR BULBS

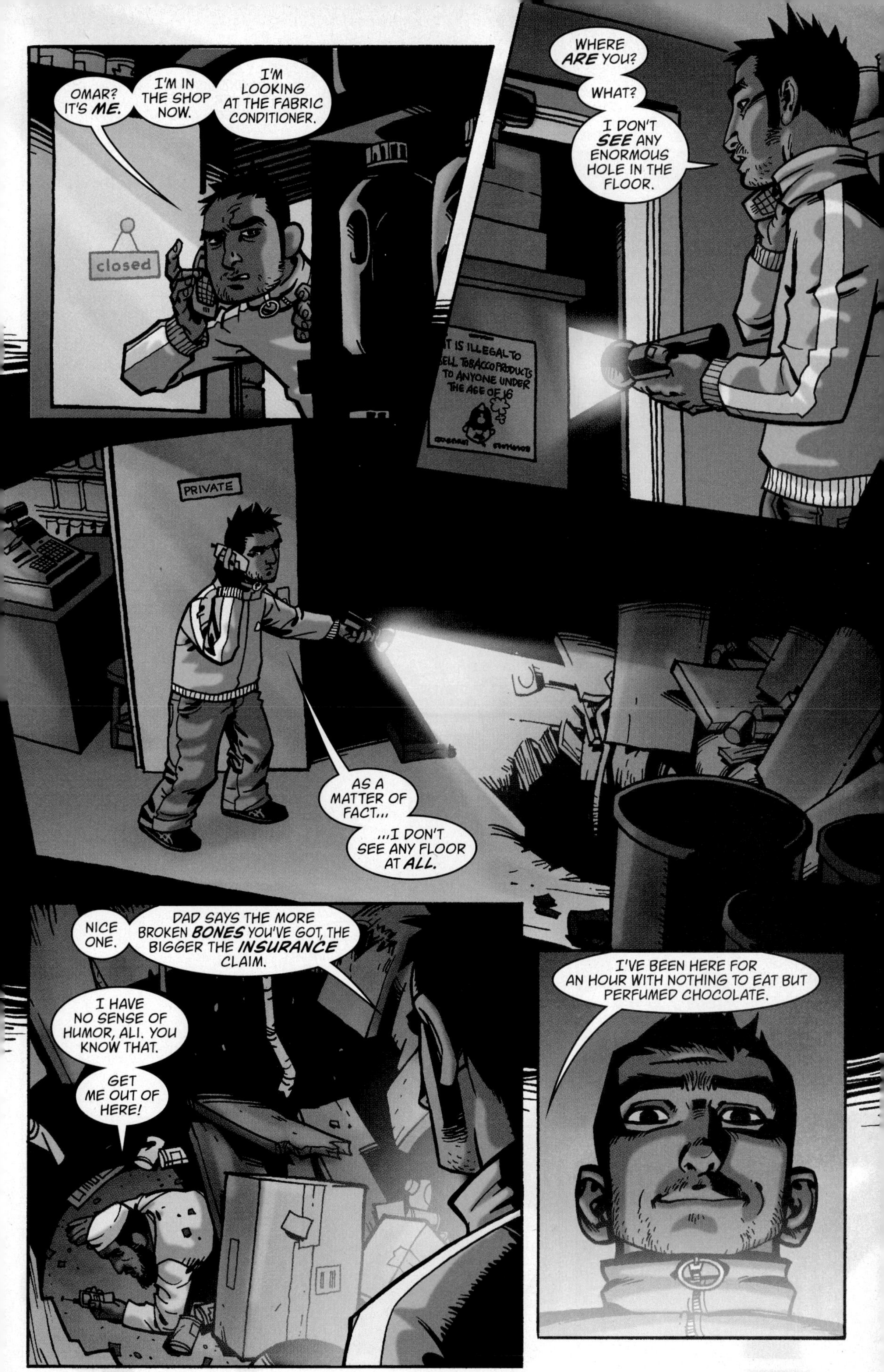

OMAR? IT'S ME.
I'M IN THE SHOP NOW.
I'M LOOKING AT THE FABRIC CONDITIONER.
closed
WHERE ARE YOU?
WHAT?
I DON'T SEE ANY ENORMOUS HOLE IN THE FLOOR.
IT IS ILLEGAL TO SELL TOBACCO PRODUCTS TO ANYONE UNDER THE AGE OF 16
PRIVATE
AS A MATTER OF FACT...
...I DON'T SEE ANY FLOOR AT ALL.
NICE ONE.
DAD SAYS THE MORE BROKEN BONES YOU'VE GOT, THE BIGGER THE INSURANCE CLAIM.
I HAVE NO SENSE OF HUMOR, ALI. YOU KNOW THAT.
GET ME OUT OF HERE!
I'VE BEEN HERE FOR AN HOUR WITH NOTHING TO EAT BUT PERFUMED CHOCOLATE.

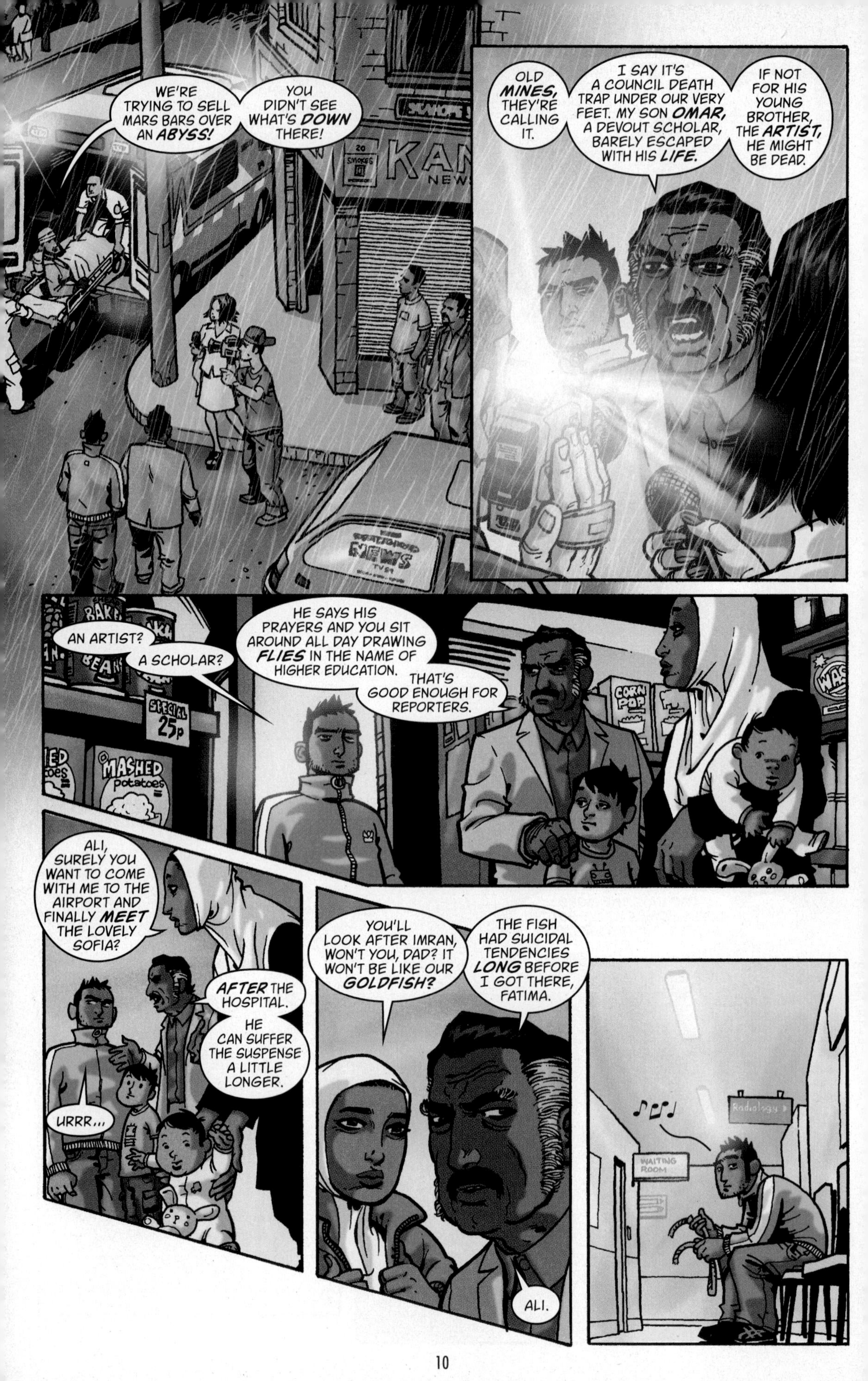
WE'RE TRYING TO SELL MARS BARS OVER AN ABYSS!
YOU DIDN'T SEE WHAT'S DOWN THERE!
KAN
NEWS
OLD MINES, THEY'RE CALLING IT.
I SAY IT'S A COUNCIL DEATH TRAP UNDER OUR VERY FEET. MY SON OMAR, A DEVOUT SCHOLAR, BARELY ESCAPED WITH HIS LIFE.
IF NOT FOR HIS YOUNG BROTHER, THE ARTIST, HE MIGHT BE DEAD.
NEWS
AN ARTIST?
A SCHOLAR?
HE SAYS HIS PRAYERS AND YOU SIT AROUND ALL DAY DRAWING FLIES IN THE NAME OF HIGHER EDUCATION.
THAT'S GOOD ENOUGH FOR REPORTERS.
SPECIAL 25p
MASHED potatoes
CORN POP
ALI, SURELY YOU WANT TO COME WITH ME TO THE AIRPORT AND FINALLY MEET THE LOVELY SOFIA?
AFTER THE HOSPITAL.
HE CAN SUFFER THE SUSPENSE A LITTLE LONGER.
URRR...
YOU'LL LOOK AFTER IMRAN, WON'T YOU, DAD? IT WON'T BE LIKE OUR GOLDFISH?
THE FISH HAD SUICIDAL TENDENCIES LONG BEFORE I GOT THERE, FATIMA.
ALI.
Radiology
WAITING ROOM

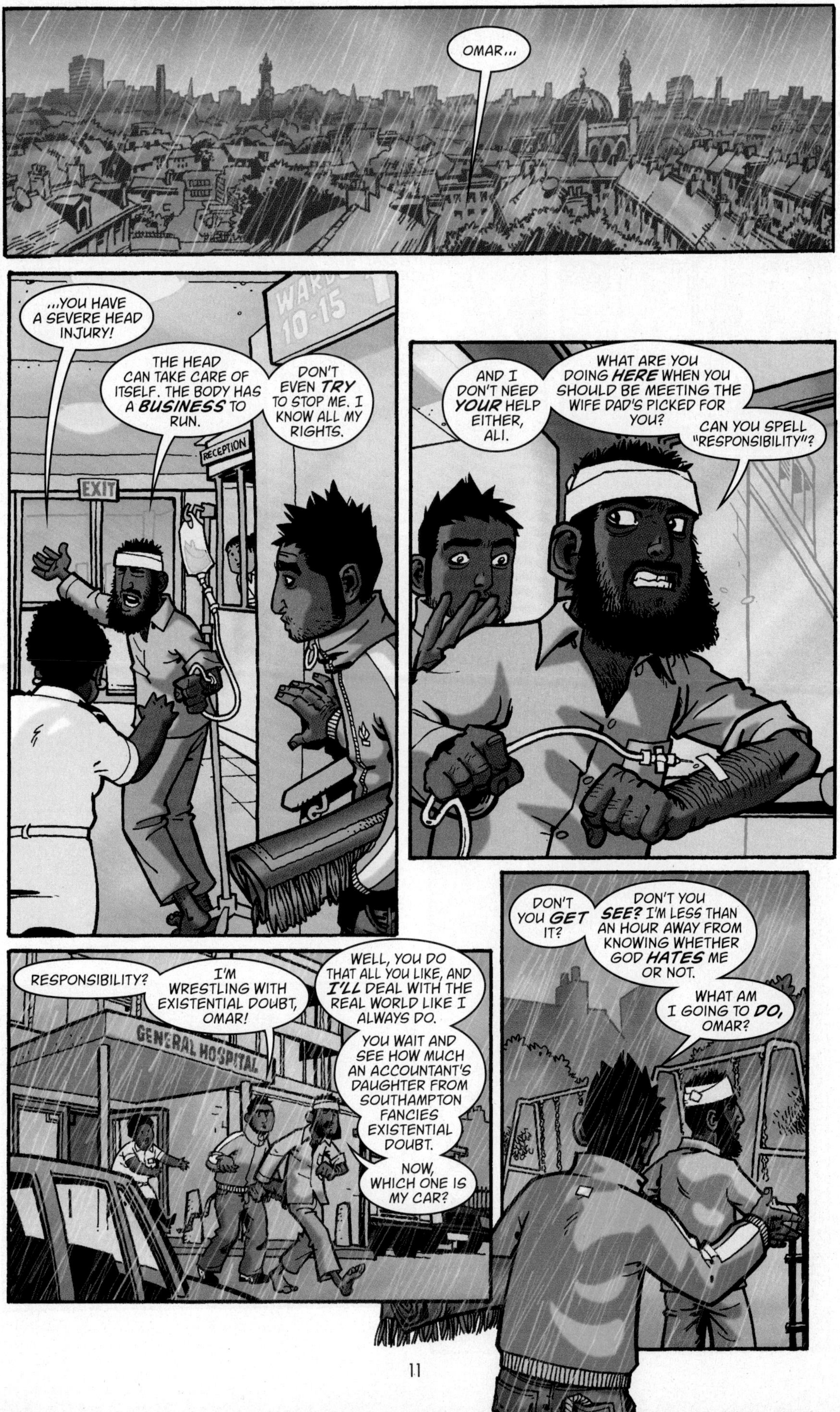

OMAR...
...YOU HAVE A SEVERE HEAD INJURY!
THE HEAD CAN TAKE CARE OF ITSELF. THE BODY HAS A BUSINESS TO RUN.
DON'T EVEN TRY TO STOP ME. I KNOW ALL MY RIGHTS.
WARD 10-15
RECEPTION
EXIT
AND I DON'T NEED YOUR HELP EITHER, ALI.
WHAT ARE YOU DOING HERE WHEN YOU SHOULD BE MEETING THE WIFE DAD'S PICKED FOR YOU?
CAN YOU SPELL "RESPONSIBILITY"?
DON'T YOU GET IT?
DON'T YOU SEE? I'M LESS THAN AN HOUR AWAY FROM KNOWING WHETHER GOD HATES ME OR NOT.
WHAT AM I GOING TO DO, OMAR?
RESPONSIBILITY?
I'M WRESTLING WITH EXISTENTIAL DOUBT, OMAR!
WELL, YOU DO THAT ALL YOU LIKE, AND I'LL DEAL WITH THE REAL WORLD LIKE I ALWAYS DO.
YOU WAIT AND SEE HOW MUCH AN ACCOUNTANT'S DAUGHTER FROM SOUTHAMPTON FANCIES EXISTENTIAL DOUBT.
NOW, WHICH ONE IS MY CAR?
GENERAL HOSPITAL

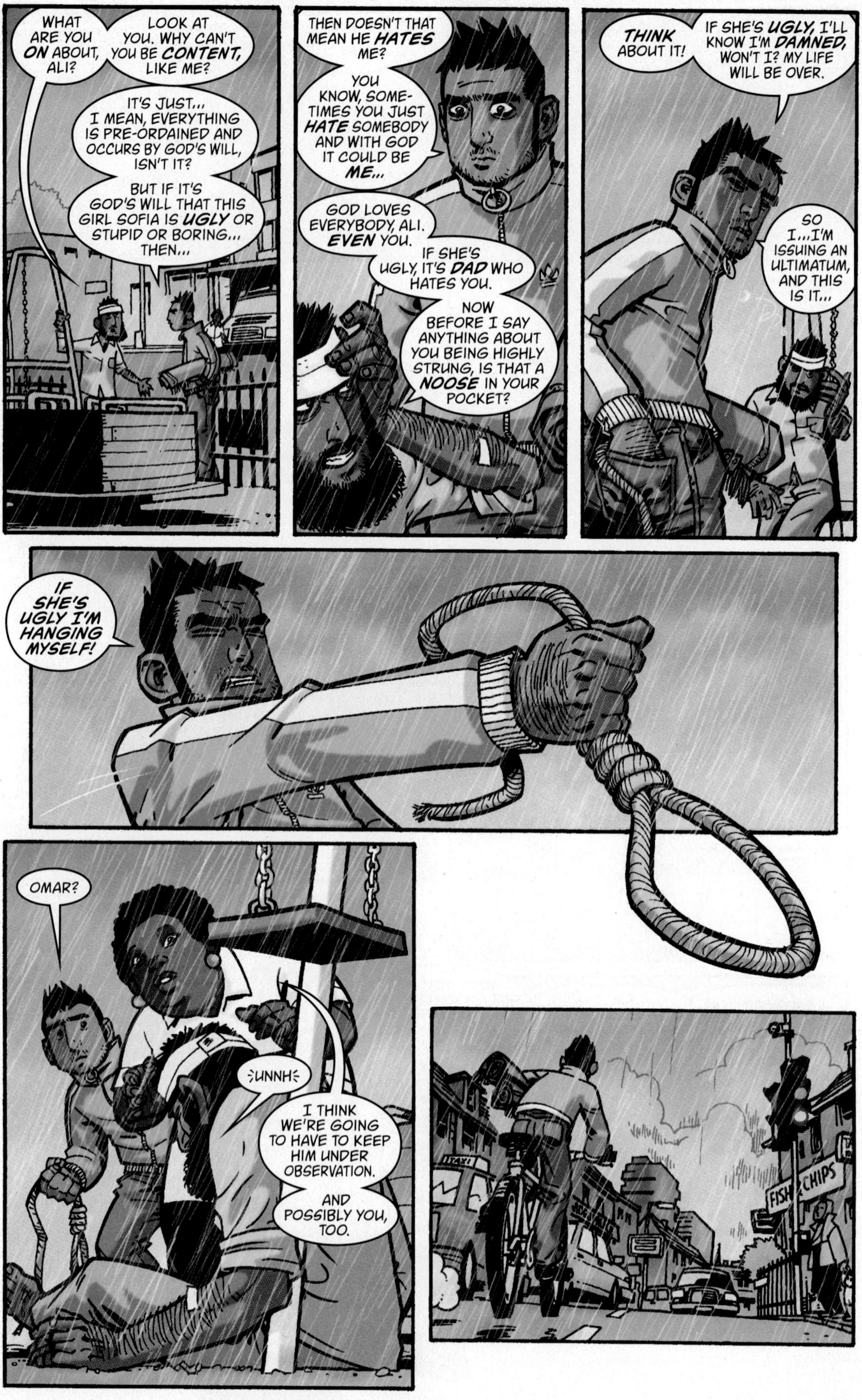
WHAT ARE YOU ON ABOUT, ALI?
LOOK AT YOU. WHY CAN'T YOU BE CONTENT, LIKE ME?
IT'S JUST... I MEAN, EVERYTHING IS PRE-ORDAINED AND OCCURS BY GOD'S WILL, ISN'T IT?
BUT IF IT'S GOD'S WILL THAT THIS GIRL SOFIA IS UGLY OR STUPID OR BORING... THEN...
THEN DOESN'T THAT MEAN HE HATES ME?
YOU KNOW, SOMETIMES YOU JUST HATE SOMEBODY AND WITH GOD IT COULD BE ME...
GOD LOVES EVERYBODY, ALI. EVEN YOU.
IF SHE'S UGLY, IT'S DAD WHO HATES YOU.
NOW BEFORE I SAY ANYTHING ABOUT YOU BEING HIGHLY STRUNG, IS THAT A NOOSE IN YOUR POCKET?
THINK ABOUT IT!
IF SHE'S UGLY, I'LL KNOW I'M DAMNED, WON'T I? MY LIFE WILL BE OVER.
SO I...I'M ISSUING AN ULTIMATUM, AND THIS IS IT...
IF SHE'S UGLY I'M HANGING MYSELF!
OMAR?
UNNH
I THINK WE'RE GOING TO HAVE TO KEEP HIM UNDER OBSERVATION.
AND POSSIBLY YOU, TOO.
TAXI
FISH CHIPS

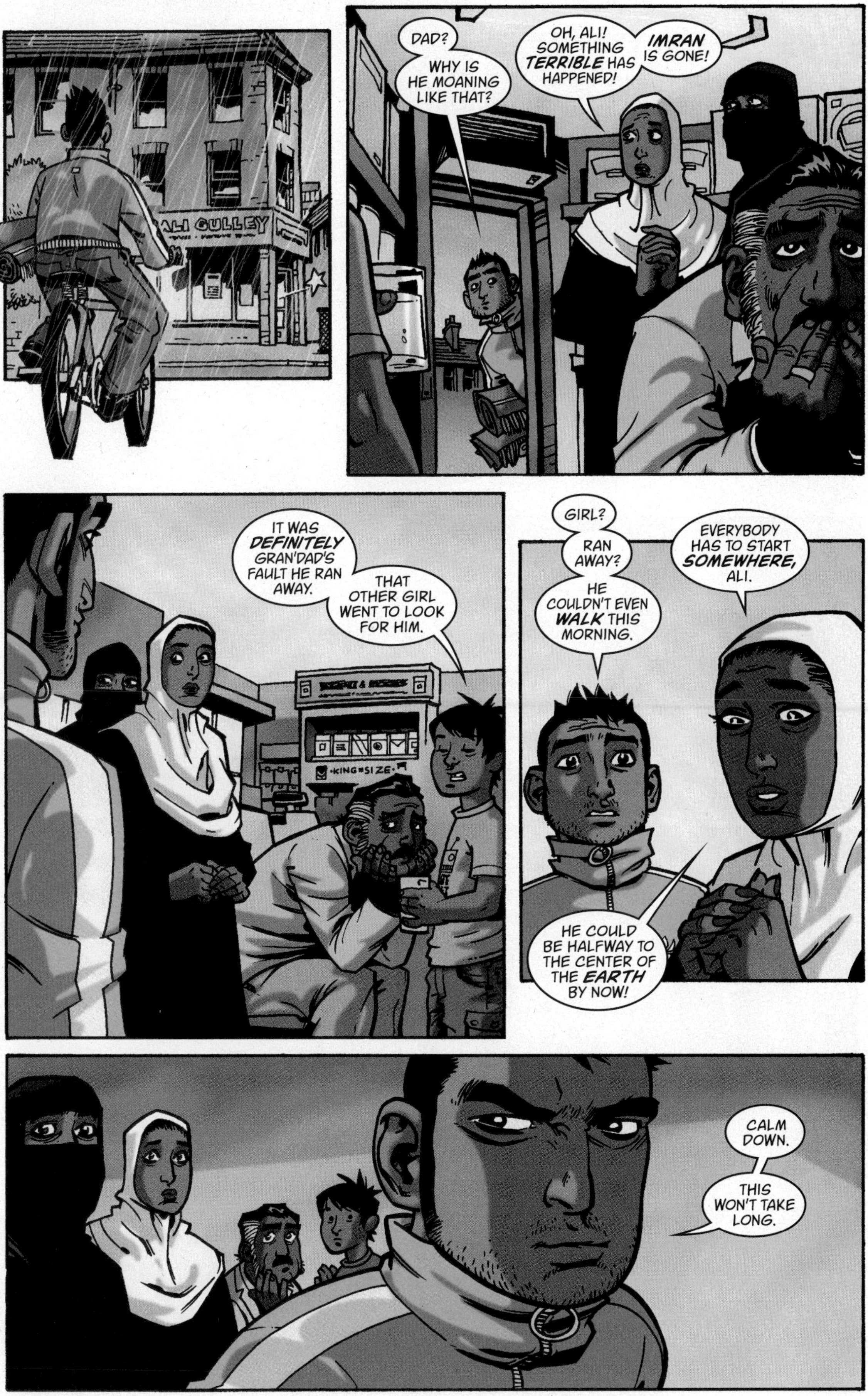
ALI GULLEY
DAD?
WHY IS HE MOANING LIKE THAT?
OH, ALI! SOMETHING TERRIBLE HAS HAPPENED!
IMRAN IS GONE!
IT WAS DEFINITELY GRAN'DAD'S FAULT HE RAN AWAY.
THAT OTHER GIRL WENT TO LOOK FOR HIM.
KING SIZE
GIRL?
RAN AWAY?
HE COULDN'T EVEN WALK THIS MORNING.
EVERYBODY HAS TO START SOMEWHERE, ALI.
HE COULD BE HALFWAY TO THE CENTER OF THE EARTH BY NOW!
CALM DOWN.
THIS WON'T TAKE LONG.

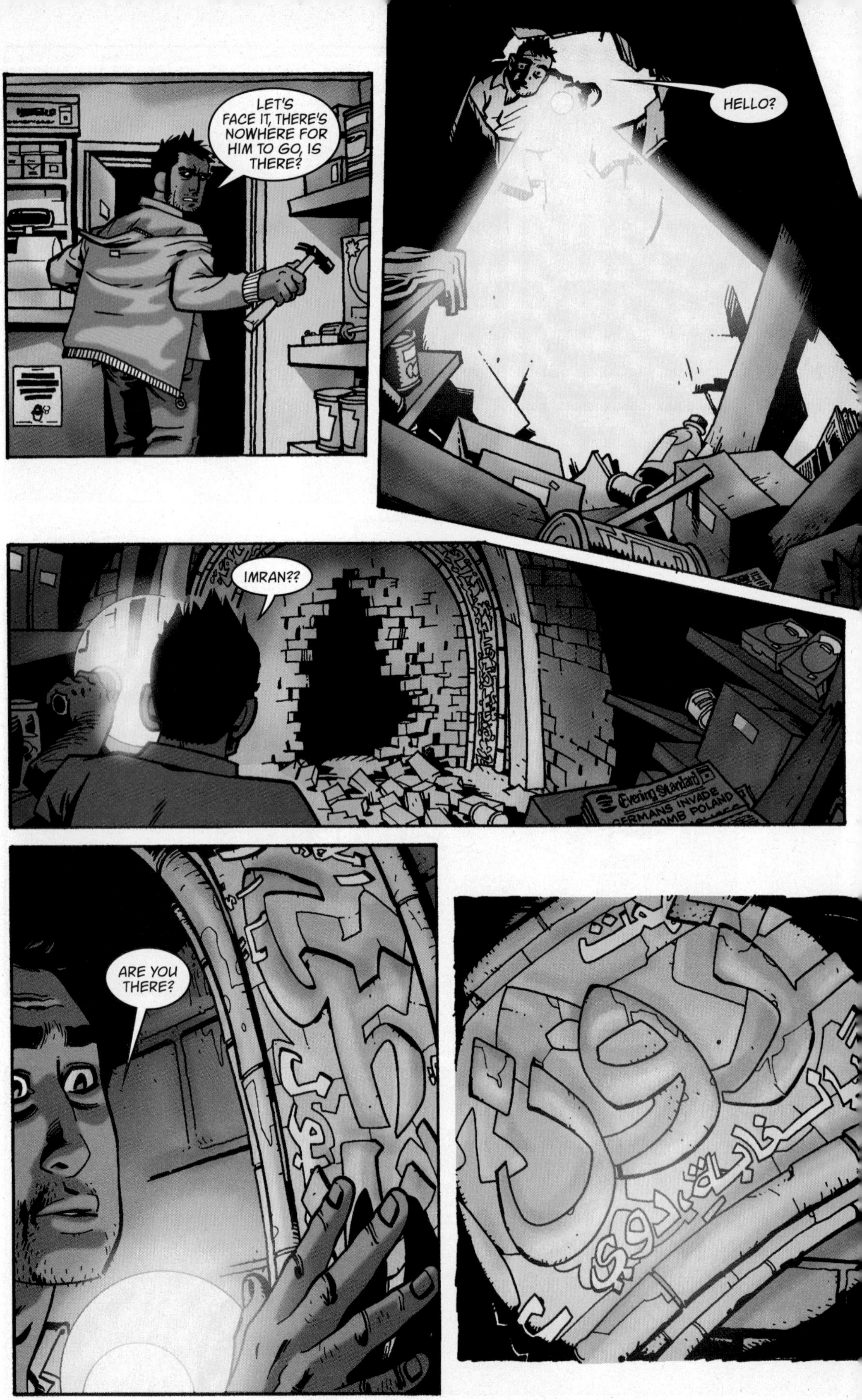

LET'S FACE IT, THERE'S NOWHERE FOR HIM TO GO, IS THERE?
HELLO?
IMRAN??
Evening Standard
GERMANS INVADE
ARE YOU THERE?

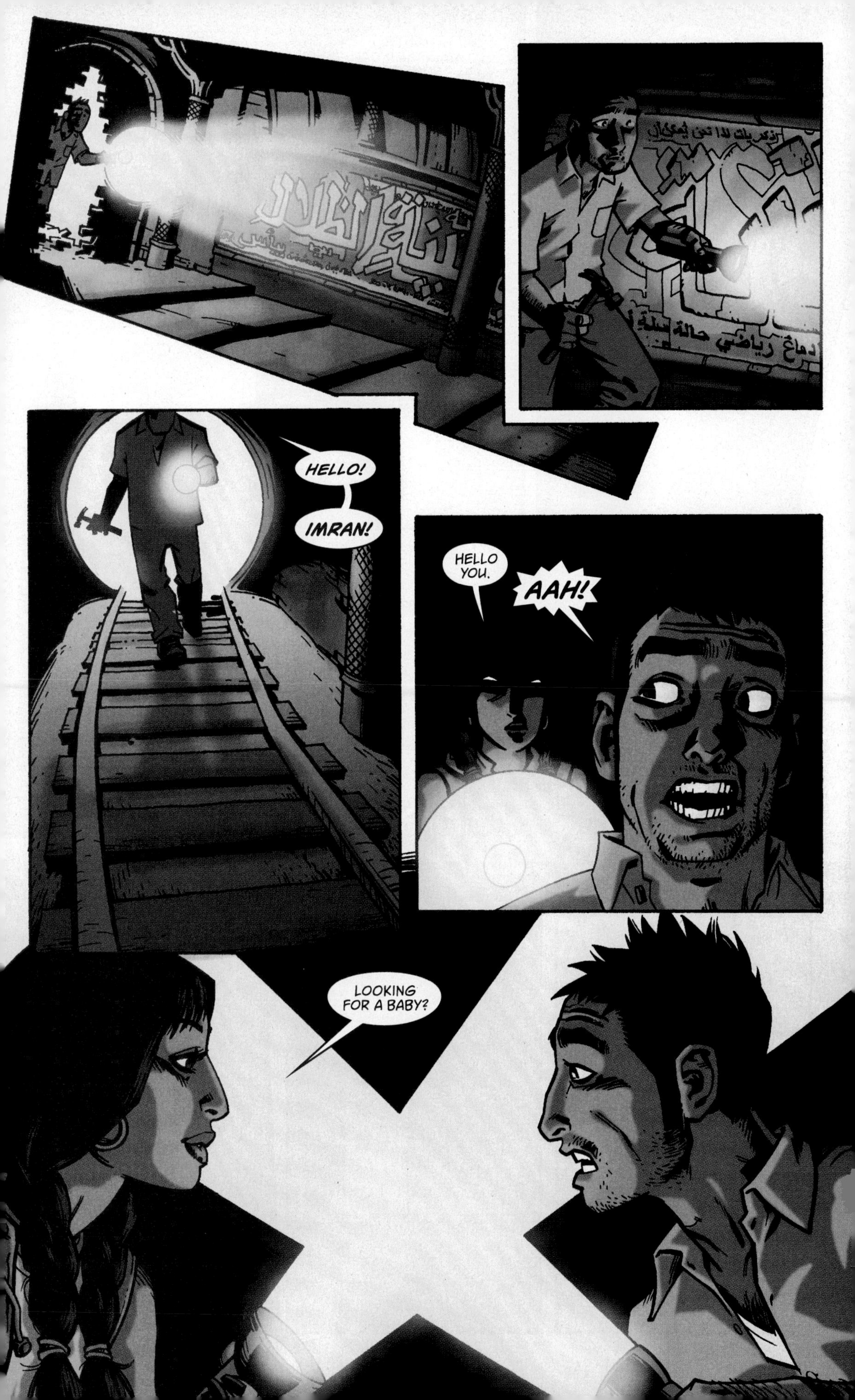
HELLO!
IMRAN!
HELLO YOU.
AAH!
LOOKING FOR A BABY?

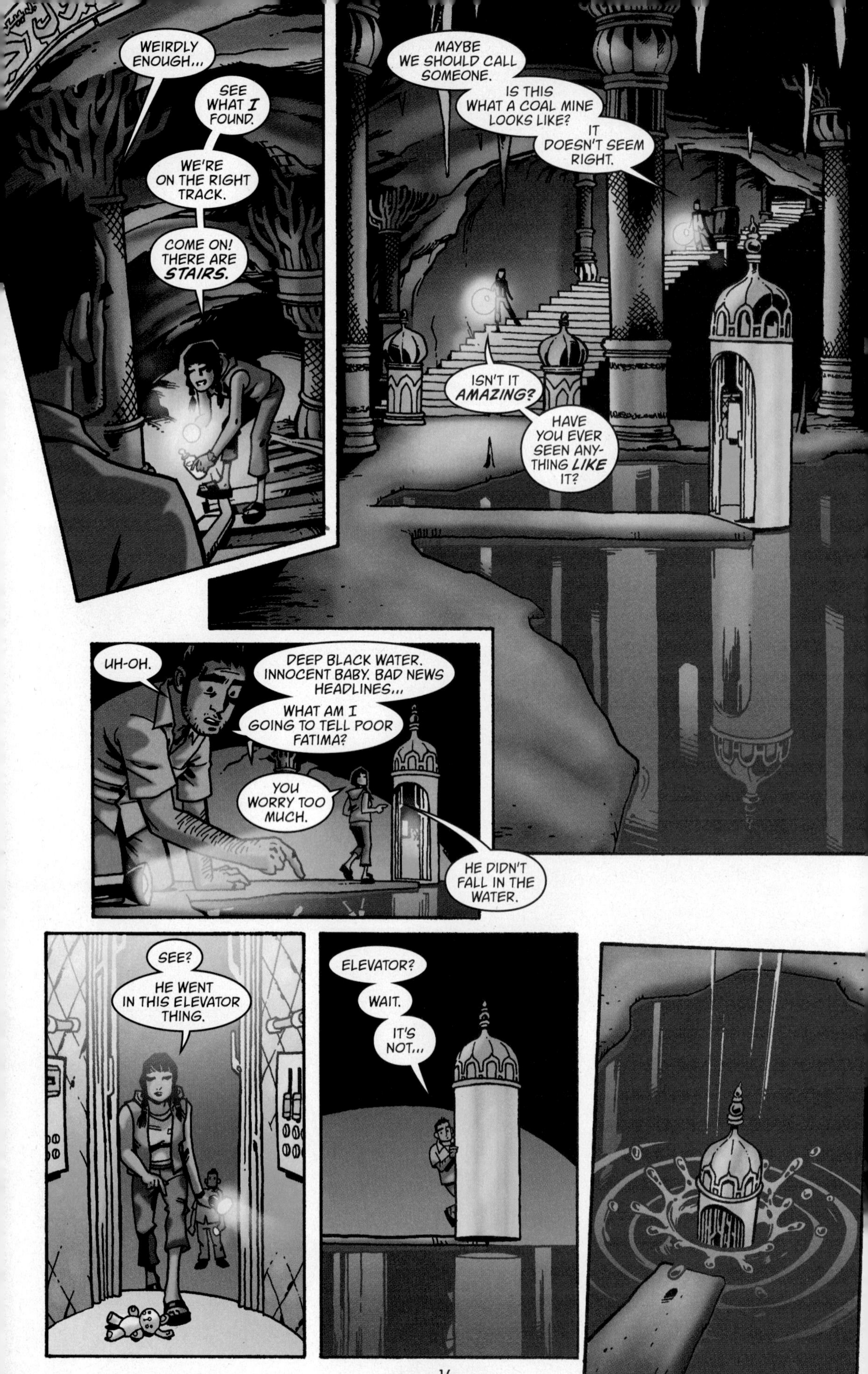
WEIRDLY ENOUGH...
SEE WHAT I FOUND.
WE'RE ON THE RIGHT TRACK.
COME ON! THERE ARE STAIRS.
MAYBE WE SHOULD CALL SOMEONE.
IS THIS WHAT A COAL MINE LOOKS LIKE?
IT DOESN'T SEEM RIGHT.
ISN'T IT AMAZING?
HAVE YOU EVER SEEN ANY-THING LIKE IT?
UH-OH.
DEEP BLACK WATER. INNOCENT BABY. BAD NEWS HEADLINES...
WHAT AM I GOING TO TELL POOR FATIMA?
YOU WORRY TOO MUCH.
HE DIDN'T FALL IN THE WATER.
SEE?
HE WENT IN THIS ELEVATOR THING.
ELEVATOR?
WAIT.
IT'S NOT...

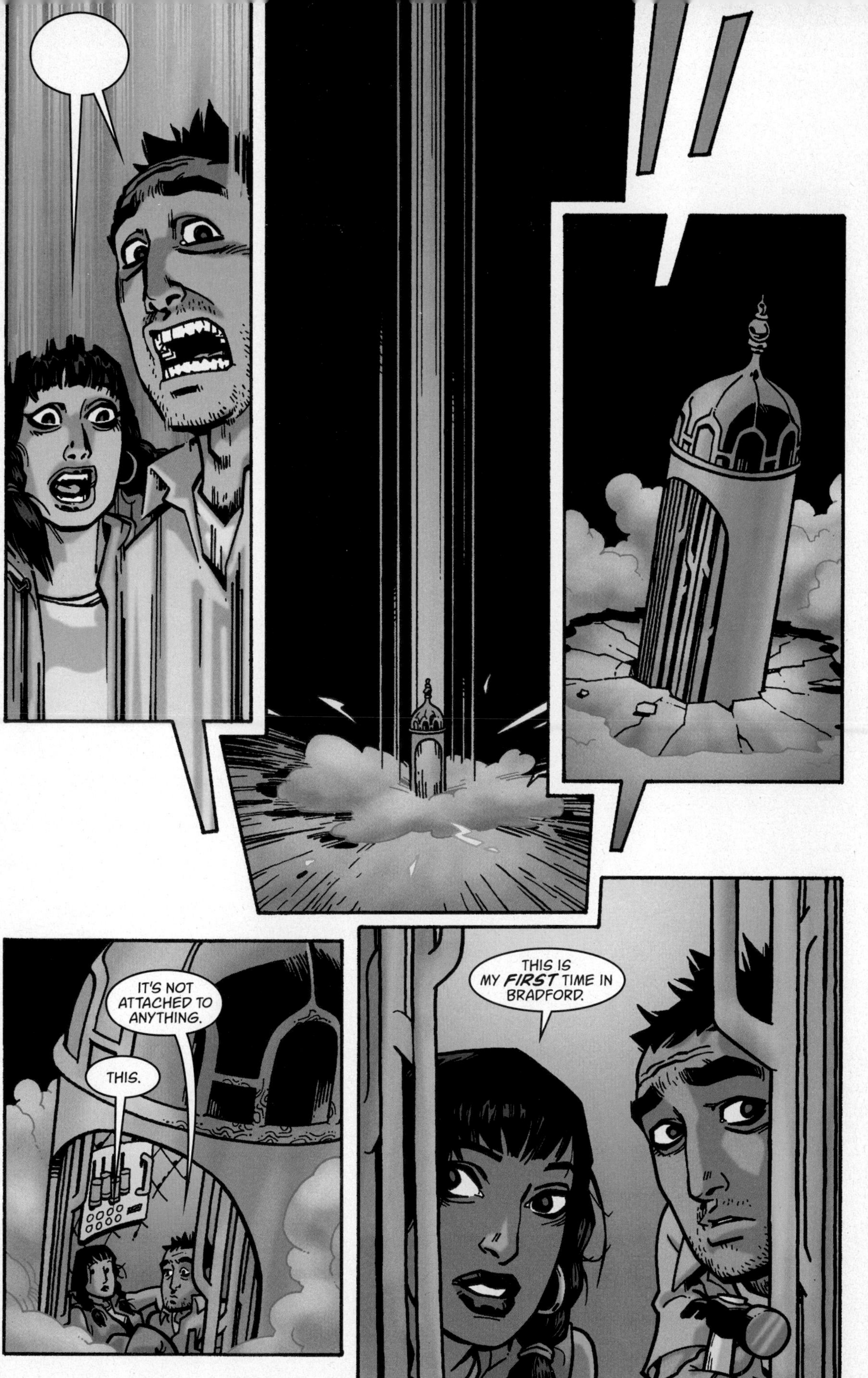
IT'S NOT ATTACHED TO ANYTHING.
THIS.
THIS IS MY FIRST TIME IN BRADFORD.

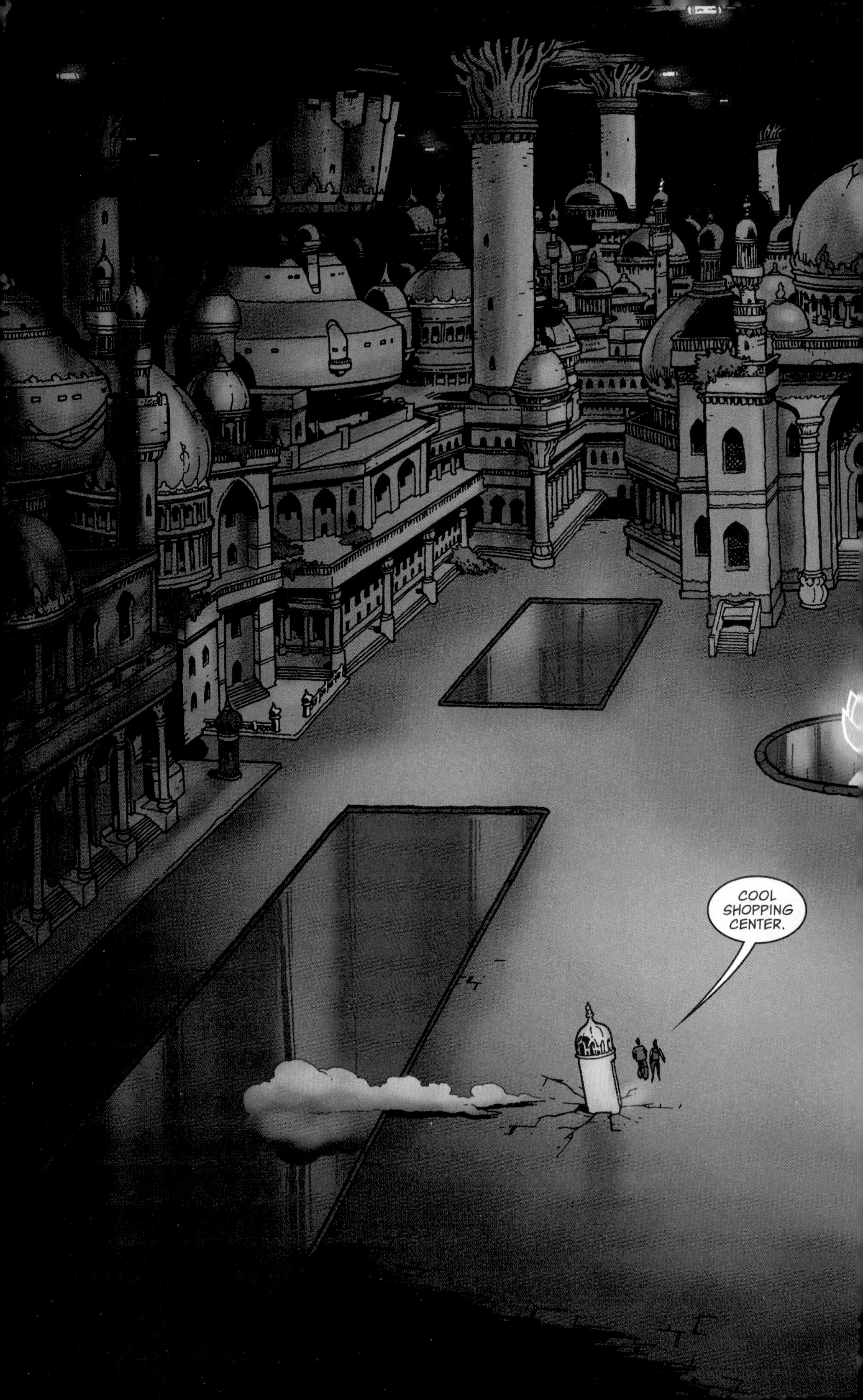
COOL SHOPPING CENTER.

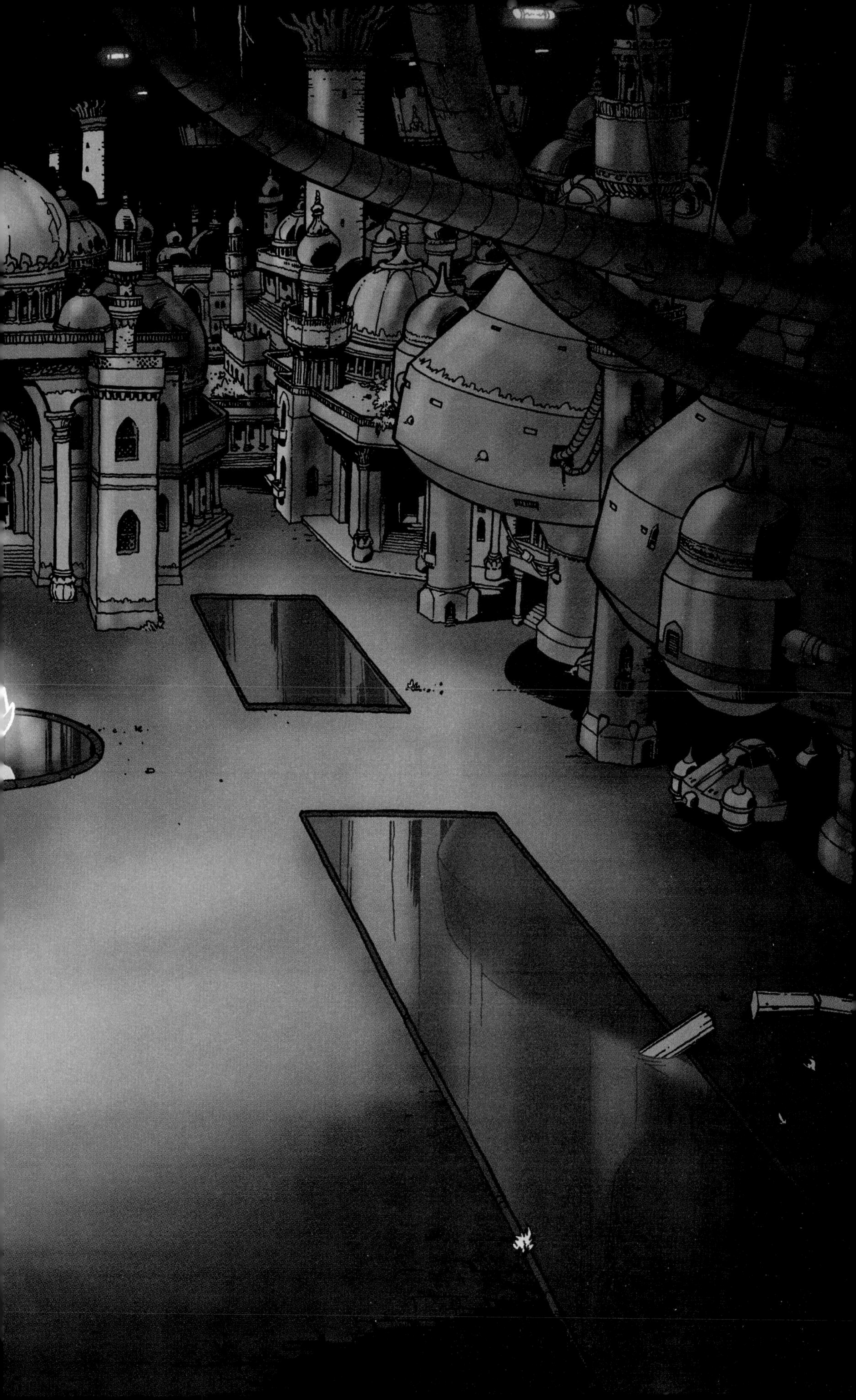

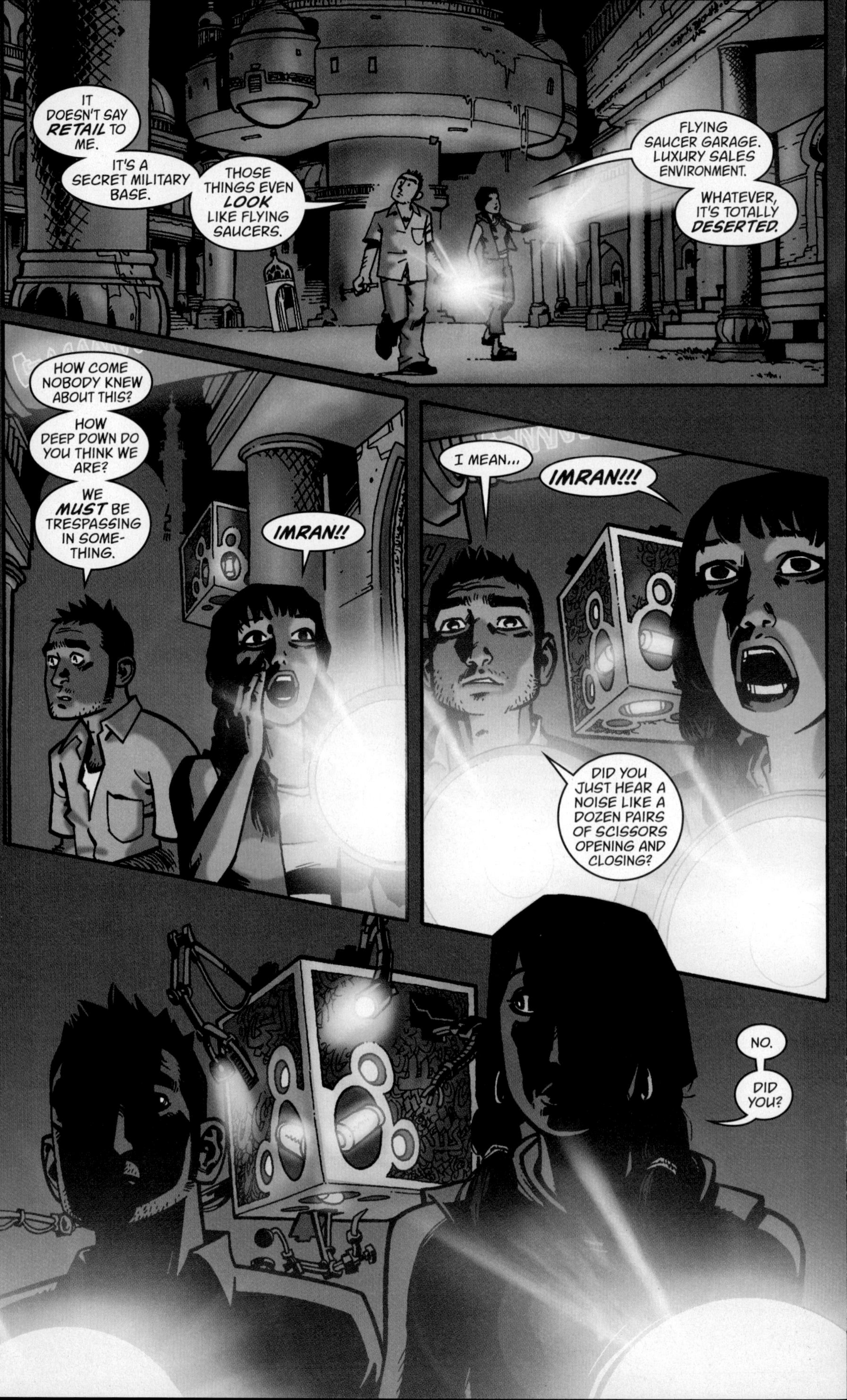
IT DOESN'T SAY **RETAIL** TO ME.
IT'S A SECRET MILITARY BASE.
THOSE THINGS EVEN **LOOK** LIKE FLYING SAUCERS.
FLYING SAUCER GARAGE. LUXURY SALES ENVIRONMENT.
WHATEVER, IT'S TOTALLY **DESERTED.**
HOW COME NOBODY KNEW ABOUT THIS?
HOW DEEP DOWN DO YOU THINK WE ARE?
WE **MUST** BE TRESPASSING IN SOME-THING.
IMRAN!!
I MEAN...
IMRAN!!!
DID YOU JUST HEAR A NOISE LIKE A DOZEN PAIRS OF SCISSORS OPENING AND CLOSING?
NO.
DID YOU?

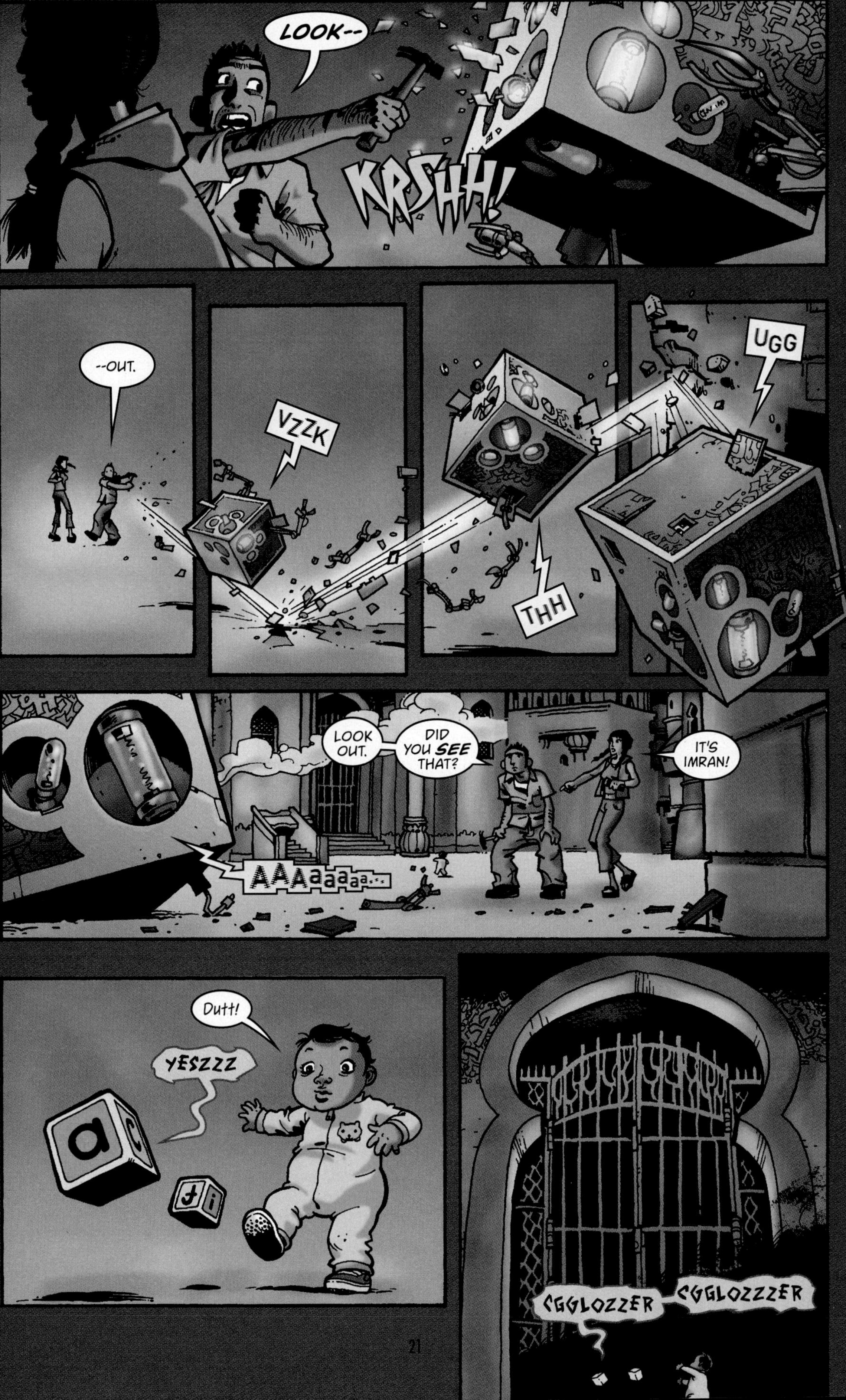
LOOK--
KRSHH!
--OUT.
VZZK
THH
UGG
AAAaaaaa...
LOOK OUT.
DID YOU SEE THAT?
IT'S IMRAN!
Dutt!
YESZZZ
CGGLOZZER
CGGLOZZZER

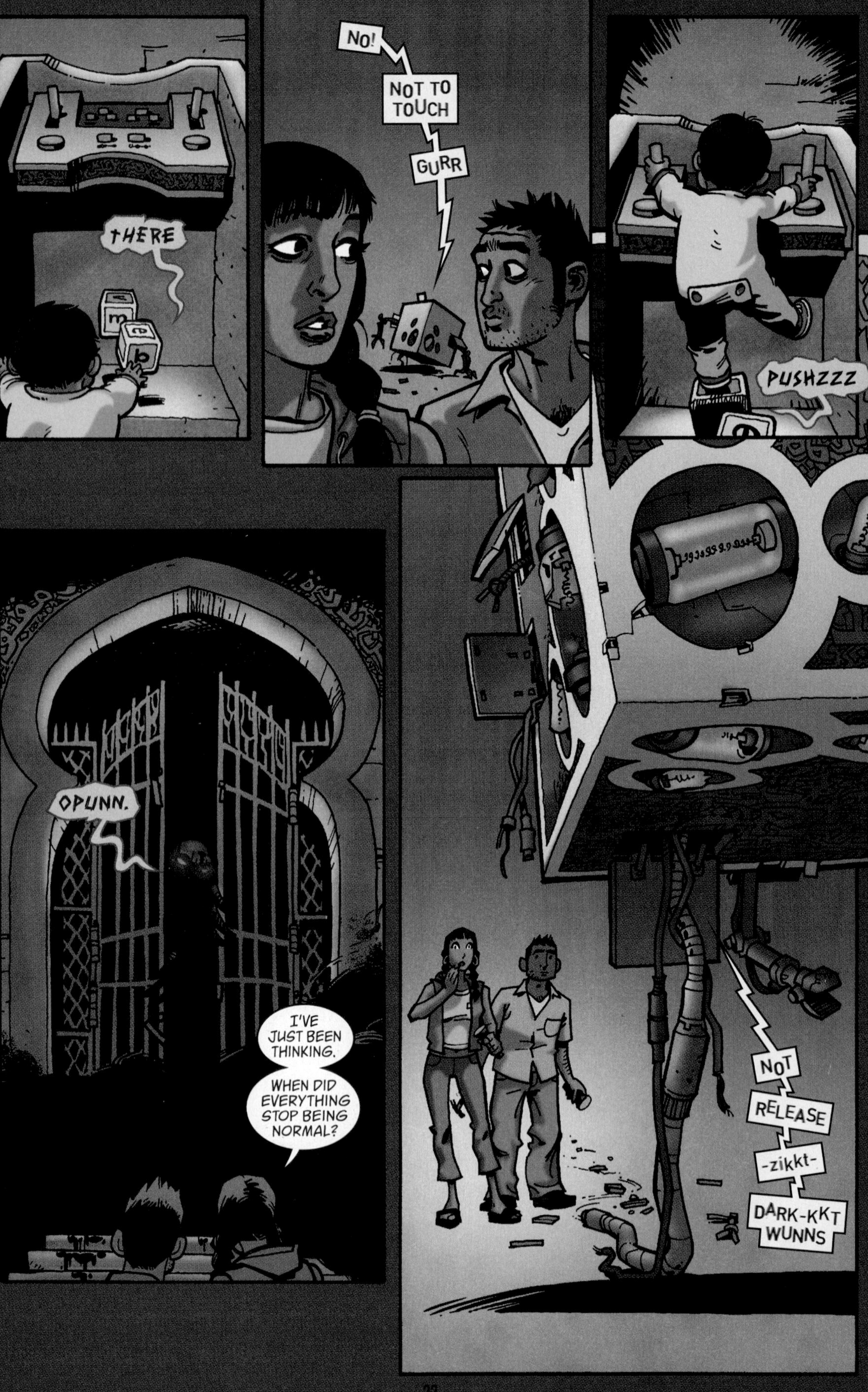
THERE
NO!
NOT TO TOUCH
GURR
PUSHZZZ
OPUNN.
I'VE JUST BEEN THINKING.
WHEN DID EVERYTHING STOP BEING NORMAL?
NOT
RELEASE
-zikkt-
DARK-KKT WUNNS

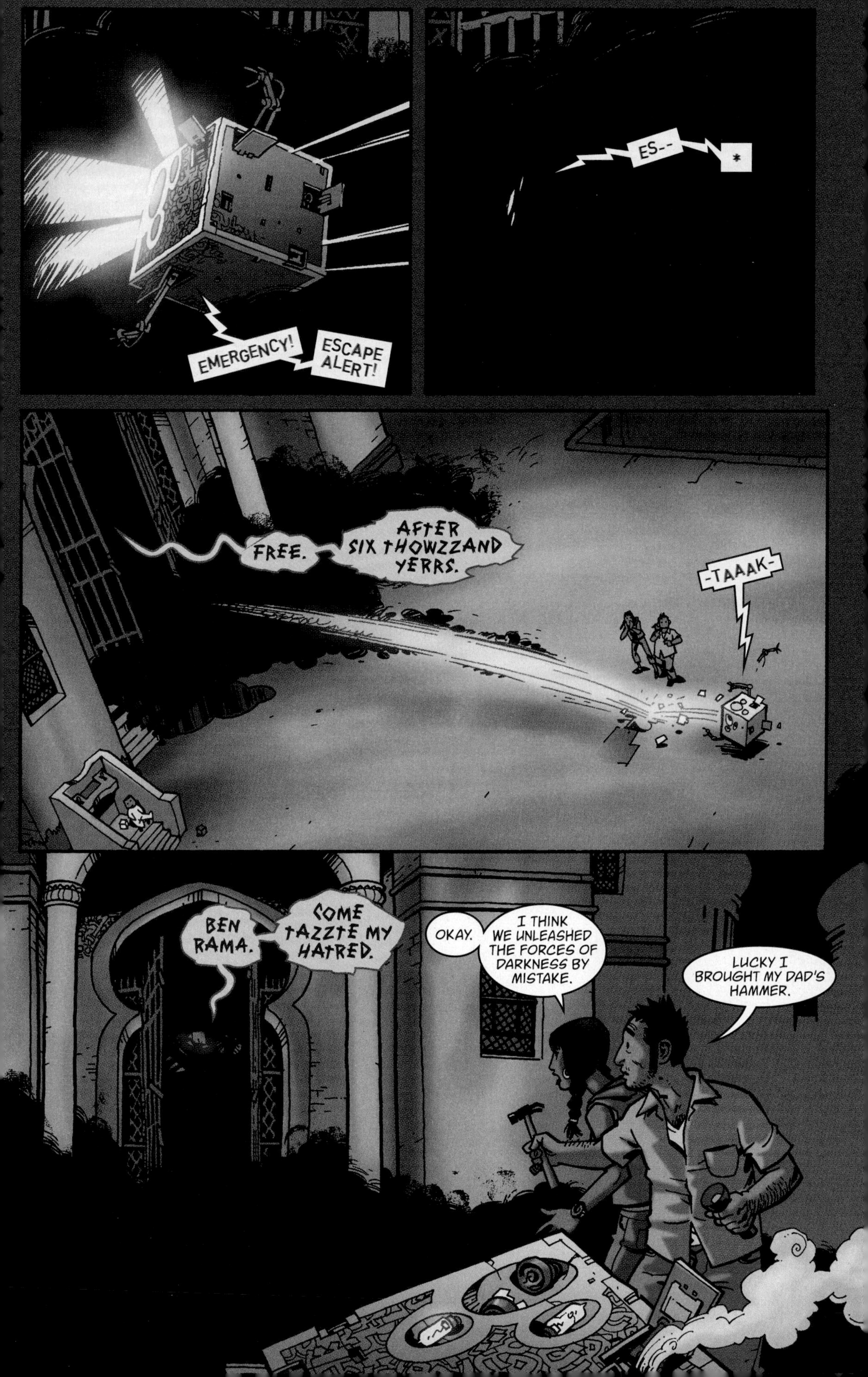
EMERGENCY!
ESCAPE ALERT!
ES--
*
FREE.
AFTER SIX THOWZZAND YERRS.
-TAAAK-
BEN RAMA.
COME TAZZTE MY HATRED.
OKAY.
I THINK WE UNLEASHED THE FORCES OF DARKNESS BY MISTAKE.
LUCKY I BROUGHT MY DAD'S HAMMER.

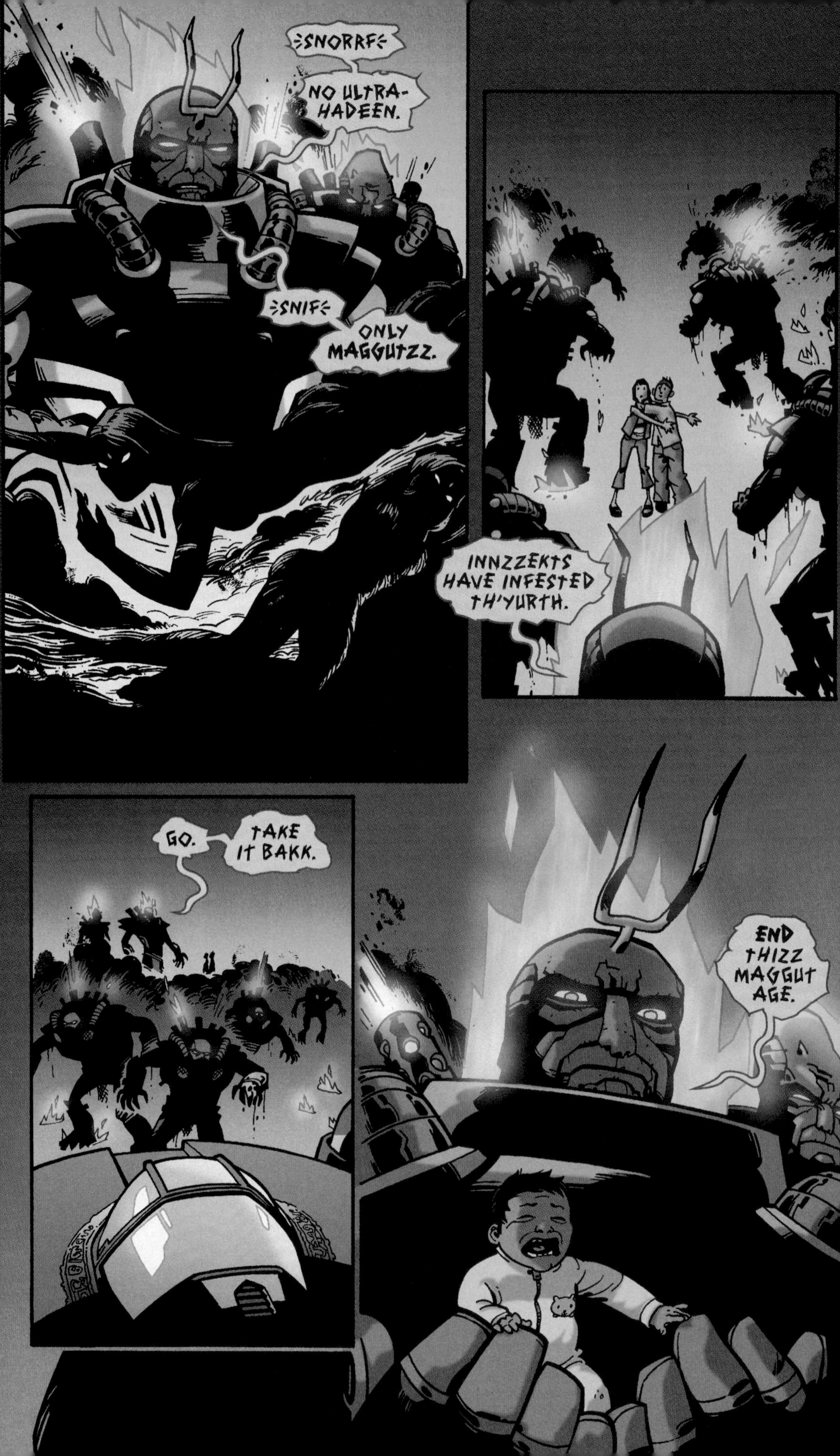
SNORRF
NO ULTRA-HADEEN.
SNIF
ONLY MAGGUTZZ.
INNZZEKTS HAVE INFESTED TH'YURTH.
GO.
TAKE IT BAKK.
END THIZZ MAGGUT AGE.

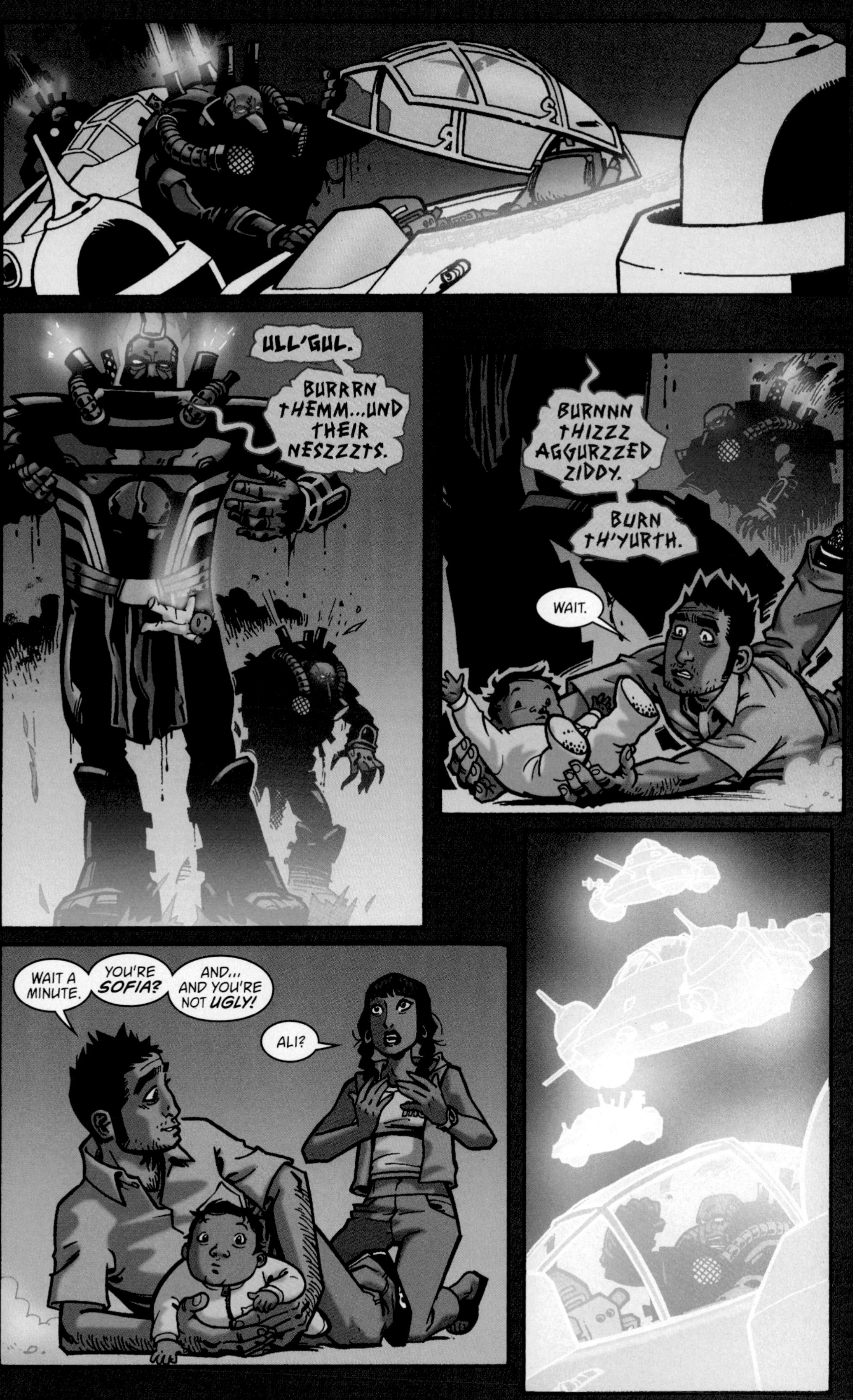
ULL'GUL.
BURRRN THEMM...UND THEIR NESZZZTS.
BURNNN THIZZZ AGGURZZED ZIDDY.
BURN TH'YURTH.
WAIT.
WAIT A MINUTE.
YOU'RE SOFIA?
AND... AND YOU'RE NOT UGLY!
ALI?

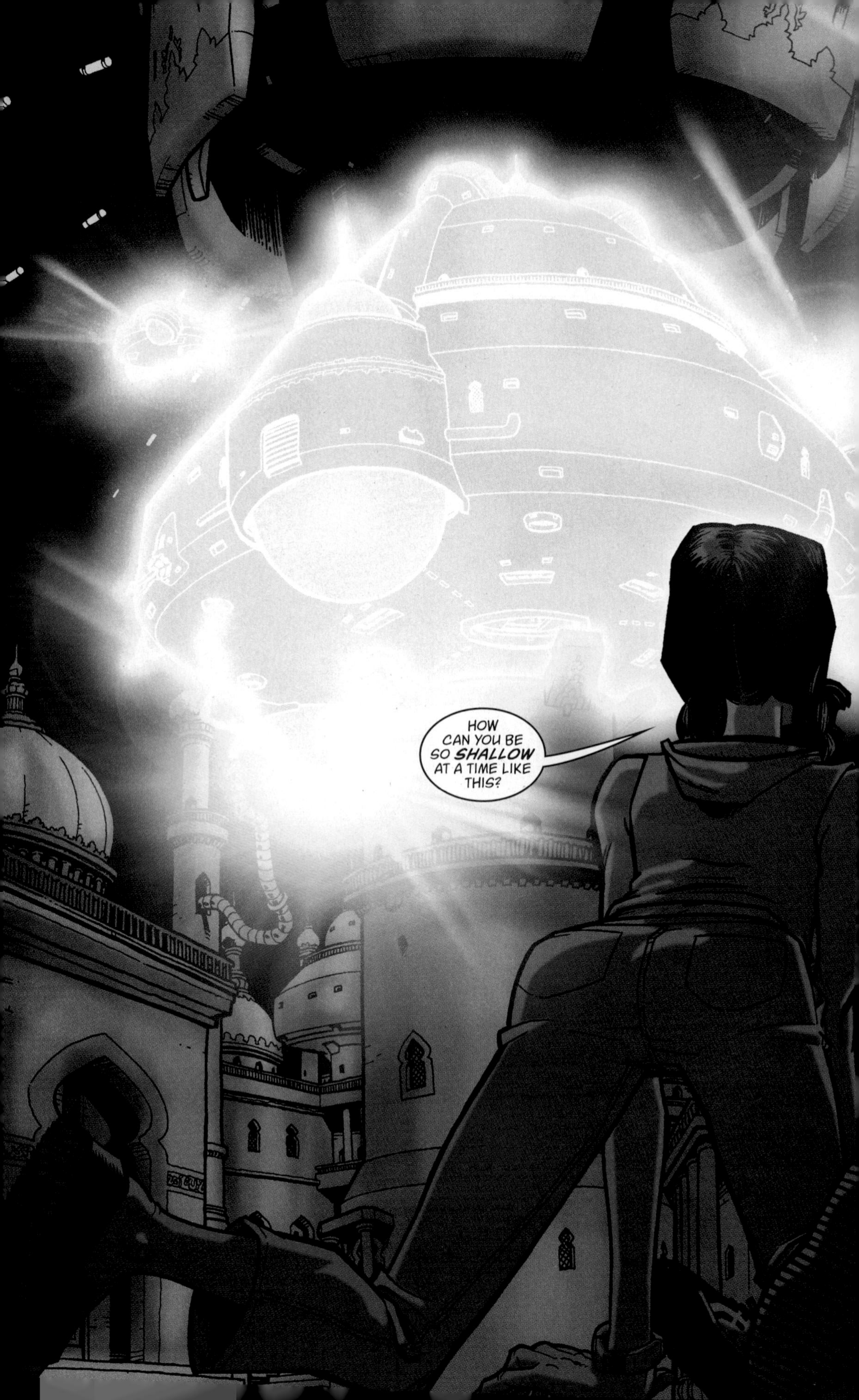
HOW CAN YOU BE SO SHALLOW AT A TIME LIKE THIS?

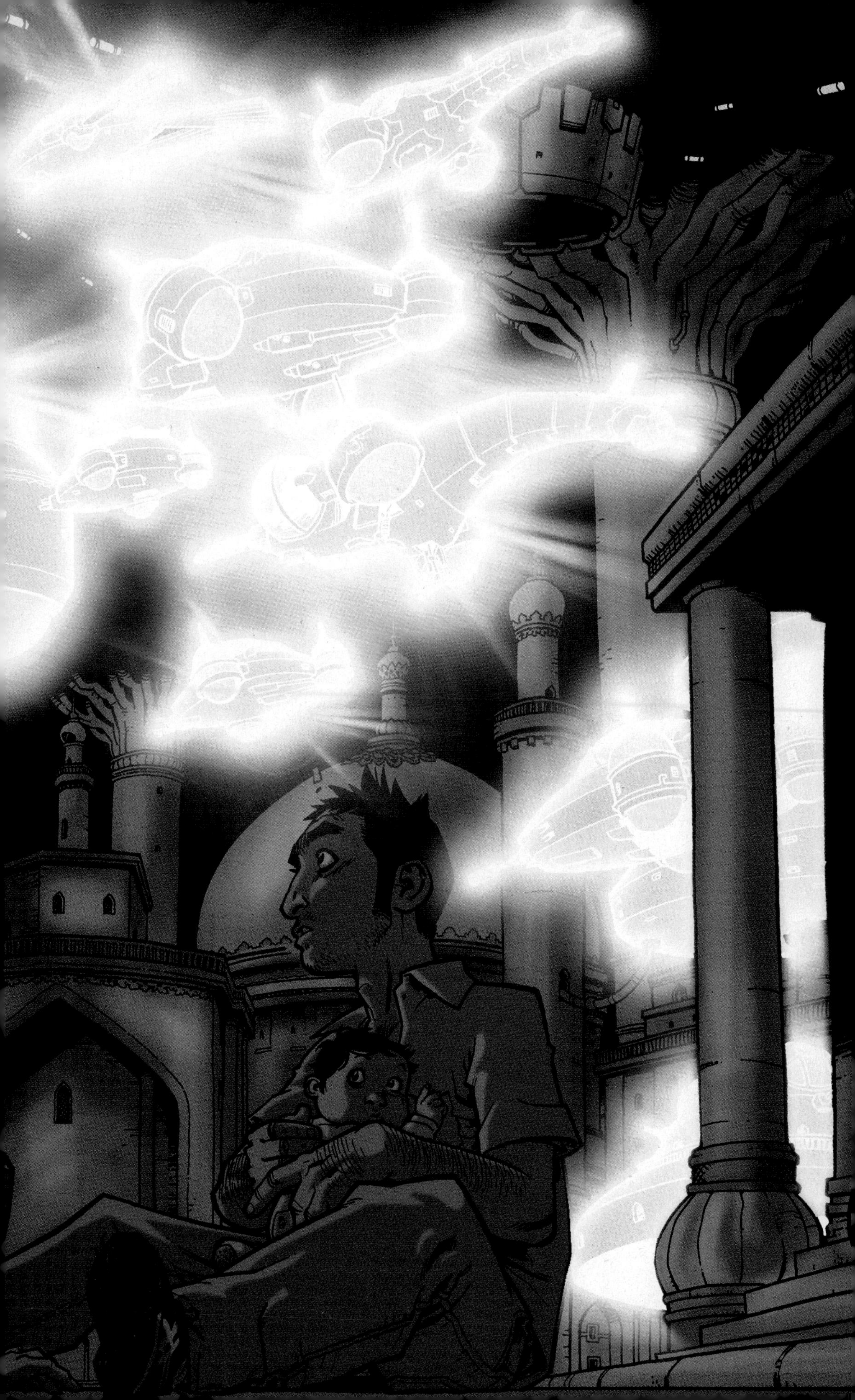

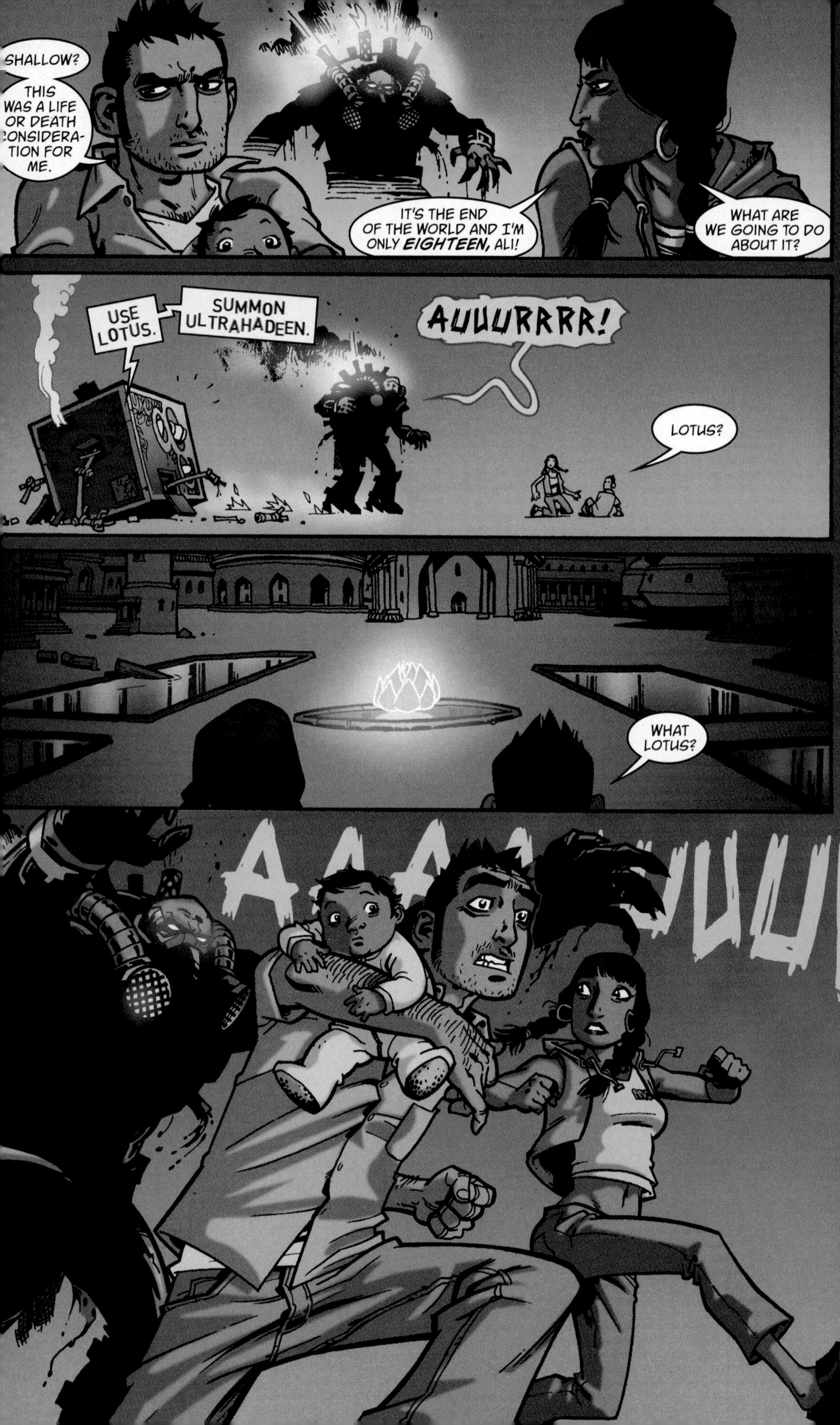
SHALLOW?
THIS WAS A LIFE OR DEATH CONSIDERATION FOR ME.
IT'S THE END OF THE WORLD AND I'M ONLY EIGHTEEN, ALI!
WHAT ARE WE GOING TO DO ABOUT IT?
USE LOTUS.
SUMMON ULTRAHADEEN.
AUUURRRR!
LOTUS?
WHAT LOTUS?

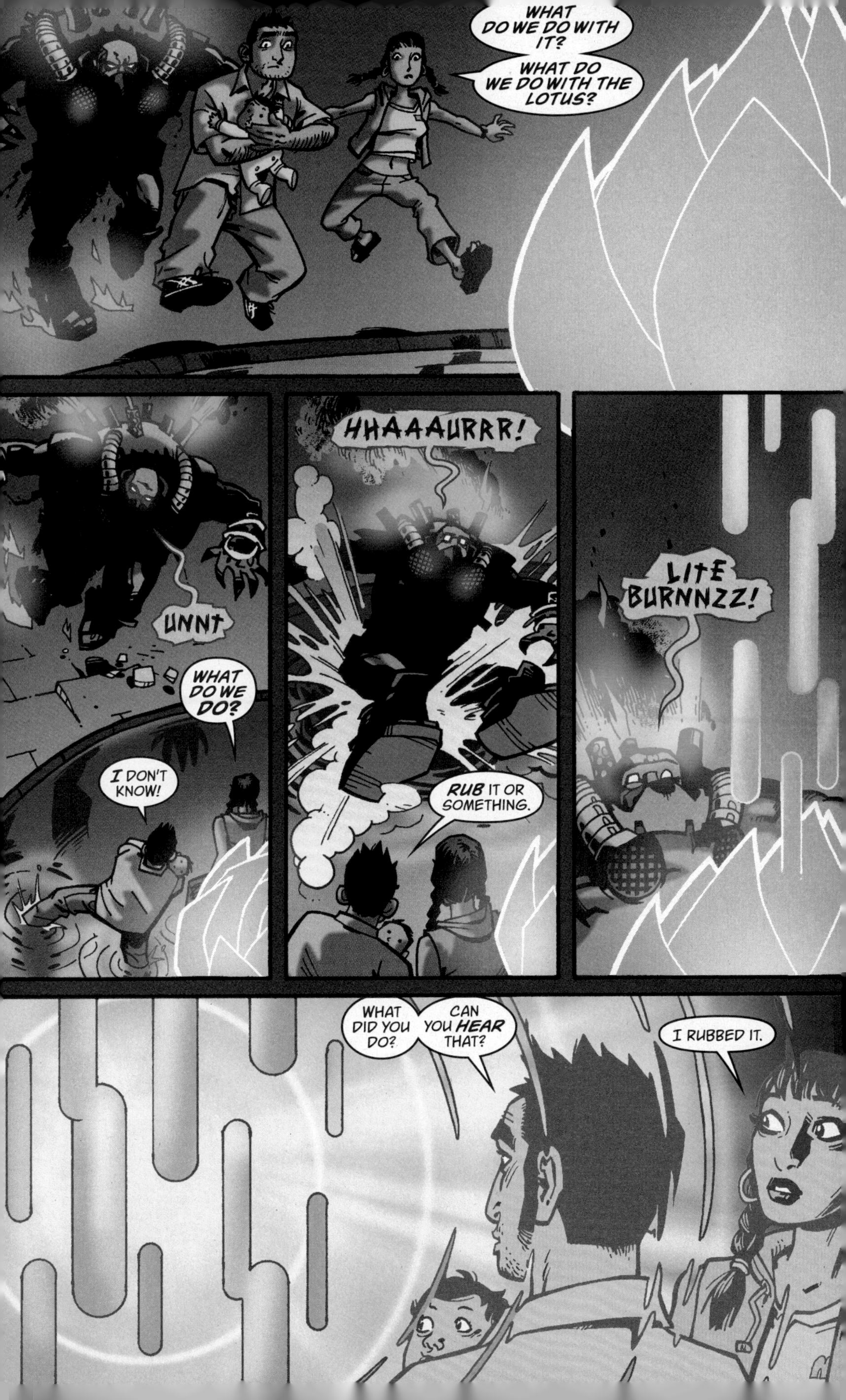
WHAT DO WE DO WITH IT?
WHAT DO WE DO WITH THE LOTUS?
UNNT
WHAT DO WE DO?
I DON'T KNOW!
HHAAAURRR!
RUB IT OR SOMETHING.
LITE BURNNZZ!
WHAT DID YOU DO?
CAN YOU HEAR THAT?
I RUBBED IT.

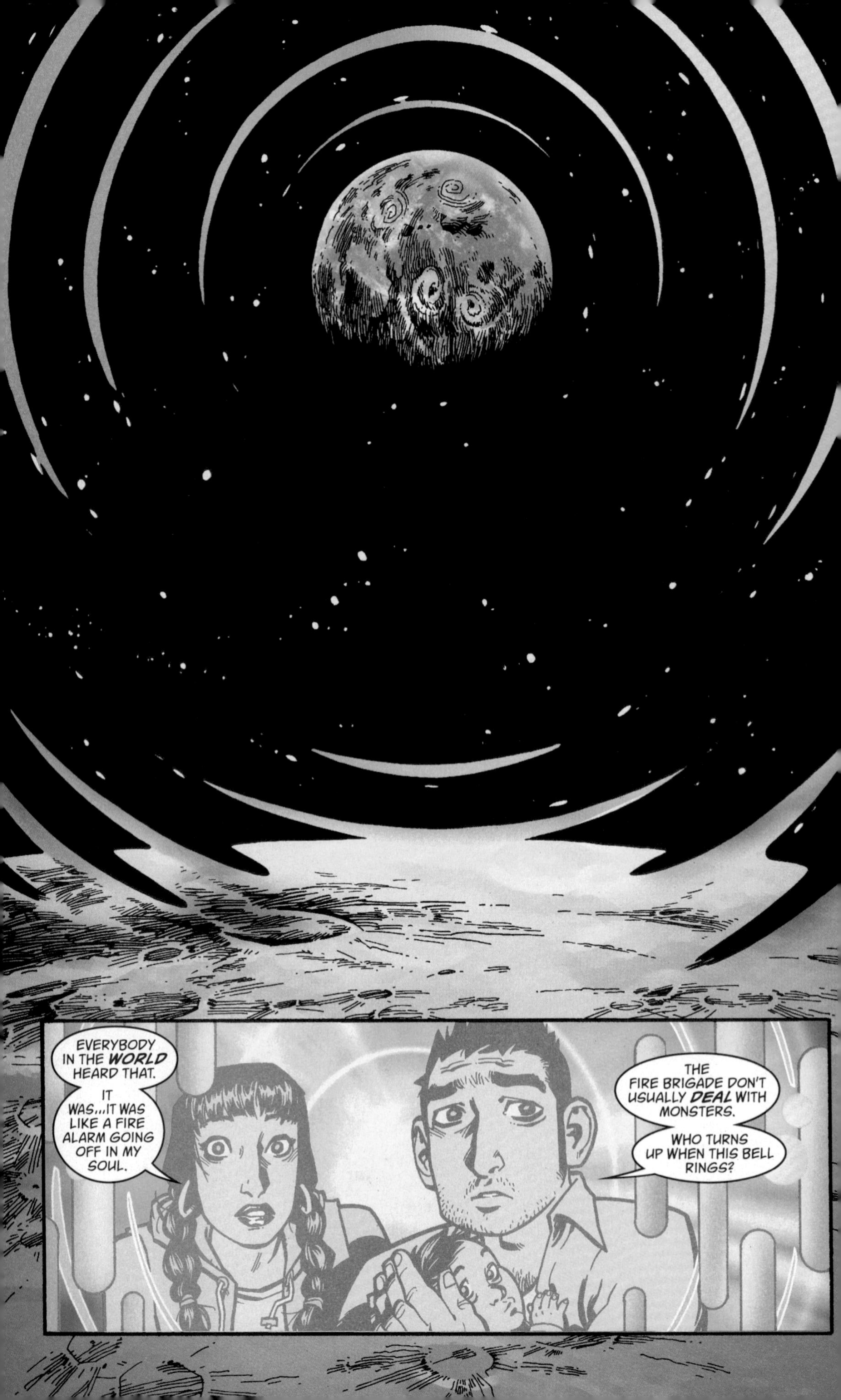

EVERYBODY IN THE *WORLD* HEARD THAT.
IT WAS...IT WAS LIKE A FIRE ALARM GOING OFF IN MY SOUL.
THE FIRE BRIGADE DON'T USUALLY *DEAL* WITH MONSTERS.
WHO TURNS UP WHEN THIS BELL RINGS?

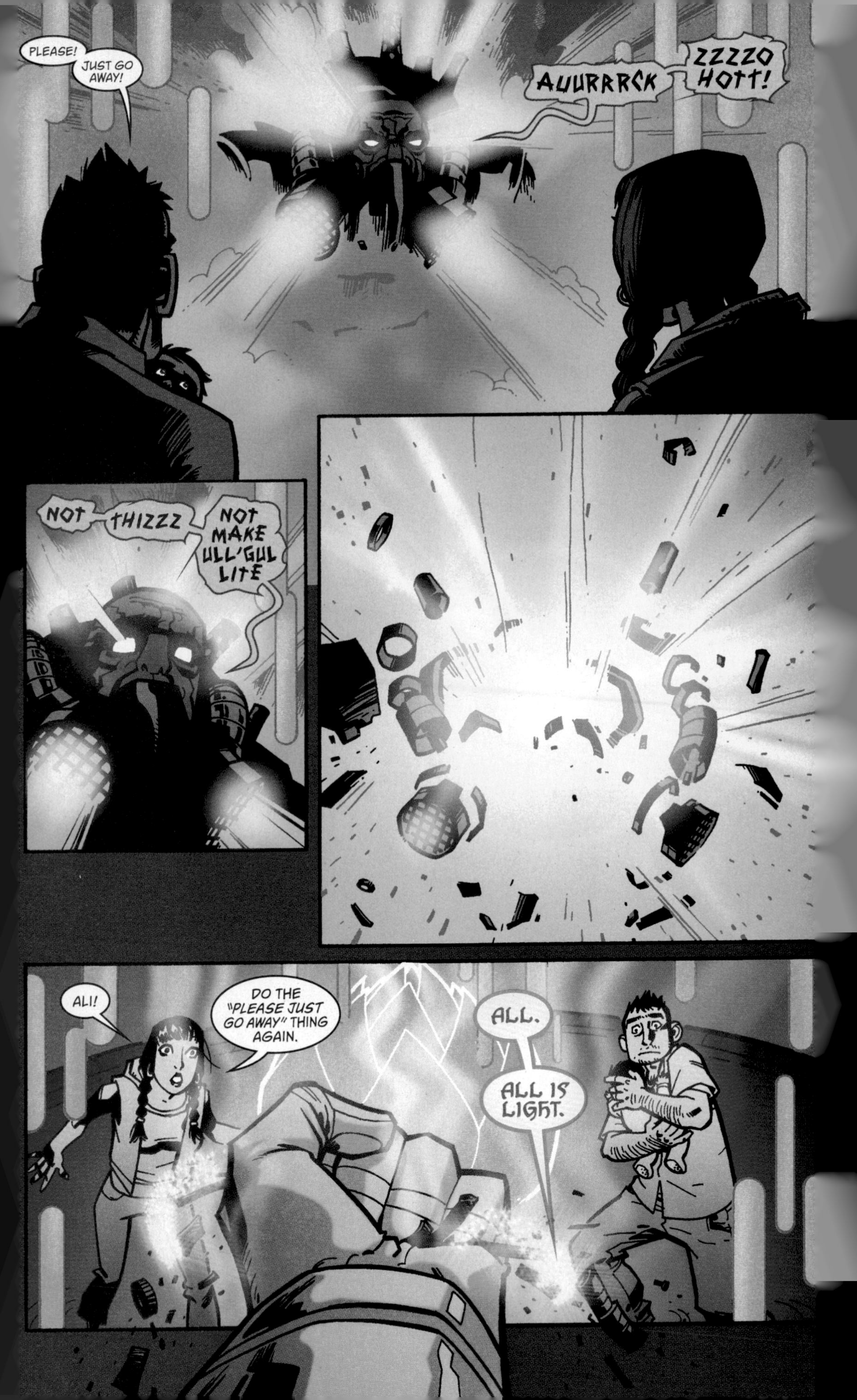
PLEASE!
JUST GO AWAY!
AUURRRCK
ZZZZO HOTT!
NOT
THIZZZ
NOT MAKE ULL'GUL LITE
ALI!
DO THE "PLEASE JUST GO AWAY" THING AGAIN.
ALL.
ALL IS LIGHT.

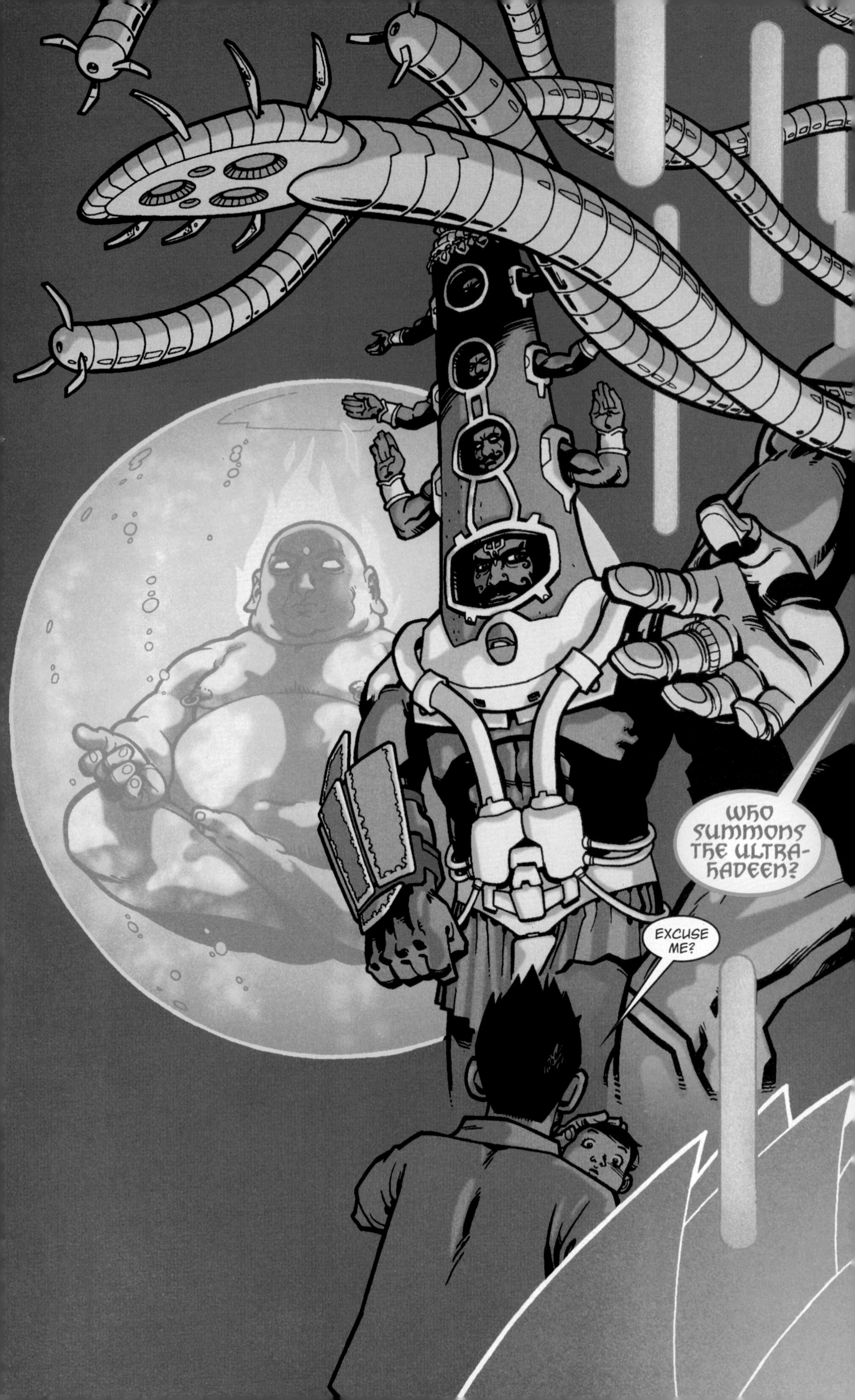
WHO SUMMONS THE ULTRA-HADEEN?
EXCUSE ME?

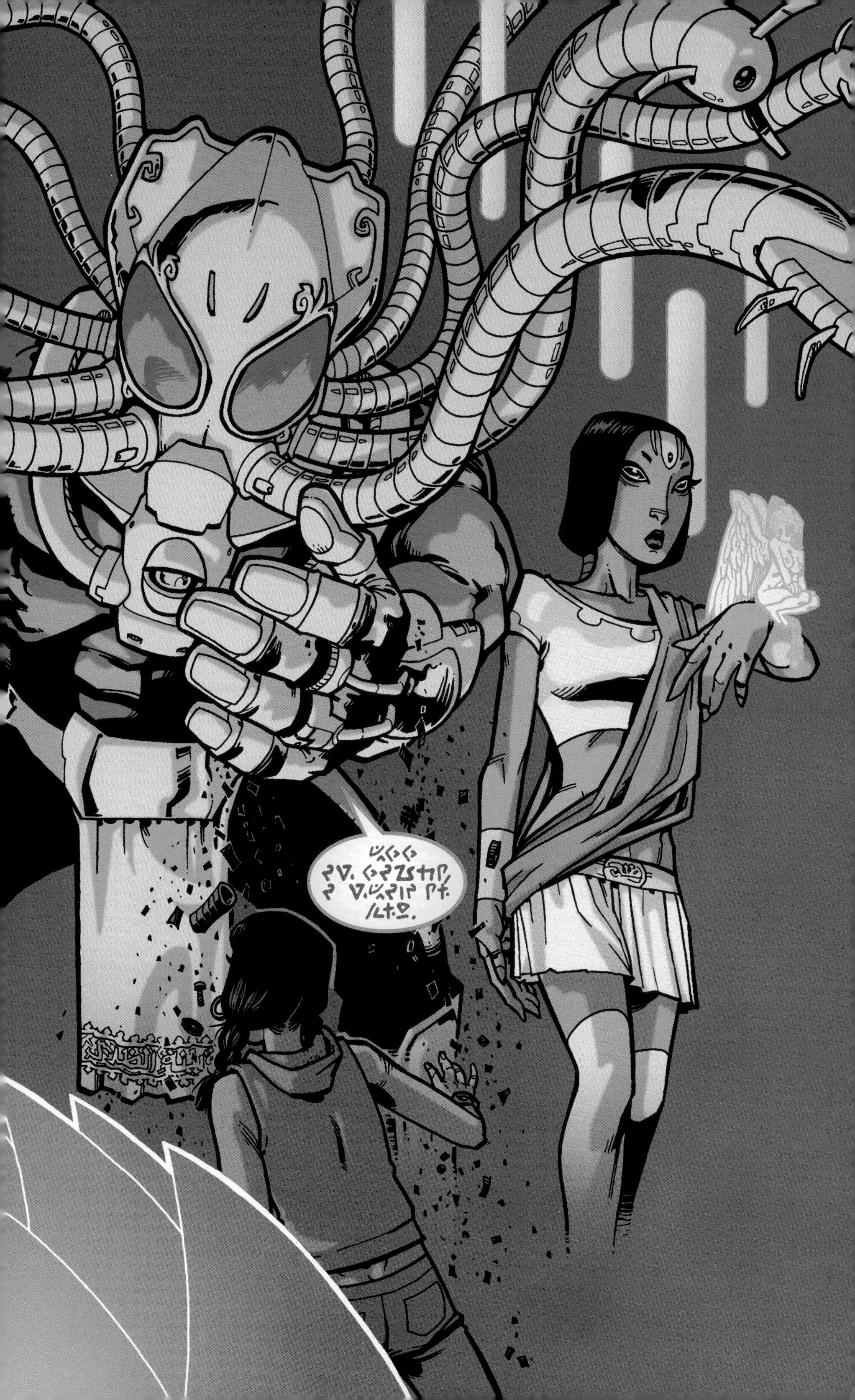

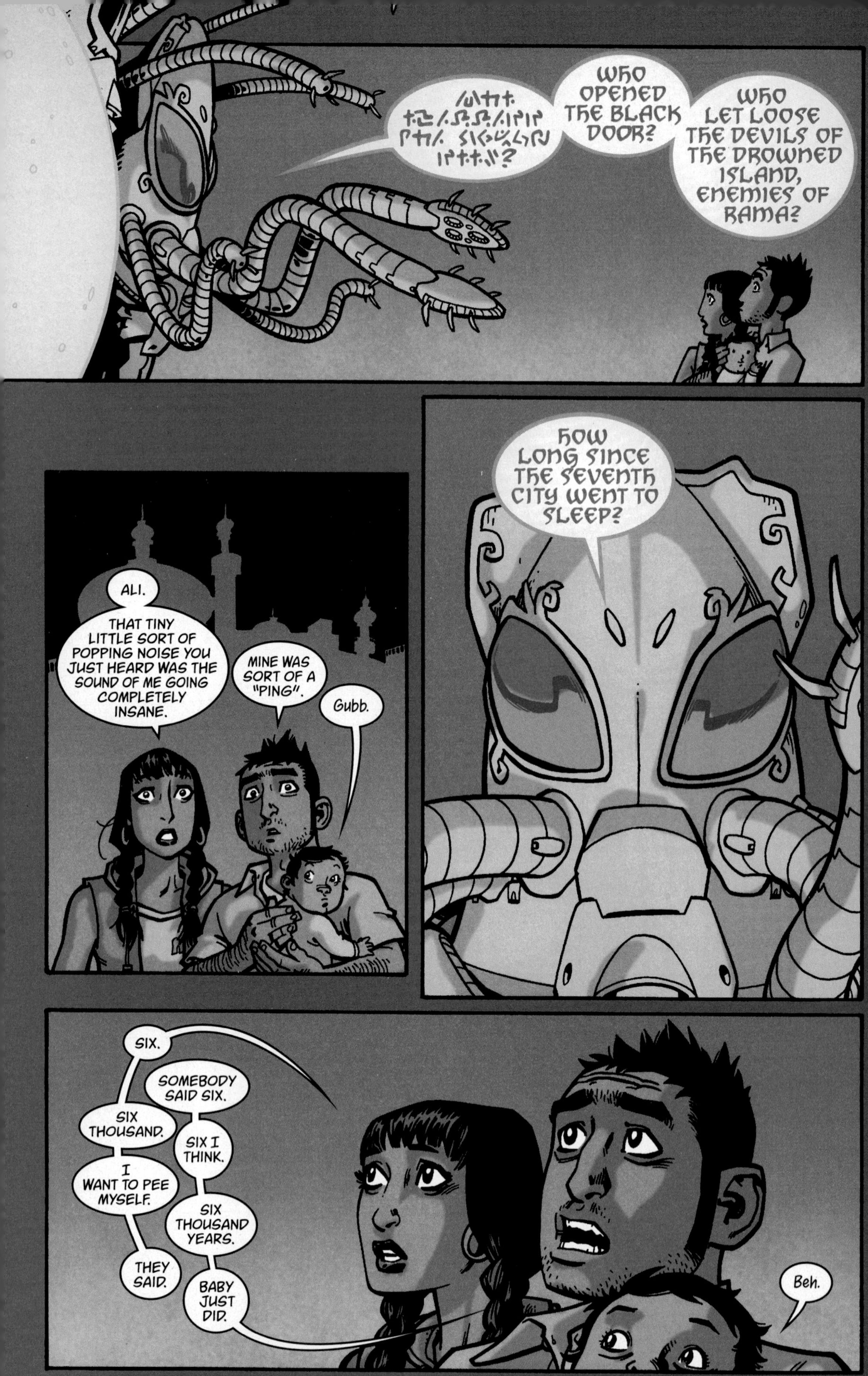
WHO OPENED THE BLACK DOOR?
WHO LET LOOSE THE DEVILS OF THE DROWNED ISLAND, ENEMIES OF RAMA?
ALI.
THAT TINY LITTLE SORT OF POPPING NOISE YOU JUST HEARD WAS THE SOUND OF ME GOING COMPLETELY INSANE.
MINE WAS SORT OF A "PING".
Gubb.
HOW LONG SINCE THE SEVENTH CITY WENT TO SLEEP?
SIX.
SOMEBODY SAID SIX.
SIX THOUSAND.
SIX I THINK.
I WANT TO PEE MYSELF.
SIX THOUSAND YEARS.
THEY SAID.
BABY JUST DID.
Beh.

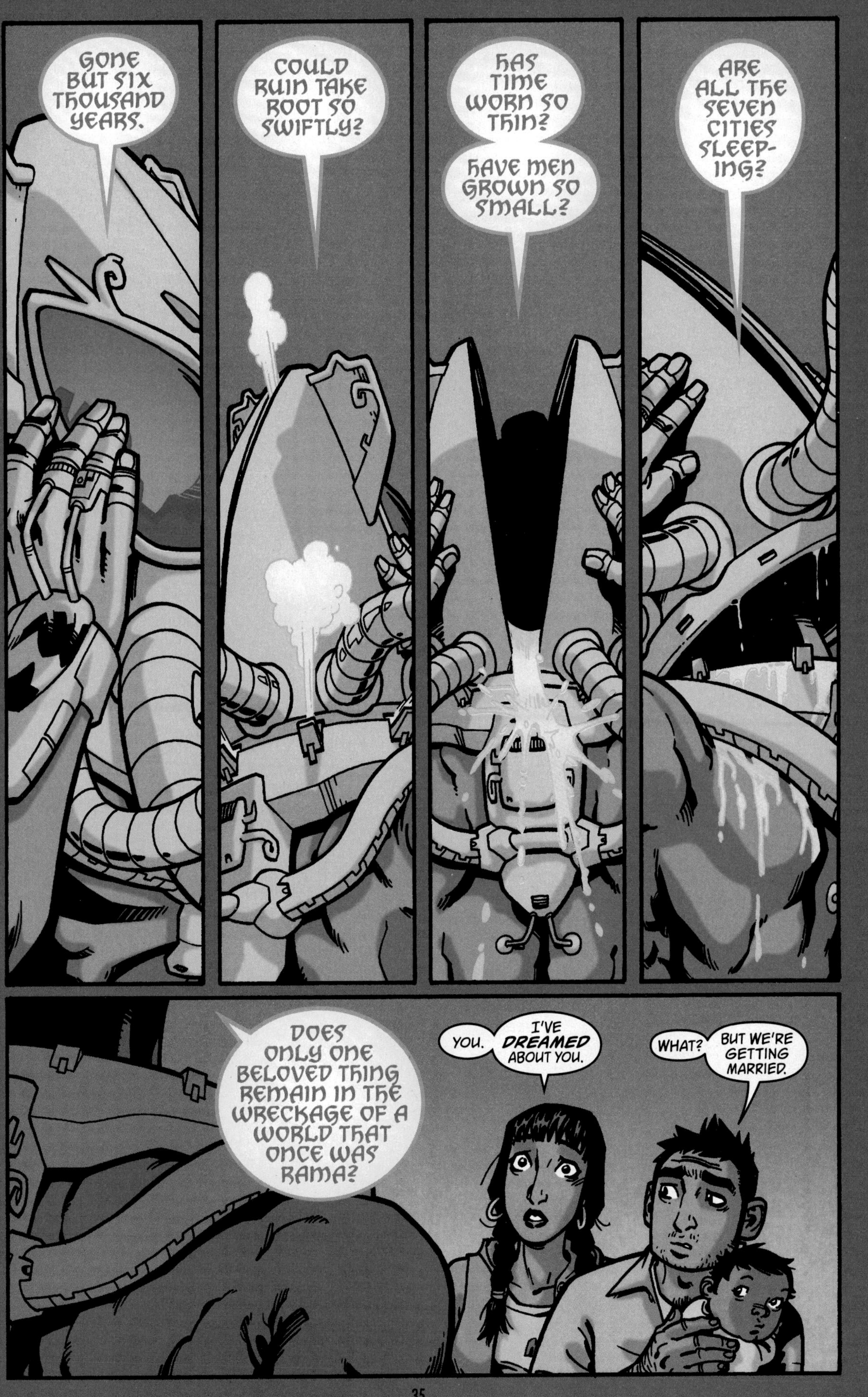
GONE BUT SIX THOUSAND YEARS.
COULD RUIN TAKE ROOT SO SWIFTLY?
HAS TIME WORN SO THIN?
HAVE MEN GROWN SO SMALL?
ARE ALL THE SEVEN CITIES SLEEPING?
DOES ONLY ONE BELOVED THING REMAIN IN THE WRECKAGE OF A WORLD THAT ONCE WAS RAMA?
YOU.
I'VE ***DREAMED*** ABOUT YOU.
WHAT?
BUT WE'RE GETTING MARRIED.

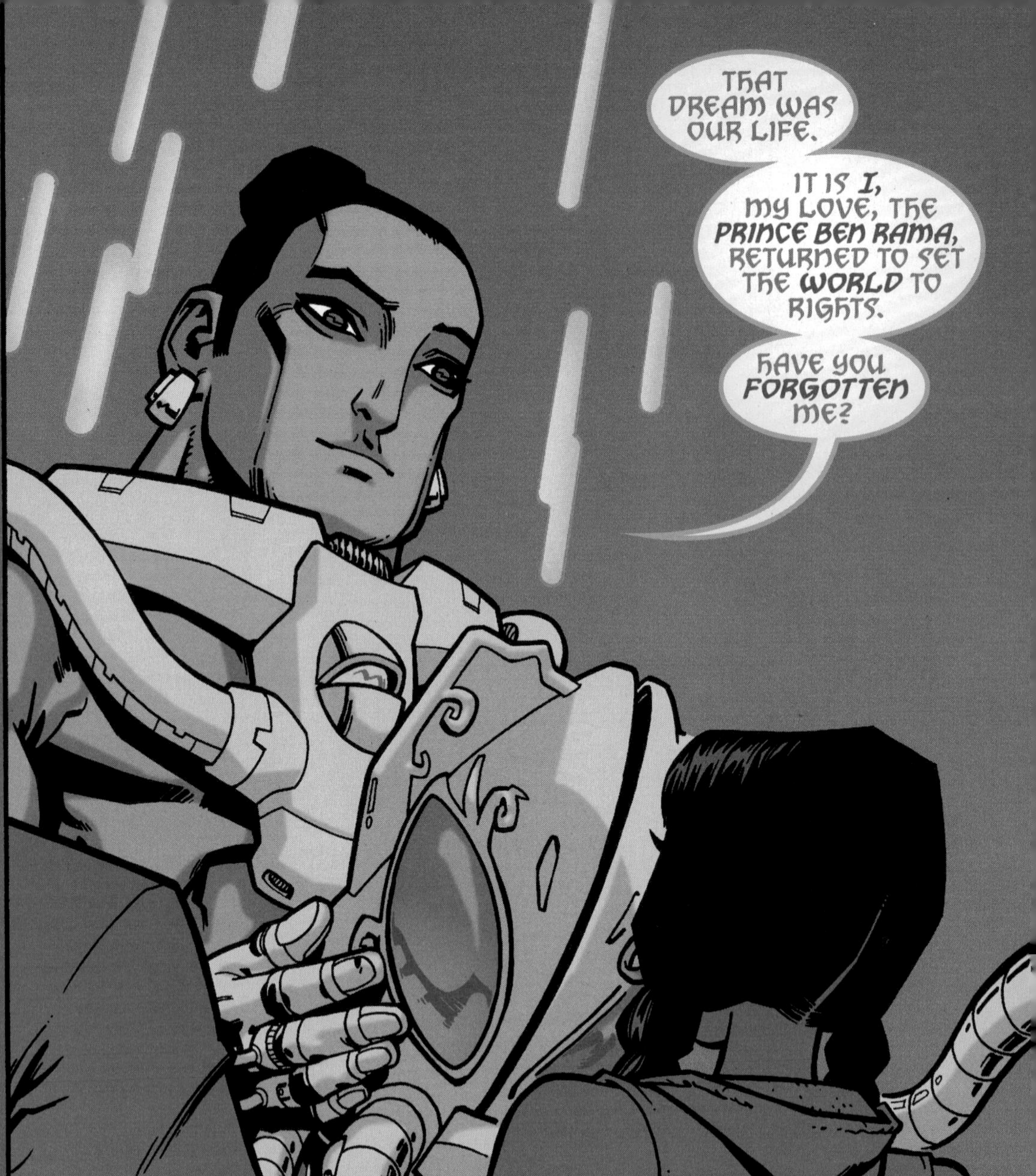
THAT DREAM WAS OUR LIFE.
IT IS *I*, MY LOVE, THE **PRINCE BEN RAMA**, RETURNED TO SET THE **WORLD** TO RIGHTS.
HAVE YOU **FORGOTTEN** ME?

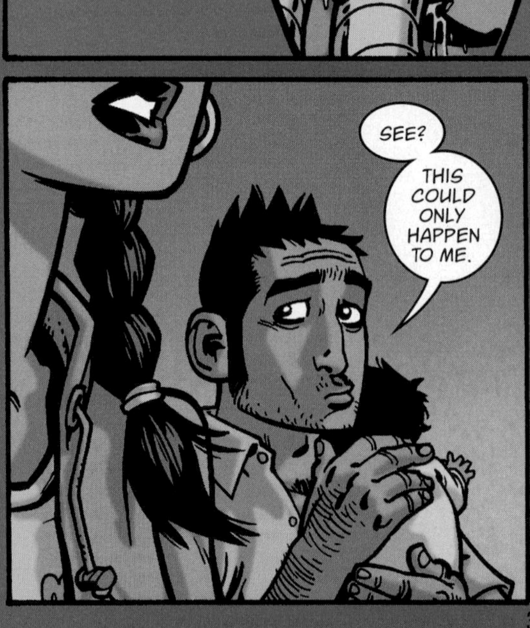
SEE?
THIS COULD ONLY HAPPEN TO ME.

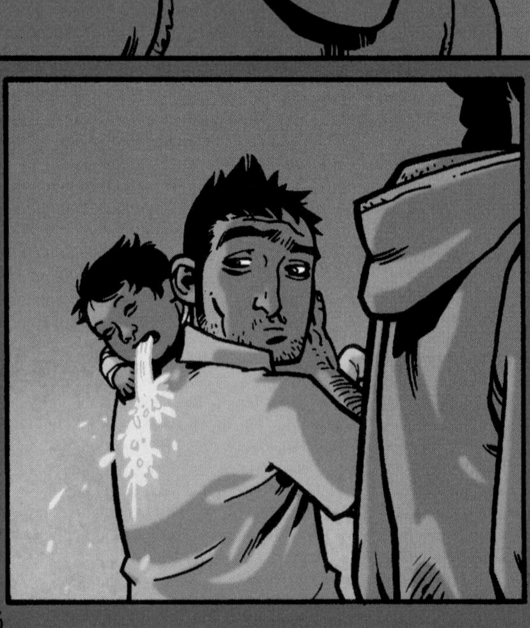

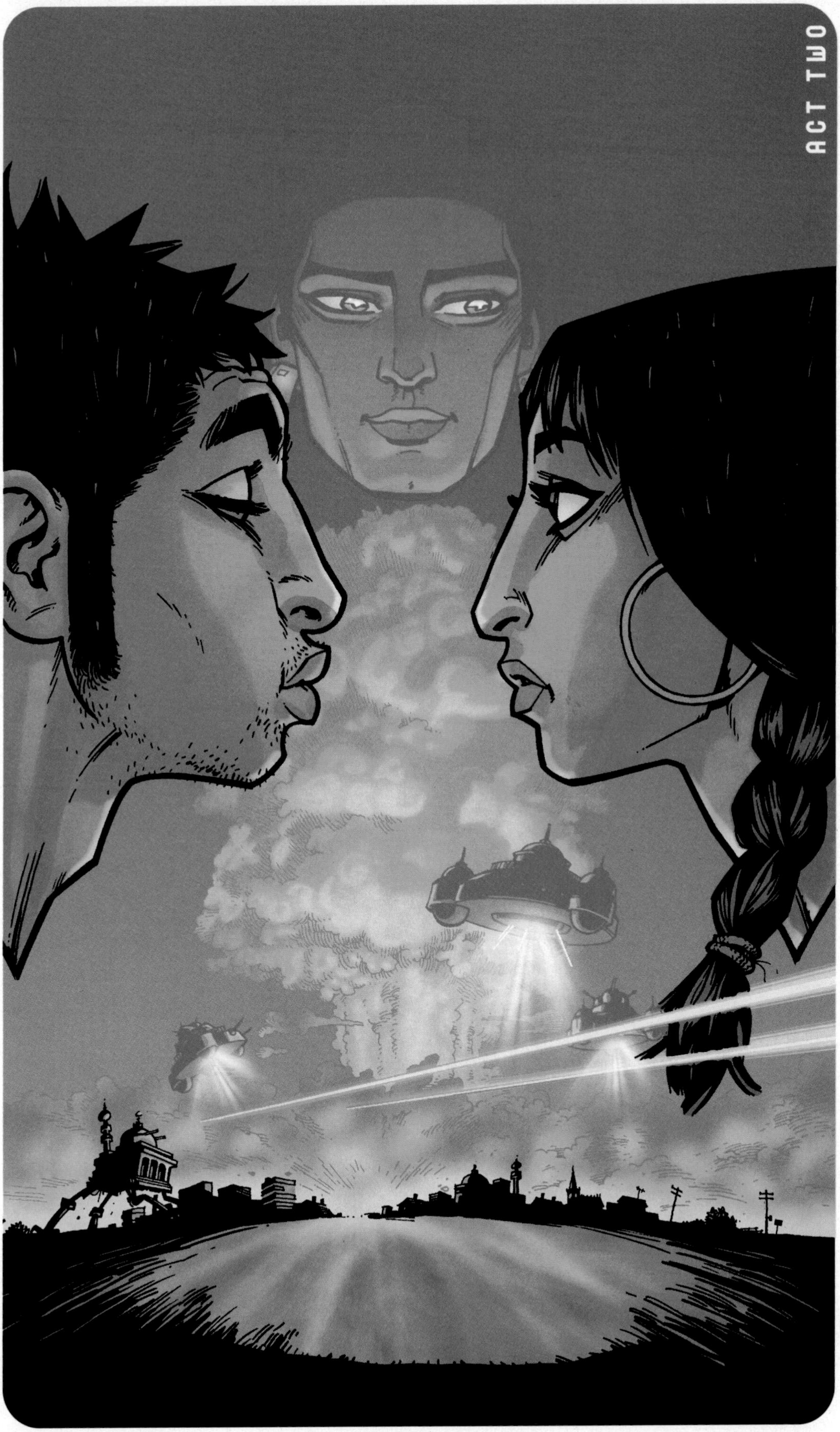
ACT TWO

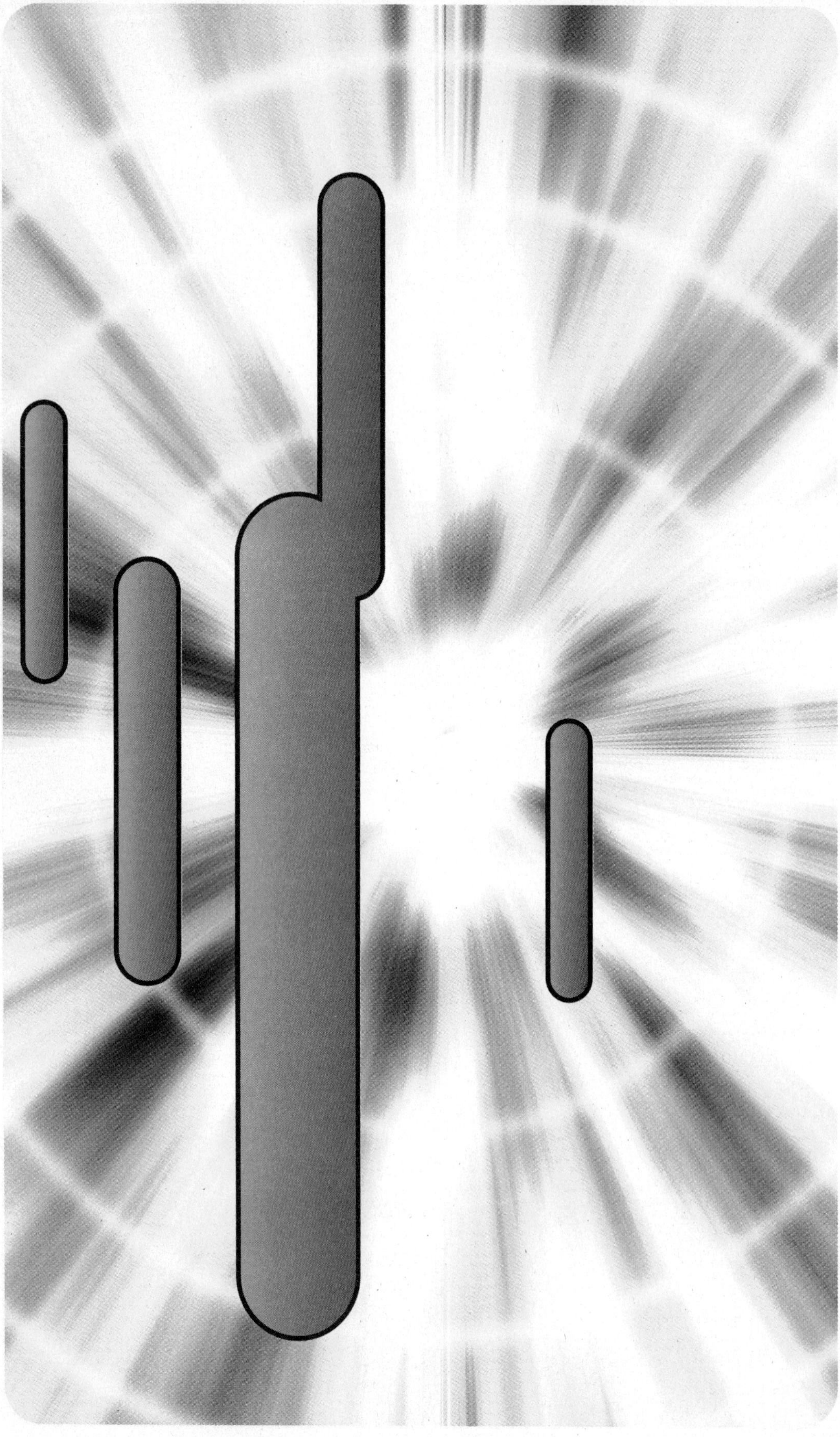

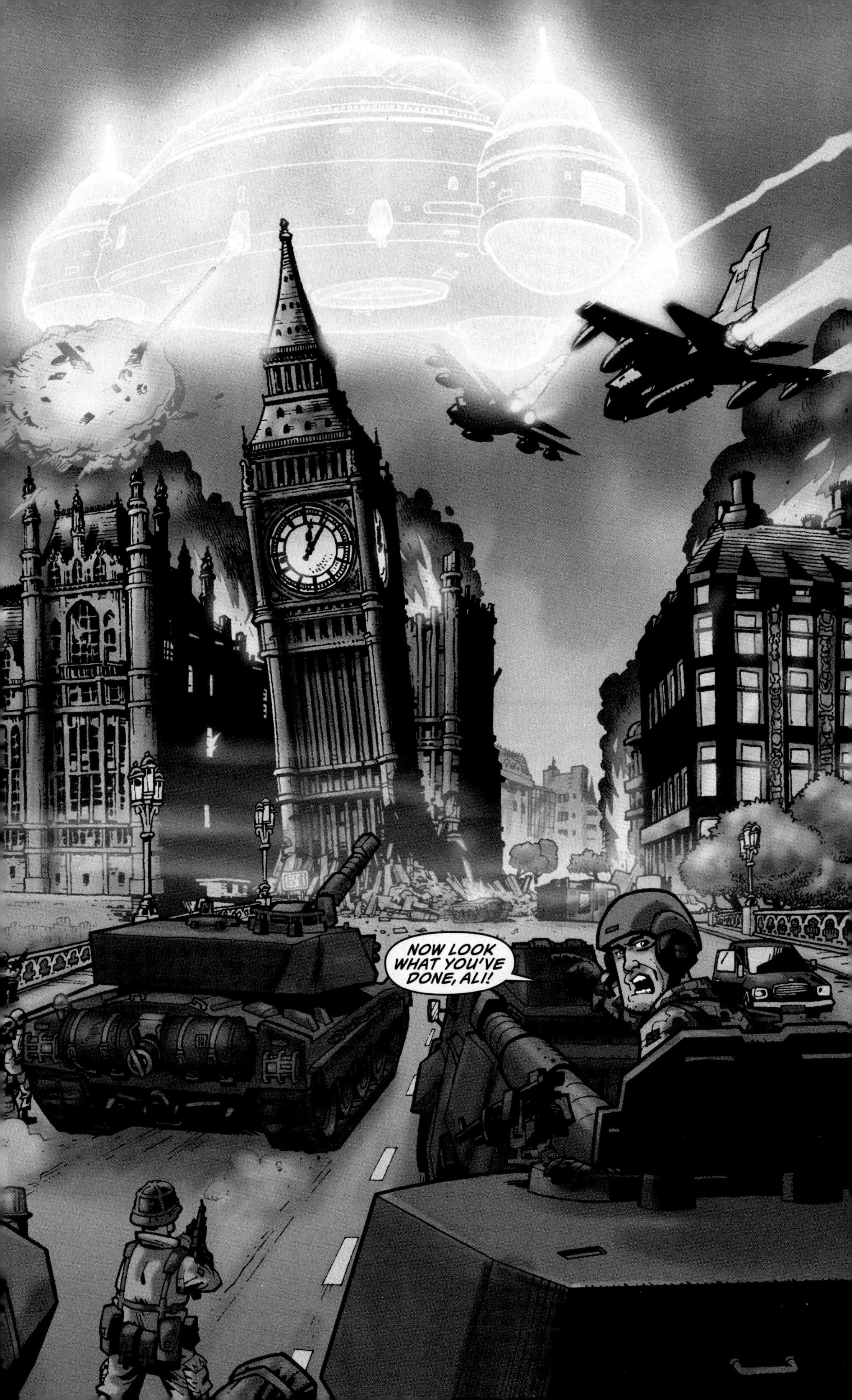
NOW LOOK WHAT YOU'VE DONE, ALI!

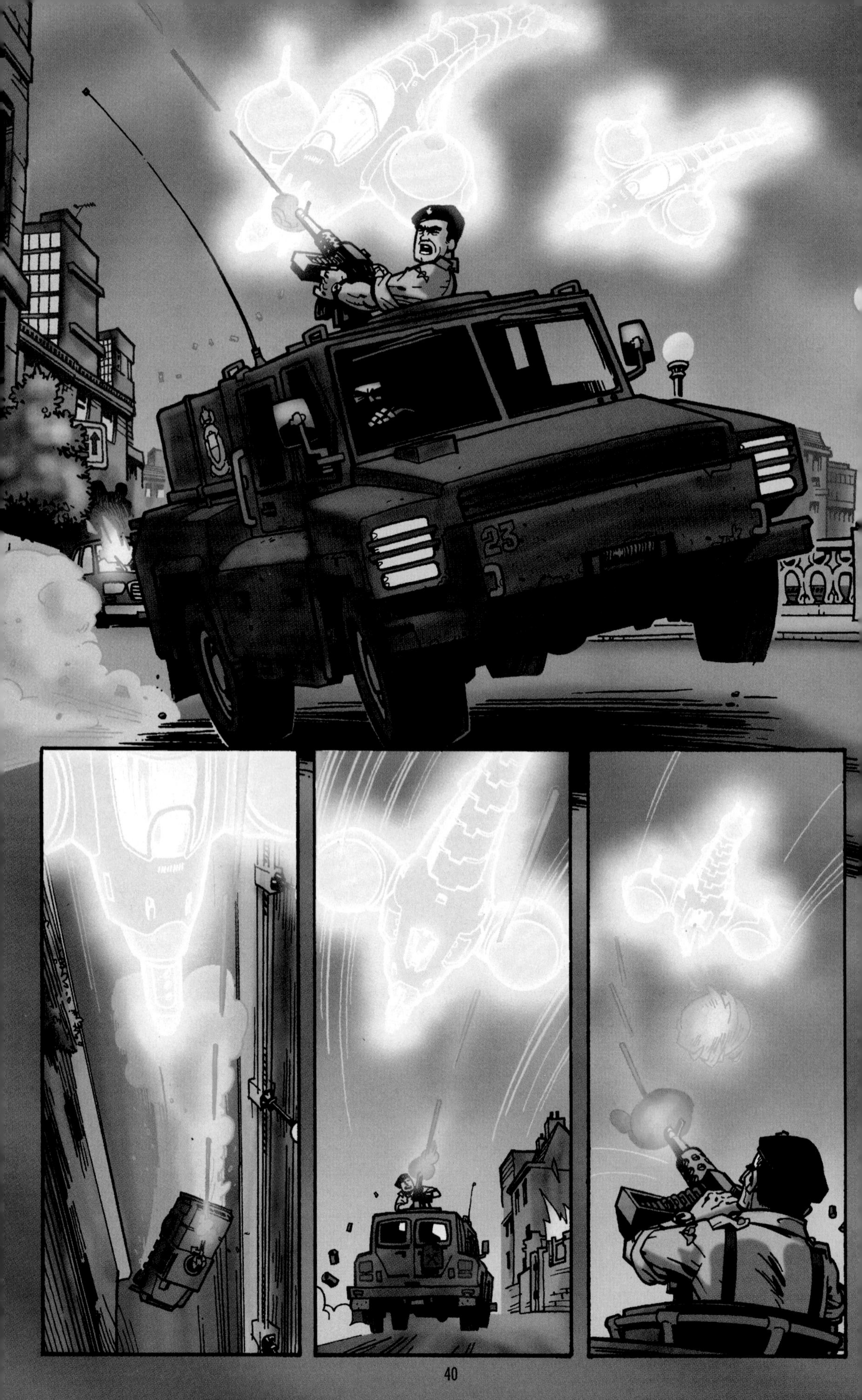
23

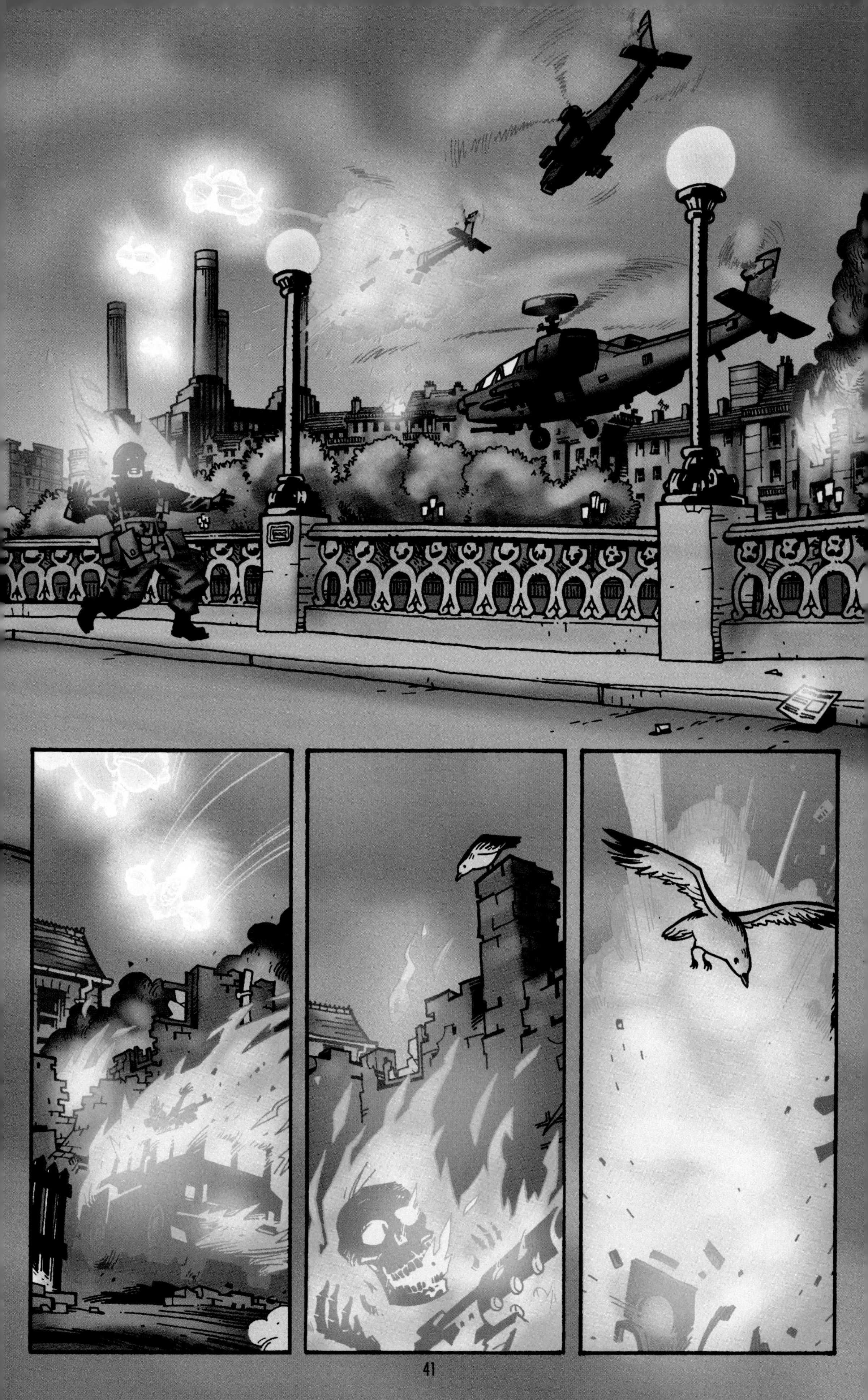

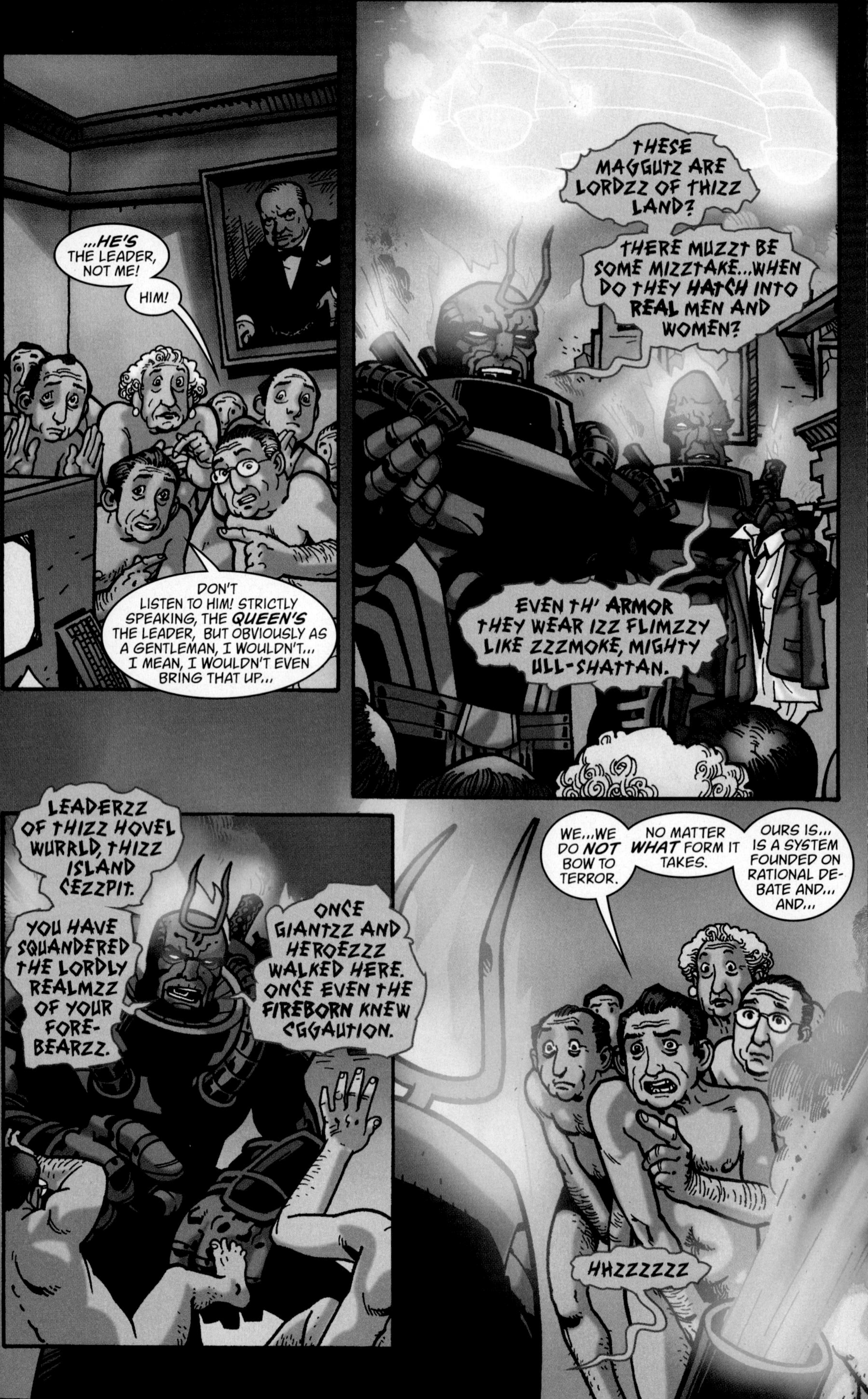
...HE'S THE LEADER, NOT ME!
HIM!
DON'T LISTEN TO HIM! STRICTLY SPEAKING, THE QUEEN'S THE LEADER, BUT OBVIOUSLY AS A GENTLEMAN, I WOULDN'T... I MEAN, I WOULDN'T EVEN BRING THAT UP...
THESE MAGGUTZ ARE LORDZZ OF THIZZ LAND?
THERE MUZZT BE SOME MIZZTAKE...WHEN DO THEY HATCH INTO REAL MEN AND WOMEN?
EVEN TH' ARMOR THEY WEAR IZZ FLIMZZY LIKE ZZZMOKE, MIGHTY ULL-SHATTAN.
LEADERZZ OF THIZZ HOVEL WURRLD, THIZZ ISLAND CEZZPIT.
YOU HAVE SQUANDERED THE LORDLY REALMZZ OF YOUR FORE-BEARZZ.
ONCE GIANTZZ AND HEROEZZZ WALKED HERE. ONCE EVEN THE FIREBORN KNEW CGGAUTION.
WE...WE DO NOT BOW TO TERROR.
NO MATTER WHAT FORM IT TAKES.
OURS IS... IS A SYSTEM FOUNDED ON RATIONAL DE-BATE AND... AND...
HHZZZZZZ

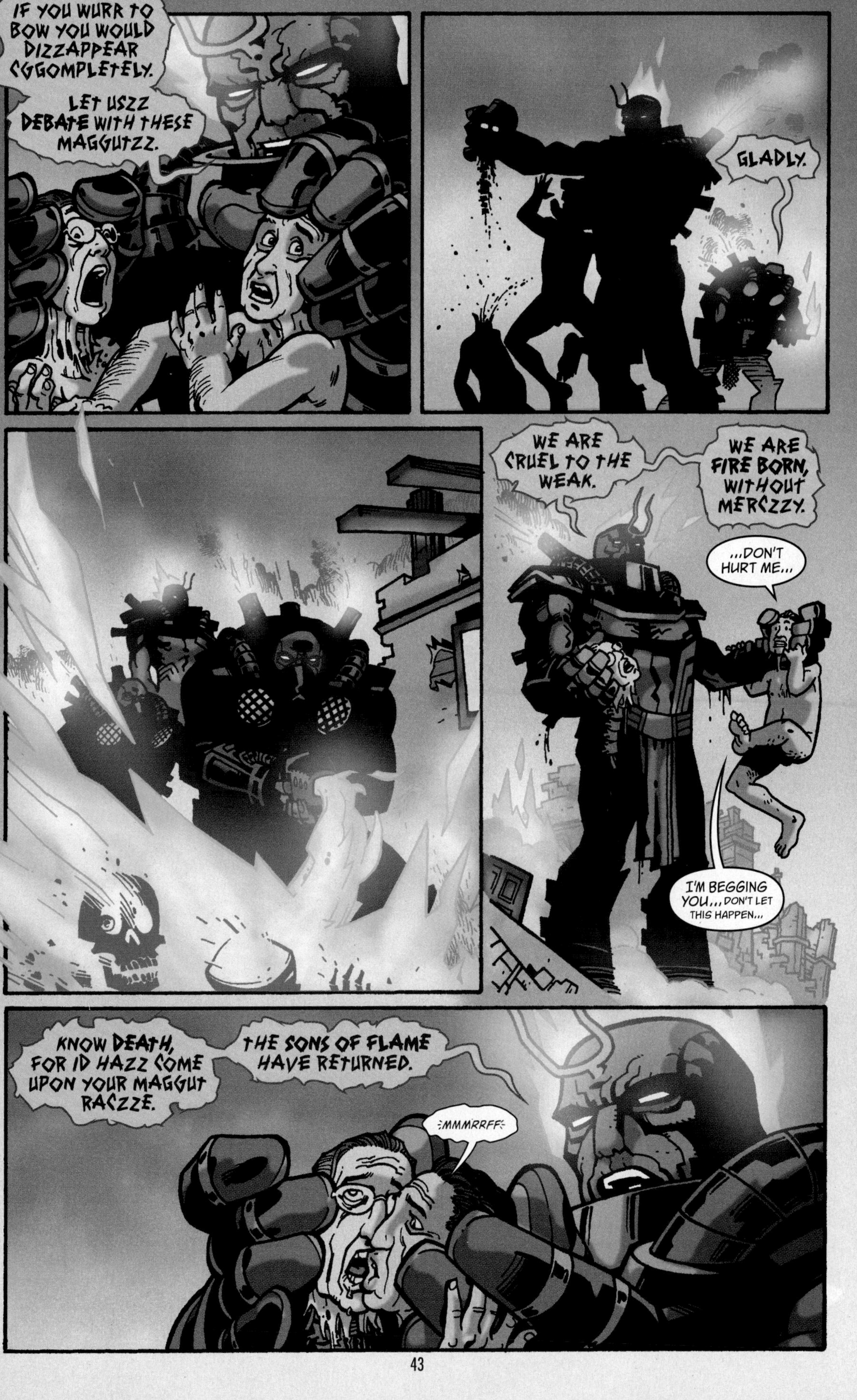
IF YOU WURR TO BOW YOU WOULD DIZZAPPEAR CGGOMPLETELY.
LET USZZ DEBATE WITH THESE MAGGUTZZ.
GLADLY.
WE ARE CRUEL TO THE WEAK.
WE ARE FIRE BORN, WITHOUT MERCZZY.
...DON'T HURT ME...
I'M BEGGING YOU... DON'T LET THIS HAPPEN...
KNOW DEATH, FOR ID HAZZ COME UPON YOUR MAGGUT RACZZE.
THE SONS OF FLAME HAVE RETURNED.
MMMRRFF

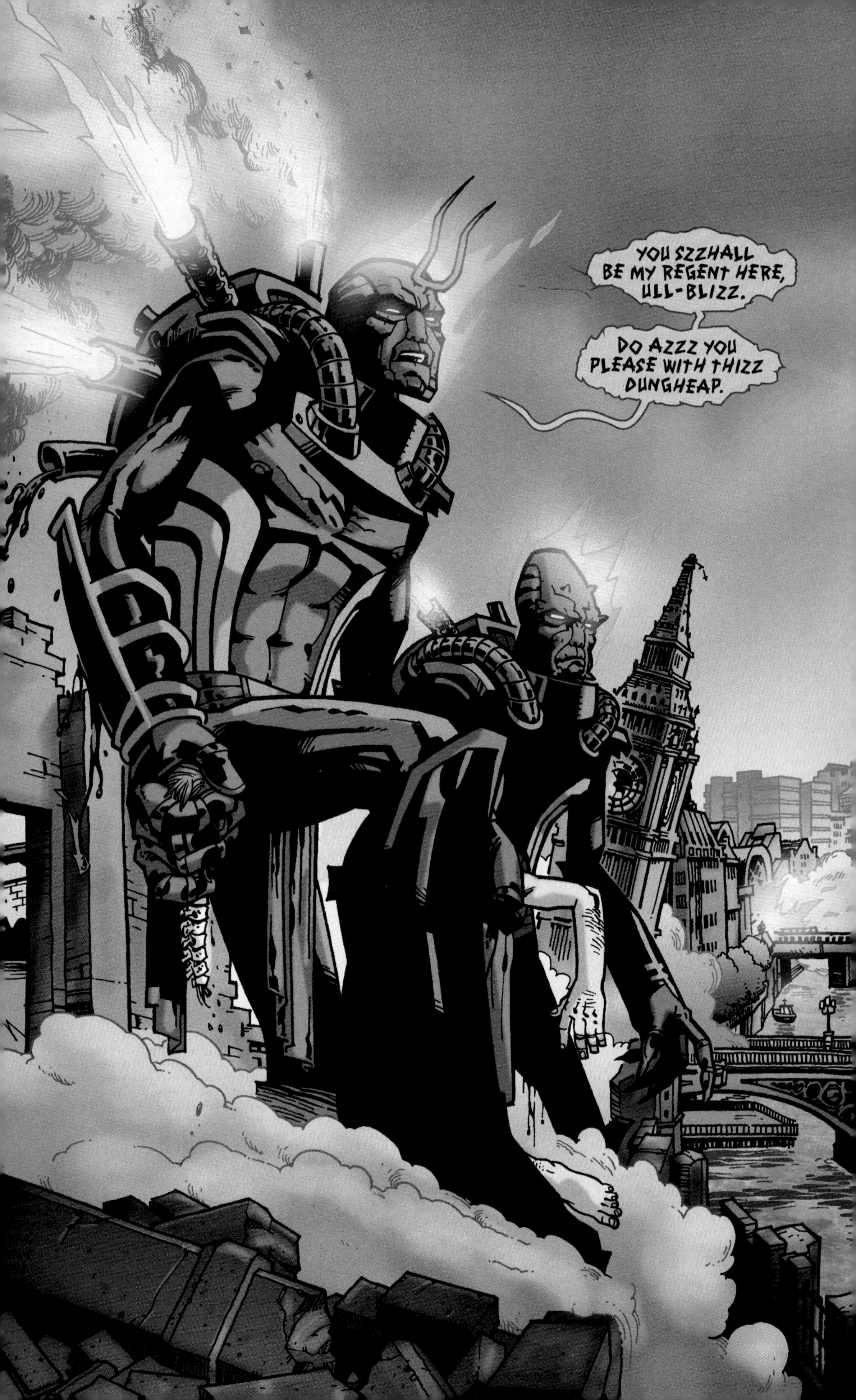
YOU SZZHALL BE MY REGENT HERE, ULL-BLIZZ.
DO AZZZ YOU PLEASE WITH THIZZ DUNGHEAP.

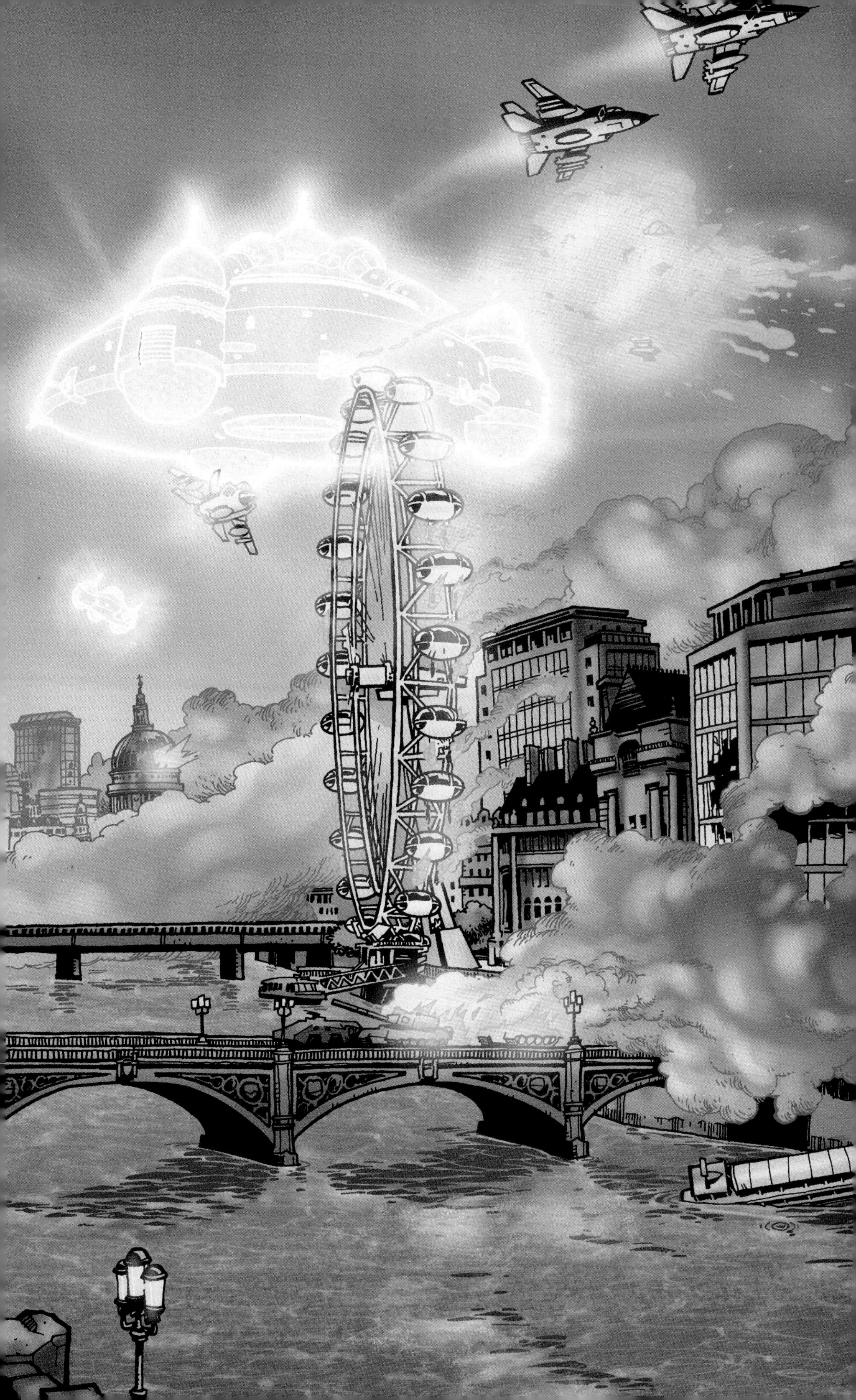

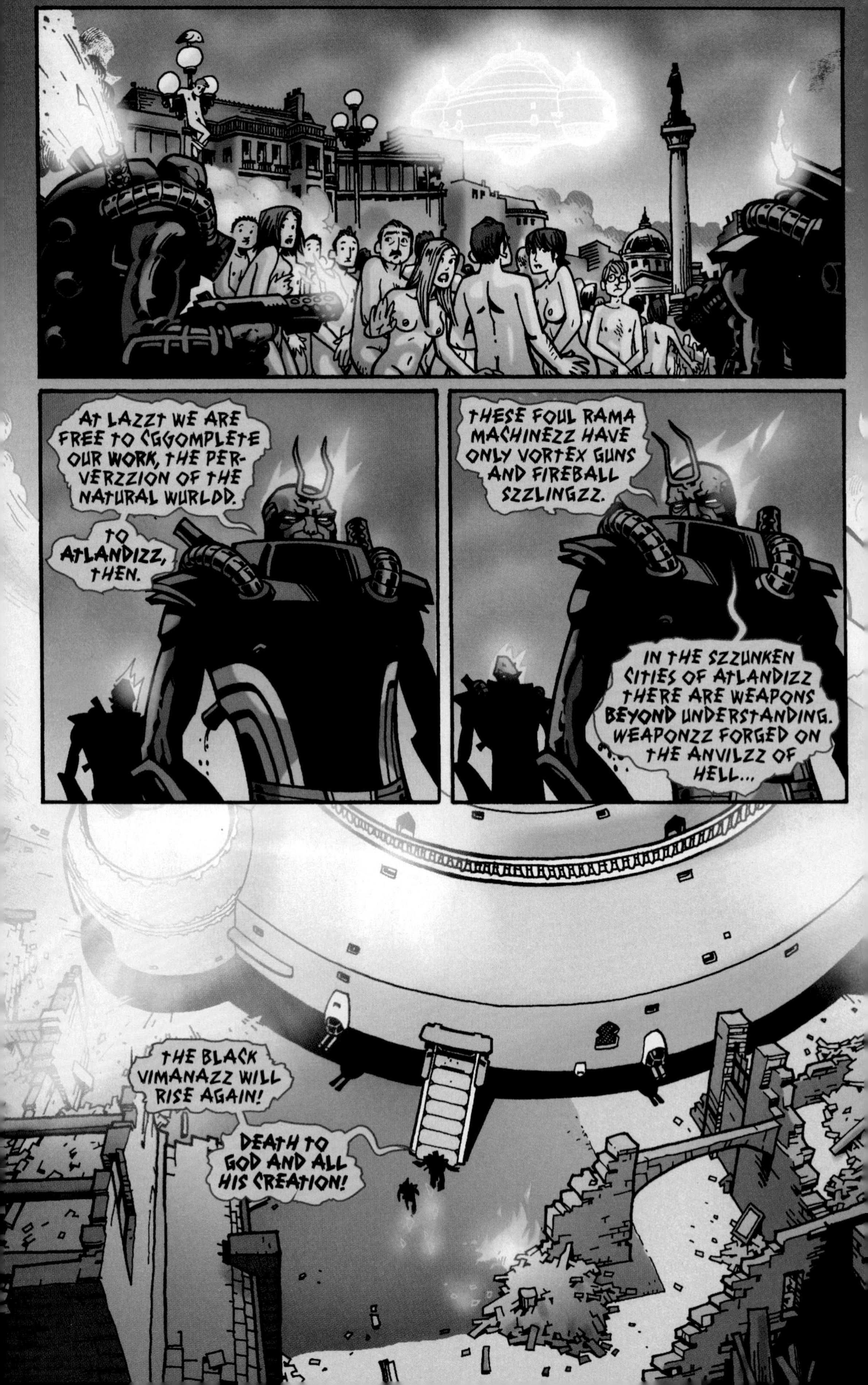
AT LAZZT WE ARE FREE TO CGGOMPLETE OUR WORK, THE PER-VERZZION OF THE NATURAL WURLDD.
TO ATLANDIZZ, THEN.
THESE FOUL RAMA MACHINEZZ HAVE ONLY VORTEX GUNS AND FIREBALL SZZLINGZZ.
IN THE SZZUNKEN CITIES OF ATLANDIZZ THERE ARE WEAPONS BEYOND UNDERSTANDING. WEAPONZZ FORGED ON THE ANVILZZ OF HELL...
THE BLACK VIMANAZZ WILL RISE AGAIN!
DEATH TO GOD AND ALL HIS CREATION!

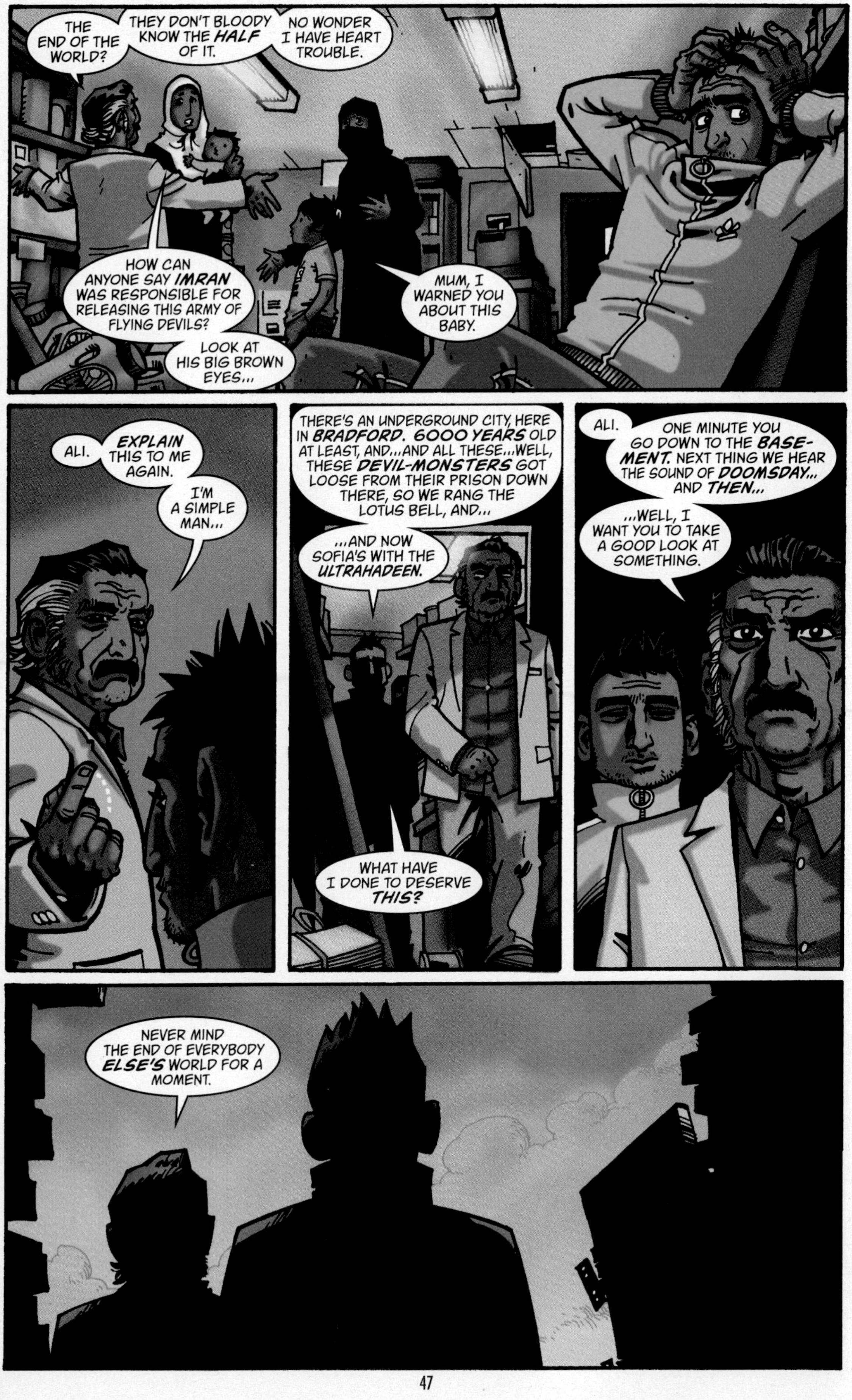
THE END OF THE WORLD?
THEY DON'T BLOODY KNOW THE HALF OF IT.
NO WONDER I HAVE HEART TROUBLE.
HOW CAN ANYONE SAY IMRAN WAS RESPONSIBLE FOR RELEASING THIS ARMY OF FLYING DEVILS?
LOOK AT HIS BIG BROWN EYES...
MUM, I WARNED YOU ABOUT THIS BABY.
ALI.
EXPLAIN THIS TO ME AGAIN.
I'M A SIMPLE MAN...
THERE'S AN UNDERGROUND CITY, HERE IN BRADFORD. 6000 YEARS OLD AT LEAST, AND...AND ALL THESE...WELL, THESE DEVIL-MONSTERS GOT LOOSE FROM THEIR PRISON DOWN THERE, SO WE RANG THE LOTUS BELL, AND...
...AND NOW SOFIA'S WITH THE ULTRAHADEEN.
WHAT HAVE I DONE TO DESERVE THIS?
ALI.
ONE MINUTE YOU GO DOWN TO THE BASE-MENT. NEXT THING WE HEAR THE SOUND OF DOOMSDAY... AND THEN...
...WELL, I WANT YOU TO TAKE A GOOD LOOK AT SOMETHING.
NEVER MIND THE END OF EVERYBODY ELSE'S WORLD FOR A MOMENT.

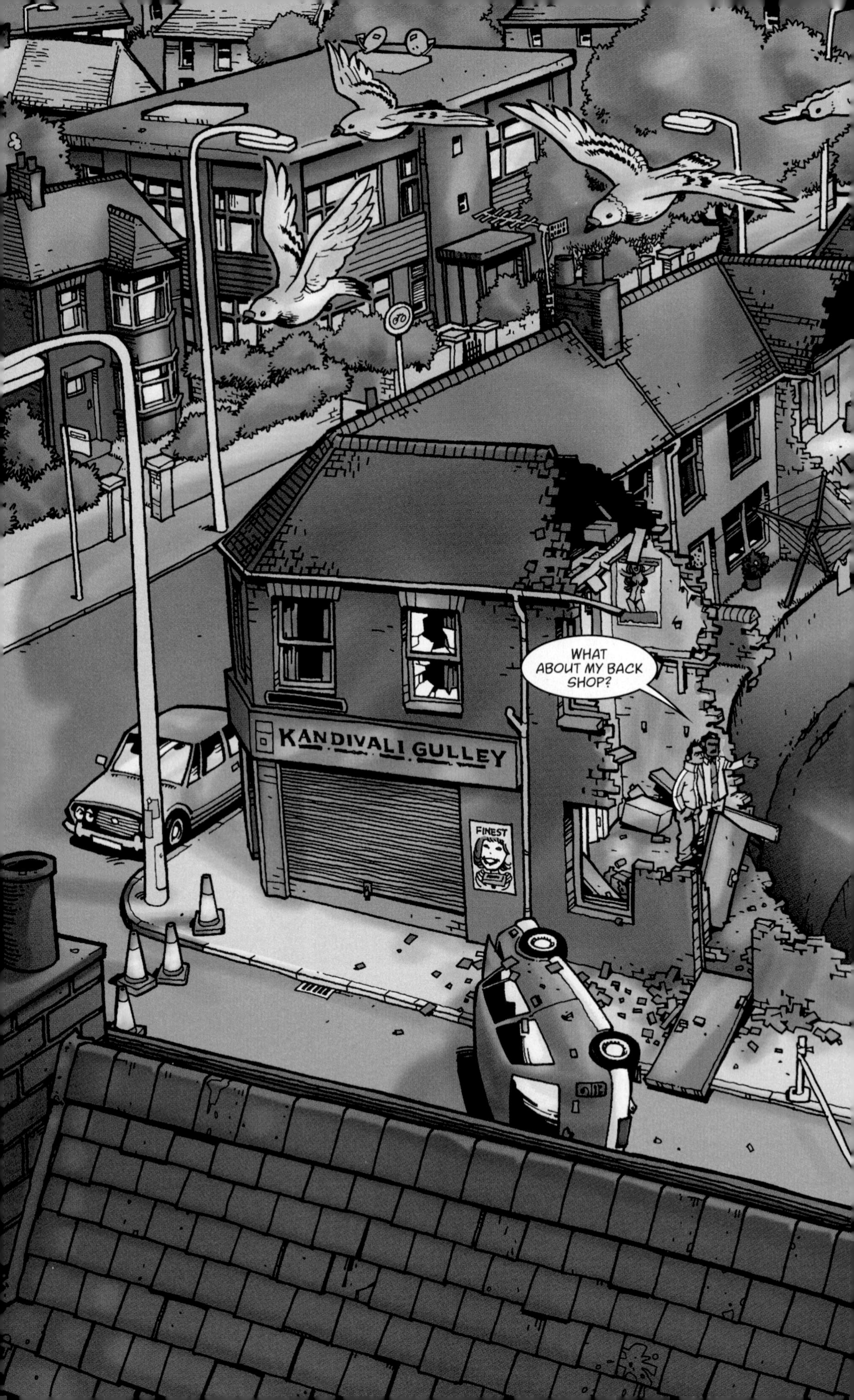
KANDIVALI GULLEY
FINEST
WHAT ABOUT MY BACK SHOP?

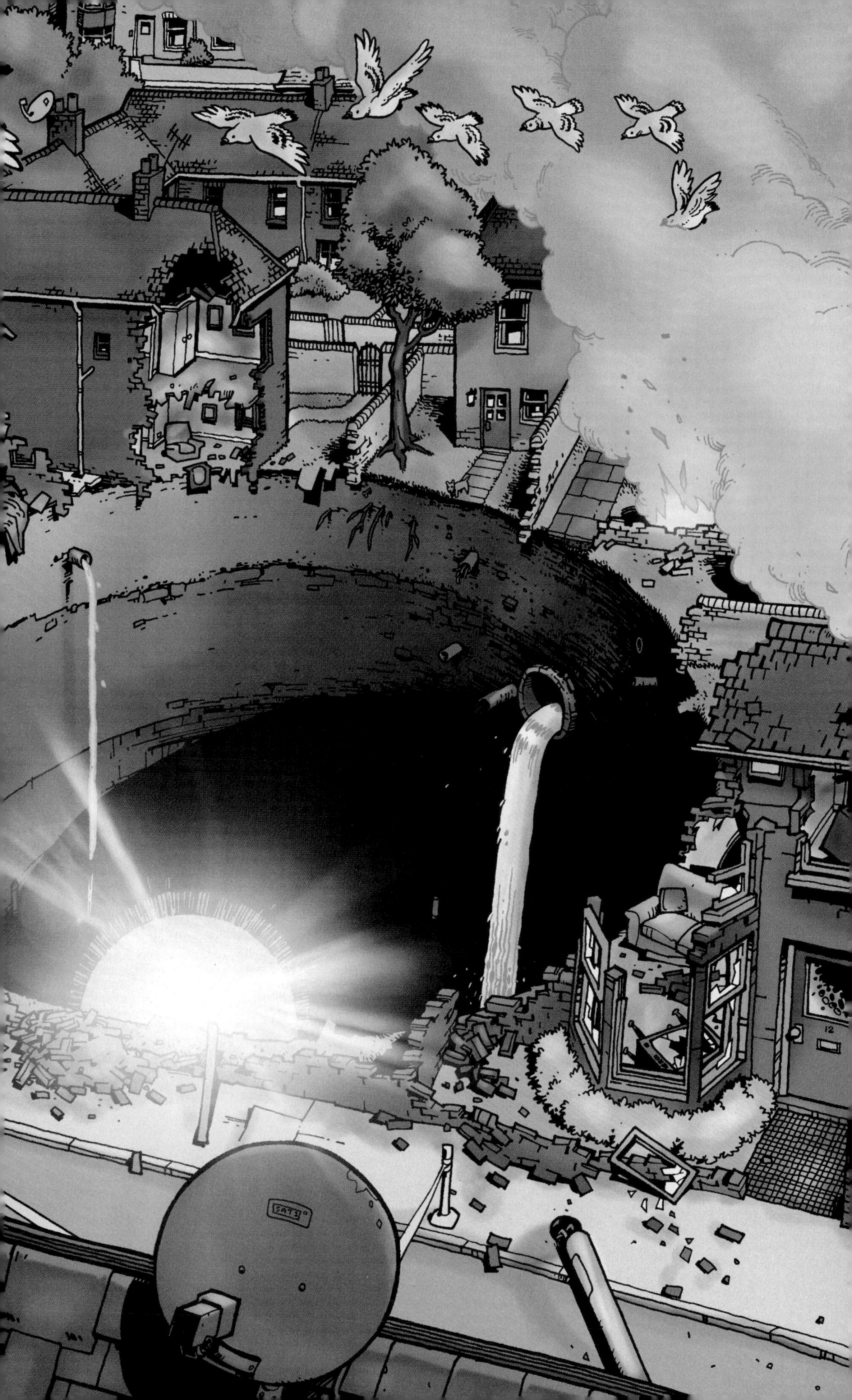
12

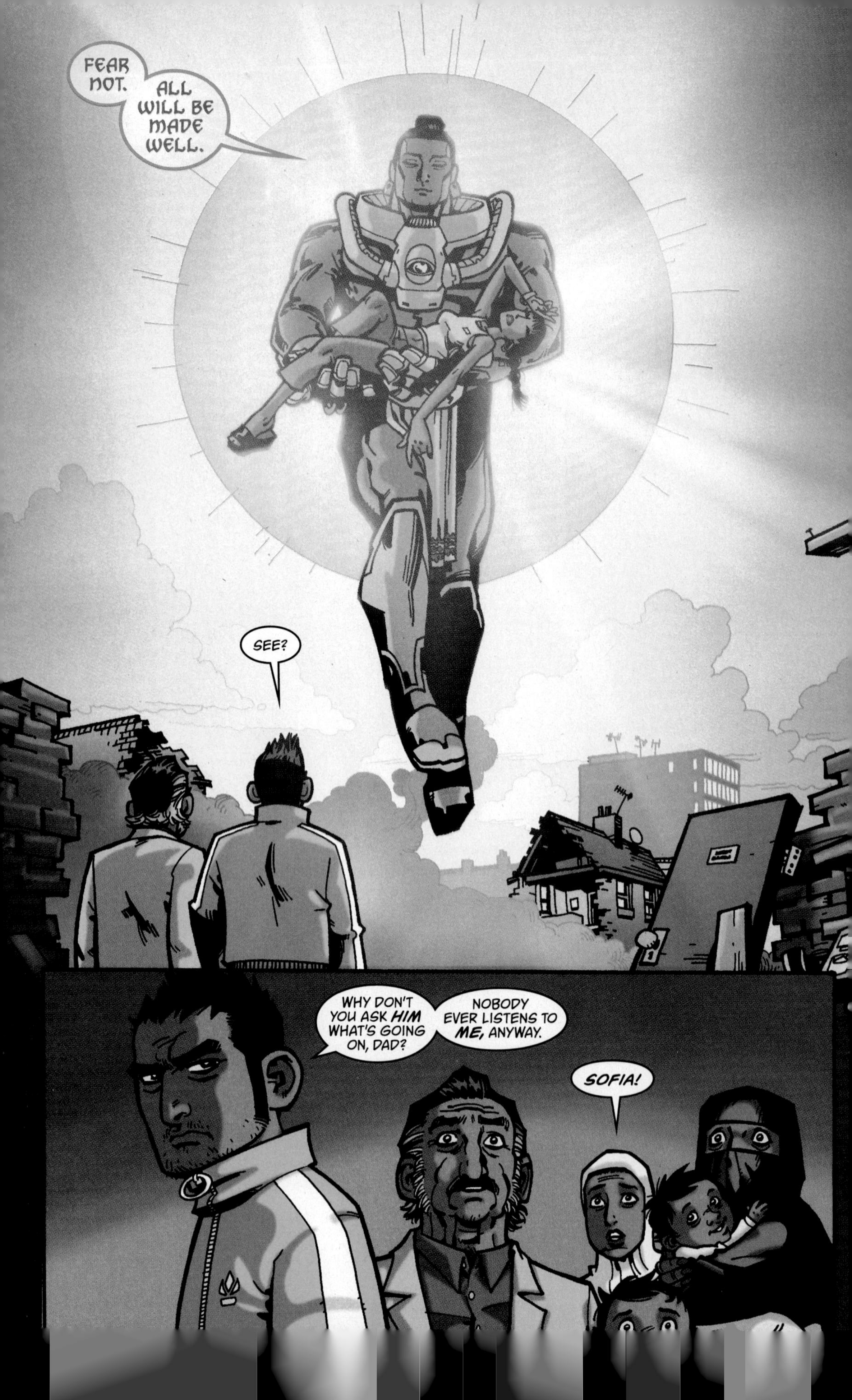
FEAR NOT.
ALL WILL BE MADE WELL.
SEE?
WHY DON'T YOU ASK HIM WHAT'S GOING ON, DAD?
NOBODY EVER LISTENS TO ME, ANYWAY.
SOFIA!

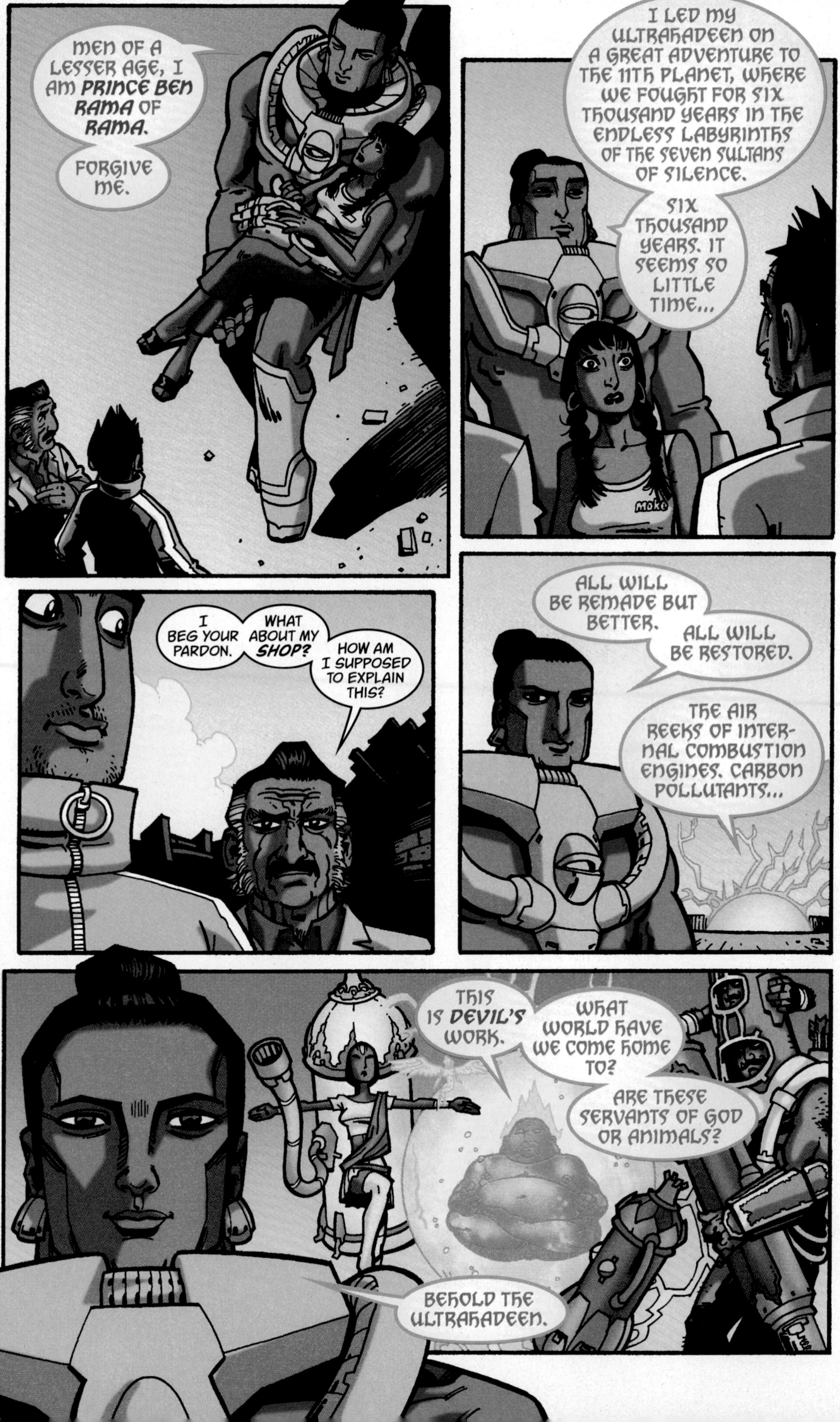
MEN OF A LESSER AGE, I AM PRINCE BEN RAMA OF RAMA.
FORGIVE ME.
I LED MY ULTRAHADEEN ON A GREAT ADVENTURE TO THE 11TH PLANET, WHERE WE FOUGHT FOR SIX THOUSAND YEARS IN THE ENDLESS LABYRINTHS OF THE SEVEN SULTANS OF SILENCE.
SIX THOUSAND YEARS. IT SEEMS SO LITTLE TIME...
MOKE
I BEG YOUR PARDON.
WHAT ABOUT MY SHOP?
HOW AM I SUPPOSED TO EXPLAIN THIS?
ALL WILL BE REMADE BUT BETTER.
ALL WILL BE RESTORED.
THE AIR REEKS OF INTERNAL COMBUSTION ENGINES. CARBON POLLUTANTS...
THIS IS DEVIL'S WORK.
WHAT WORLD HAVE WE COME HOME TO?
ARE THESE SERVANTS OF GOD OR ANIMALS?
BEHOLD THE ULTRAHADEEN.

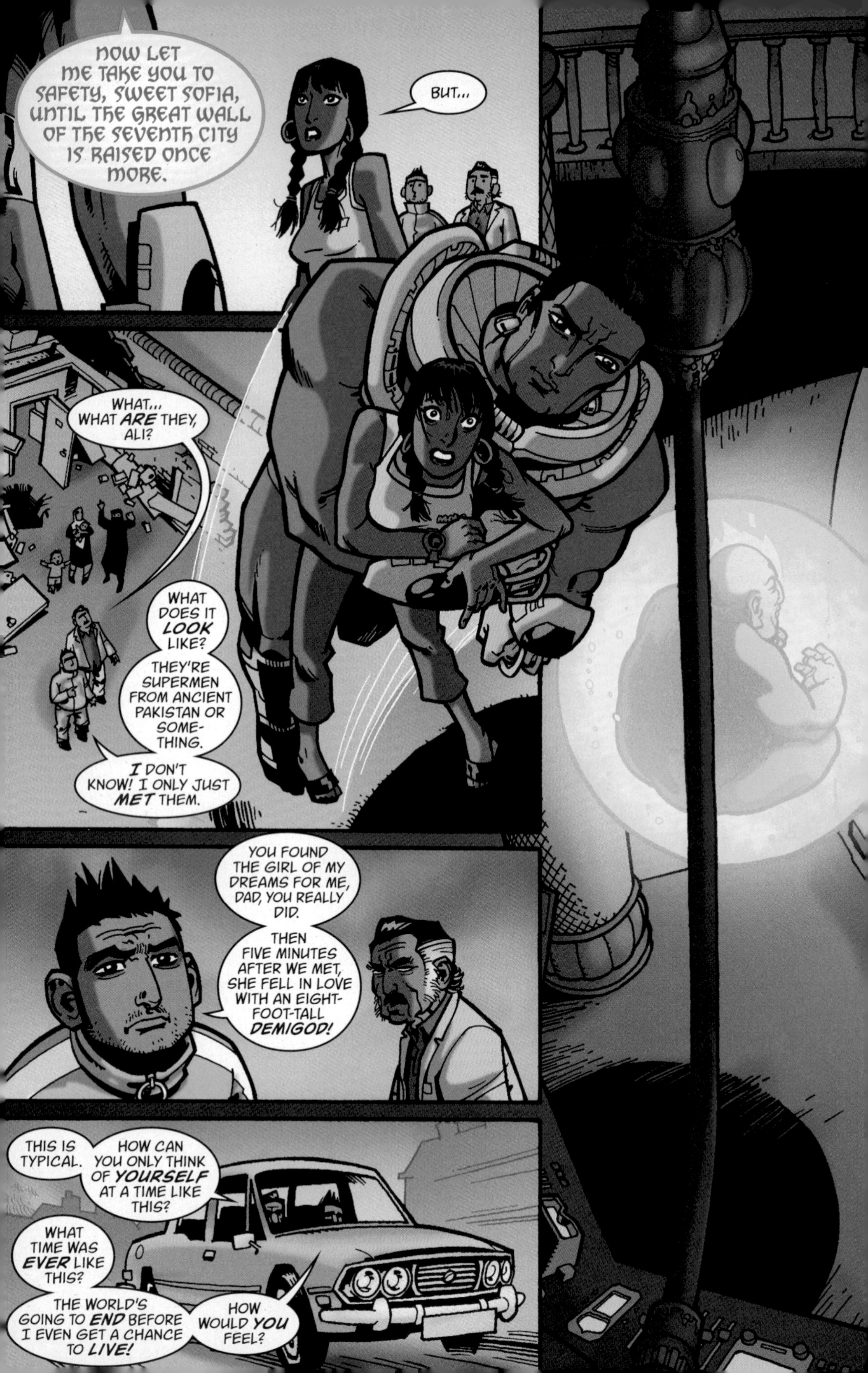
NOW LET ME TAKE YOU TO SAFETY, SWEET SOFIA, UNTIL THE GREAT WALL OF THE SEVENTH CITY IS RAISED ONCE MORE.
BUT...
WHAT... WHAT ARE THEY, ALI?
WHAT DOES IT LOOK LIKE?
THEY'RE SUPERMEN FROM ANCIENT PAKISTAN OR SOME-THING.
I DON'T KNOW! I ONLY JUST MET THEM.
YOU FOUND THE GIRL OF MY DREAMS FOR ME, DAD, YOU REALLY DID.
THEN FIVE MINUTES AFTER WE MET, SHE FELL IN LOVE WITH AN EIGHT-FOOT-TALL DEMIGOD!
THIS IS TYPICAL.
HOW CAN YOU ONLY THINK OF YOURSELF AT A TIME LIKE THIS?
WHAT TIME WAS EVER LIKE THIS?
THE WORLD'S GOING TO END BEFORE I EVEN GET A CHANCE TO LIVE!
HOW WOULD YOU FEEL?

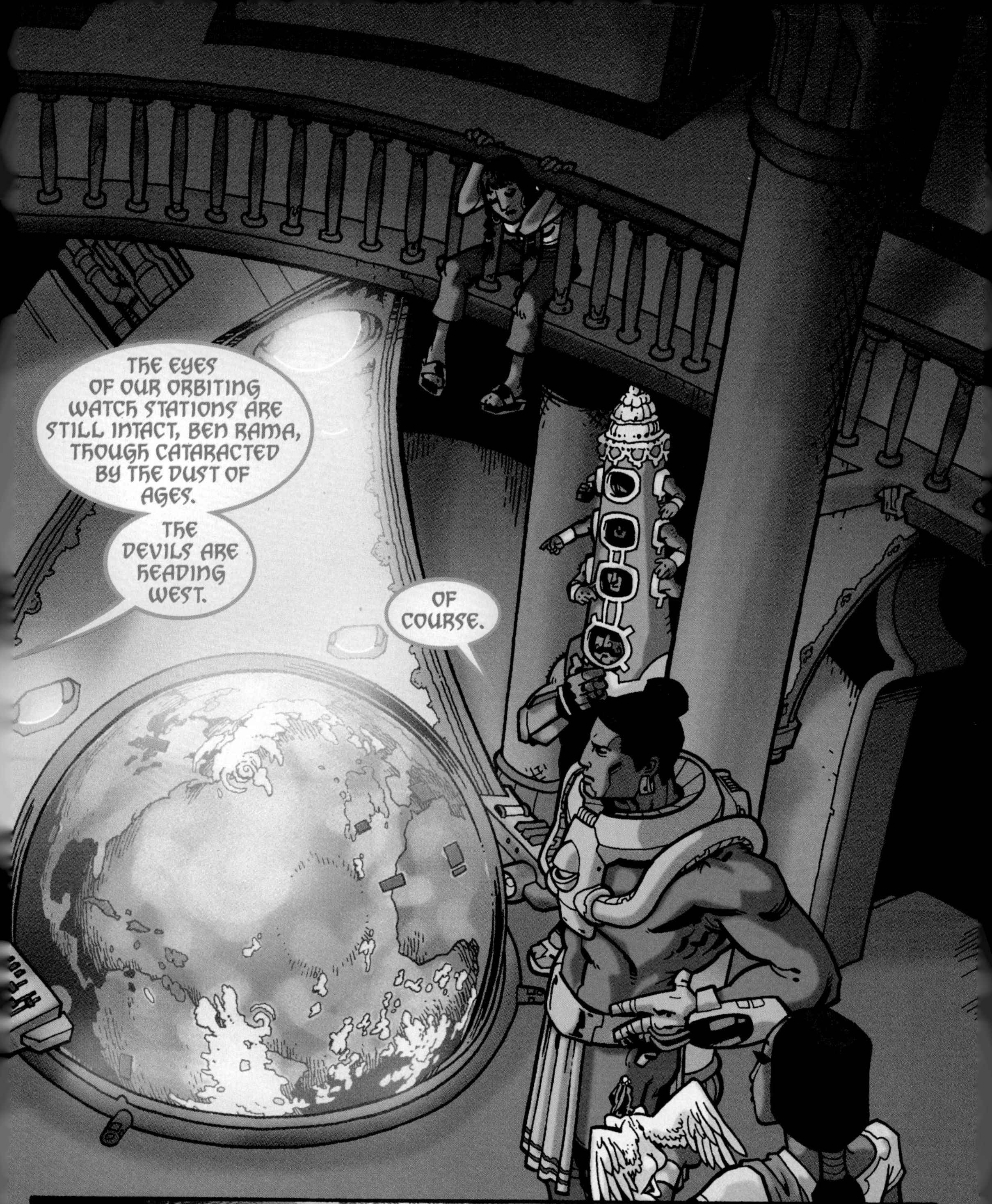
THE EYES OF OUR ORBITING WATCH STATIONS ARE STILL INTACT, BEN RAMA, THOUGH CATARACTED BY THE DUST OF AGES.
THE DEVILS ARE HEADING WEST.
OF COURSE.

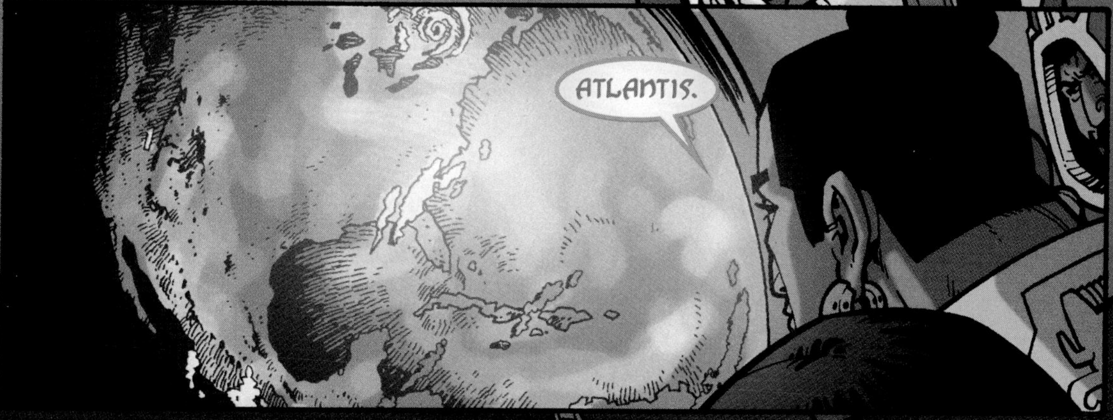
ATLANTIS.

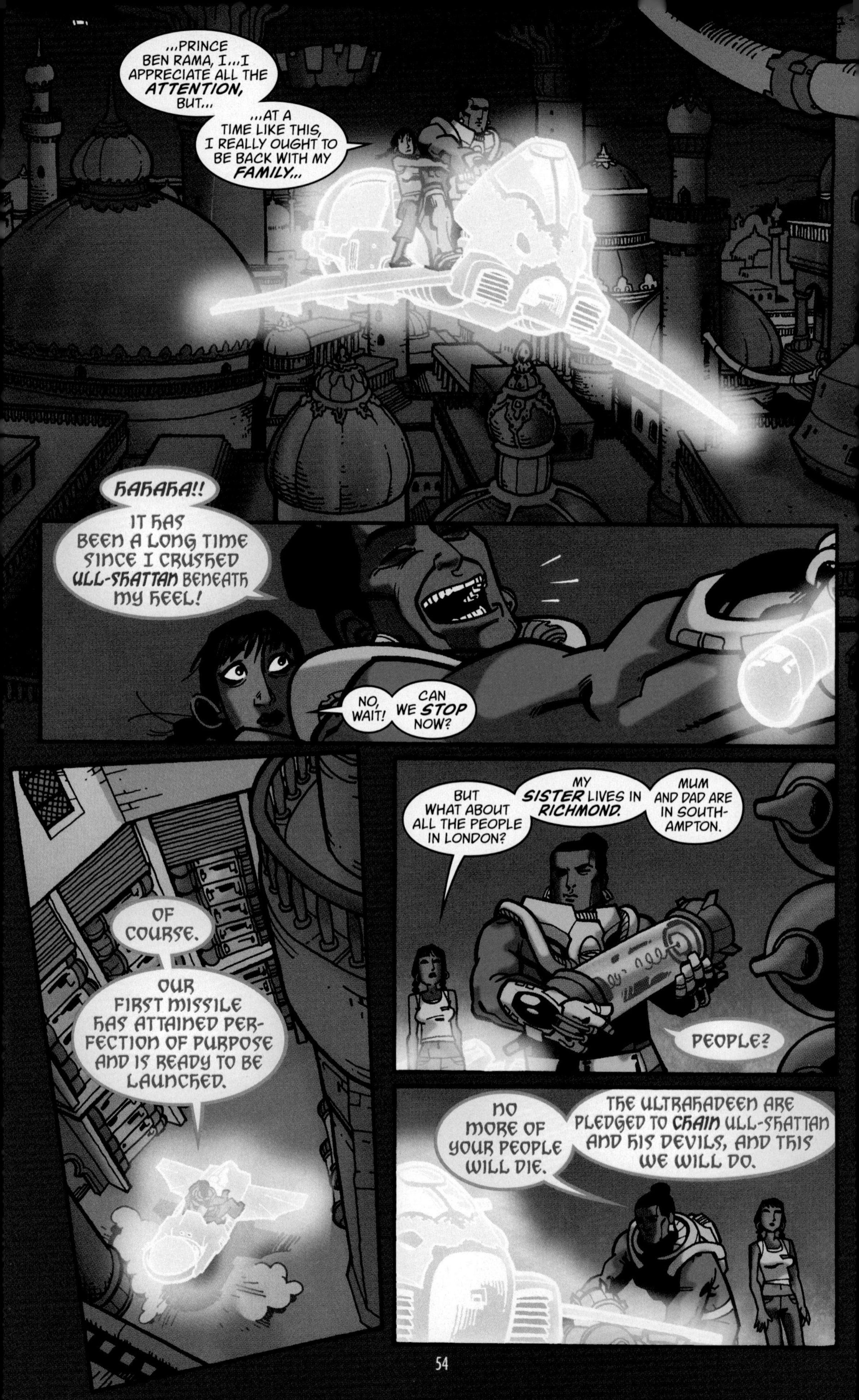

...PRINCE BEN RAMA, I...I APPRECIATE ALL THE ATTENTION, BUT...
...AT A TIME LIKE THIS, I REALLY OUGHT TO BE BACK WITH MY FAMILY...
HAHAHA!!
IT HAS BEEN A LONG TIME SINCE I CRUSHED ULL-SHATTAN BENEATH MY HEEL!
NO, WAIT!
CAN WE STOP NOW?
OF COURSE.
OUR FIRST MISSILE HAS ATTAINED PER-FECTION OF PURPOSE AND IS READY TO BE LAUNCHED.
BUT WHAT ABOUT ALL THE PEOPLE IN LONDON?
MY SISTER LIVES IN RICHMOND.
MUM AND DAD ARE IN SOUTH-AMPTON.
PEOPLE?
NO MORE OF YOUR PEOPLE WILL DIE.
THE ULTRAHADEEN ARE PLEDGED TO CHAIN ULL-SHATTAN AND HIS DEVILS, AND THIS WE WILL DO.

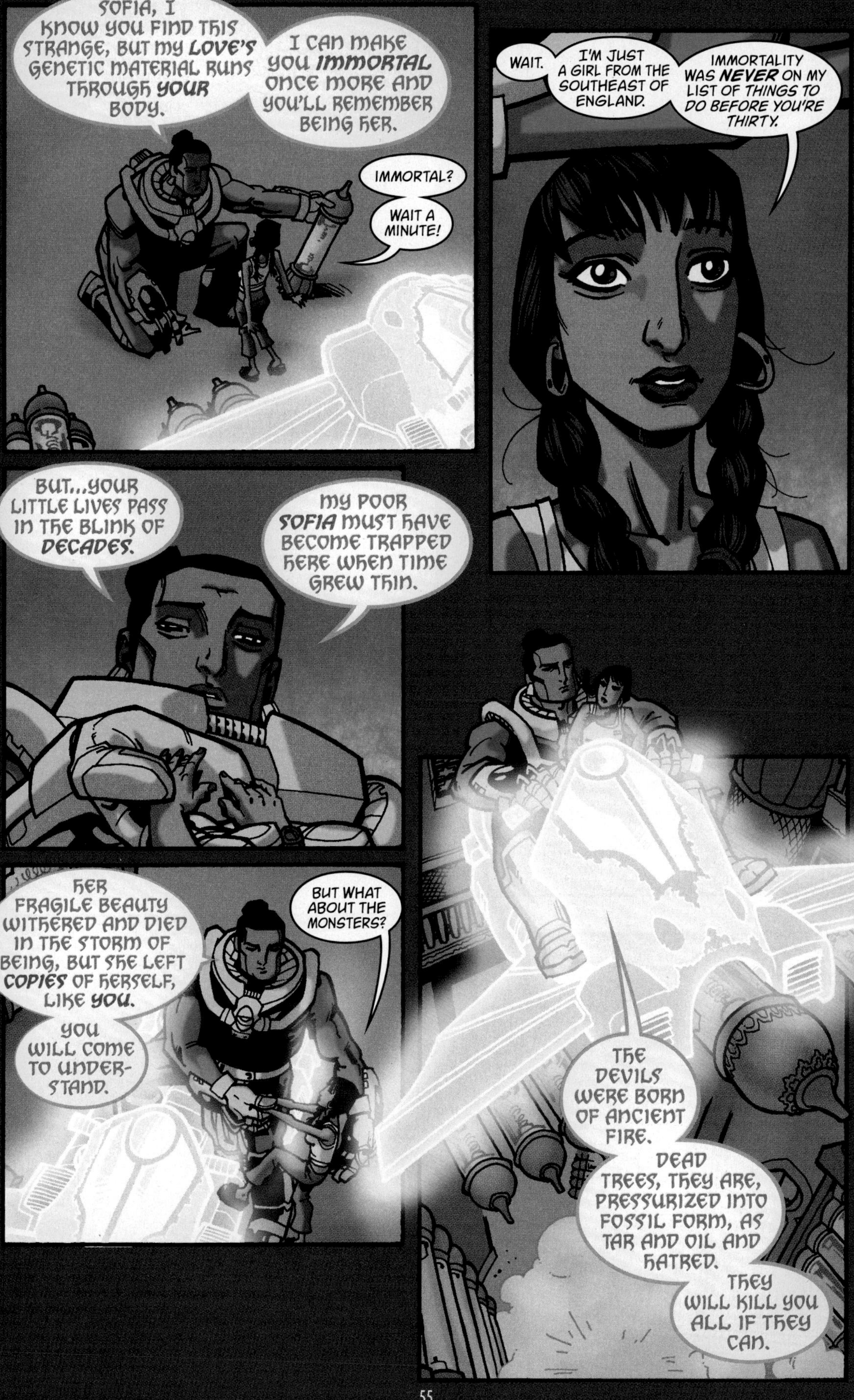

SOFIA, I KNOW YOU FIND THIS STRANGE, BUT MY LOVE'S GENETIC MATERIAL RUNS THROUGH YOUR BODY.
I CAN MAKE YOU IMMORTAL ONCE MORE AND YOU'LL REMEMBER BEING HER.
IMMORTAL?
WAIT A MINUTE!
WAIT.
I'M JUST A GIRL FROM THE SOUTHEAST OF ENGLAND.
IMMORTALITY WAS NEVER ON MY LIST OF THINGS TO DO BEFORE YOU'RE THIRTY.
BUT...YOUR LITTLE LIVES PASS IN THE BLINK OF DECADES.
MY POOR SOFIA MUST HAVE BECOME TRAPPED HERE WHEN TIME GREW THIN.
HER FRAGILE BEAUTY WITHERED AND DIED IN THE STORM OF BEING, BUT SHE LEFT COPIES OF HERSELF, LIKE YOU.
YOU WILL COME TO UNDER-STAND.
BUT WHAT ABOUT THE MONSTERS?
THE DEVILS WERE BORN OF ANCIENT FIRE.
DEAD TREES, THEY ARE, PRESSURIZED INTO FOSSIL FORM, AS TAR AND OIL AND HATRED.
THEY WILL KILL YOU ALL IF THEY CAN.

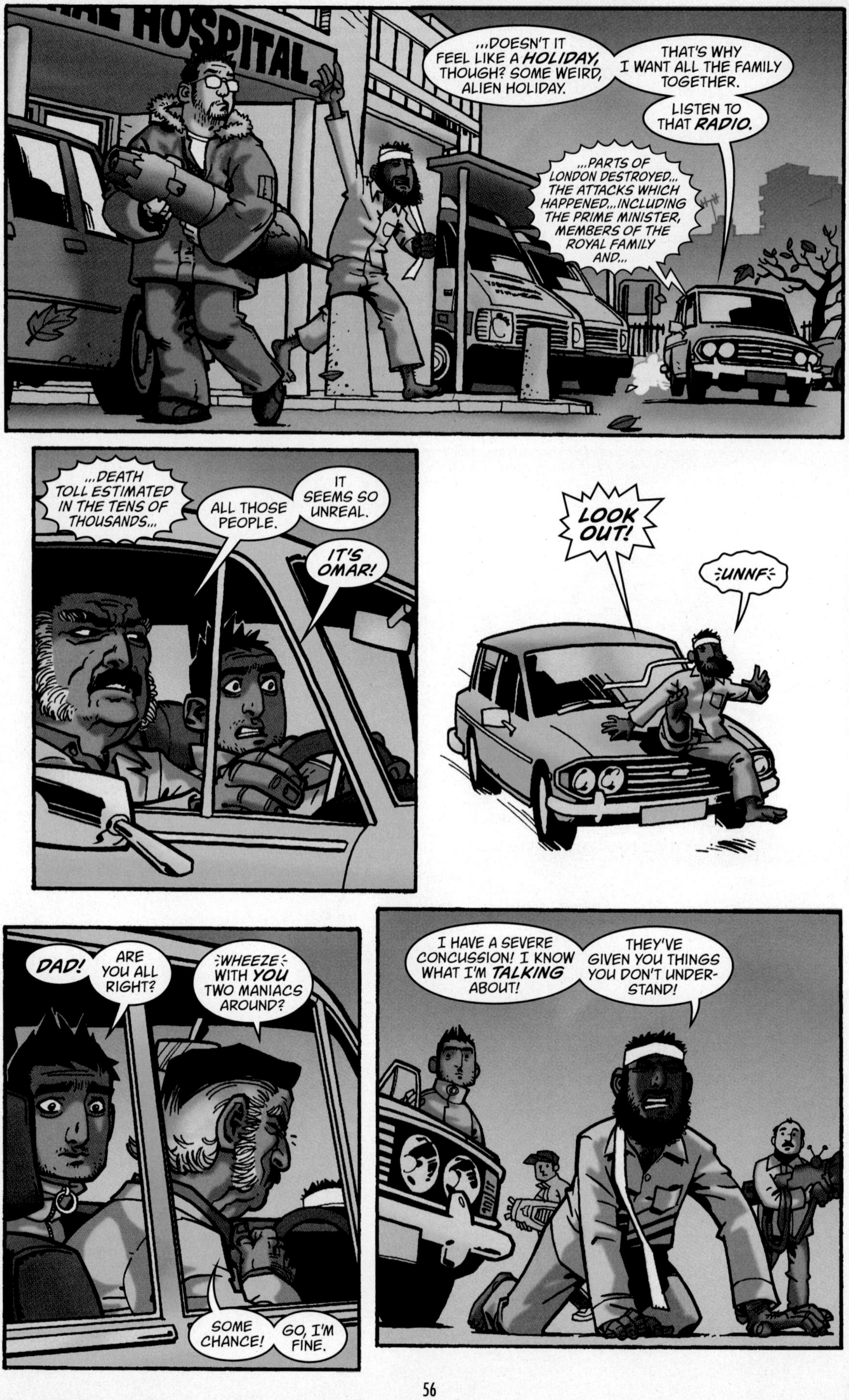
...DOESN'T IT FEEL LIKE A HOLIDAY, THOUGH? SOME WEIRD, ALIEN HOLIDAY.
THAT'S WHY I WANT ALL THE FAMILY TOGETHER.
LISTEN TO THAT RADIO.
...PARTS OF LONDON DESTROYED... THE ATTACKS WHICH HAPPENED...INCLUDING THE PRIME MINISTER, MEMBERS OF THE ROYAL FAMILY AND...
HOSPITAL
...DEATH TOLL ESTIMATED IN THE TENS OF THOUSANDS...
ALL THOSE PEOPLE.
IT SEEMS SO UNREAL.
IT'S OMAR!
LOOK OUT!
UNNF
DAD!
ARE YOU ALL RIGHT?
WHEEZE WITH YOU TWO MANIACS AROUND?
SOME CHANCE!
GO, I'M FINE.
I HAVE A SEVERE CONCUSSION! I KNOW WHAT I'M TALKING ABOUT!
THEY'VE GIVEN YOU THINGS YOU DON'T UNDER-STAND!

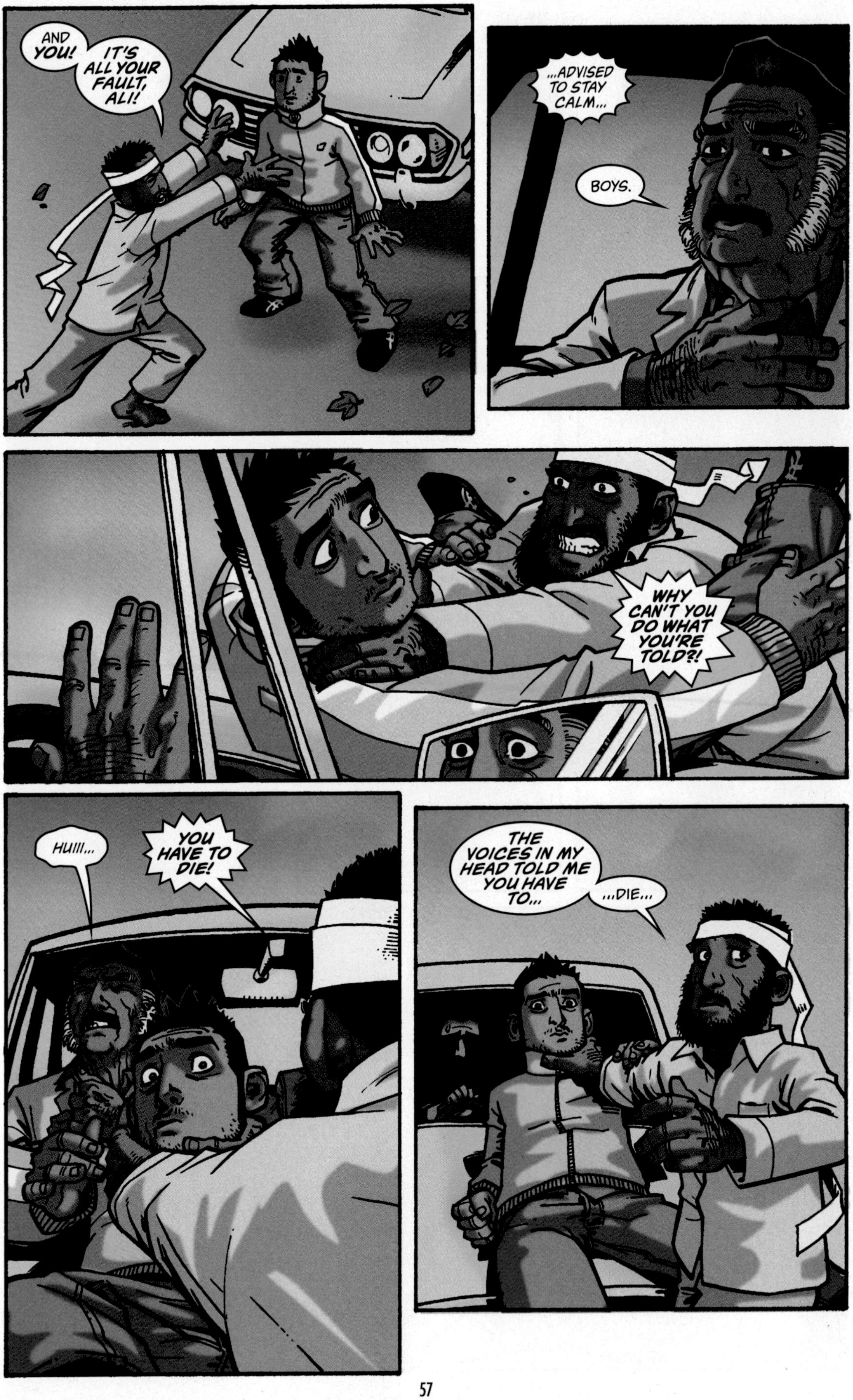
AND YOU!
IT'S ALL YOUR FAULT, ALI!
...ADVISED TO STAY CALM...
BOYS.
WHY CAN'T YOU DO WHAT YOU'RE TOLD?!
HUIII...
YOU HAVE TO DIE!
THE VOICES IN MY HEAD TOLD ME YOU HAVE TO...
...DIE...

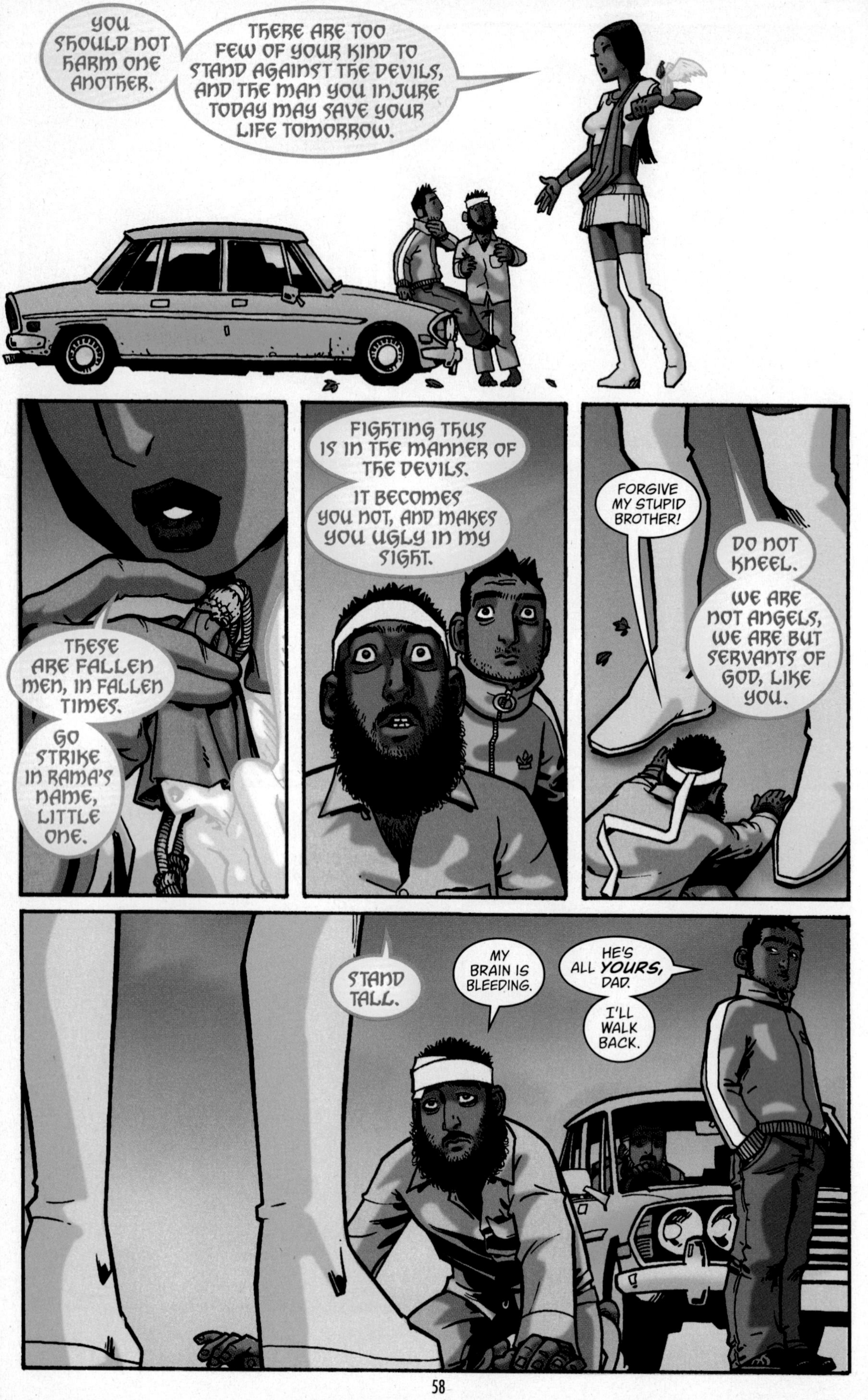
YOU SHOULD NOT HARM ONE ANOTHER.
THERE ARE TOO FEW OF YOUR KIND TO STAND AGAINST THE DEVILS, AND THE MAN YOU INJURE TODAY MAY SAVE YOUR LIFE TOMORROW.
THESE ARE FALLEN MEN, IN FALLEN TIMES.
GO STRIKE IN RAMA'S NAME, LITTLE ONE.
FIGHTING THUS IS IN THE MANNER OF THE DEVILS.
IT BECOMES YOU NOT, AND MAKES YOU UGLY IN MY SIGHT.
FORGIVE MY STUPID BROTHER!
DO NOT KNEEL.
WE ARE NOT ANGELS, WE ARE BUT SERVANTS OF GOD, LIKE YOU.
STAND TALL.
MY BRAIN IS BLEEDING.
HE'S ALL *YOURS*, DAD.
I'LL WALK BACK.

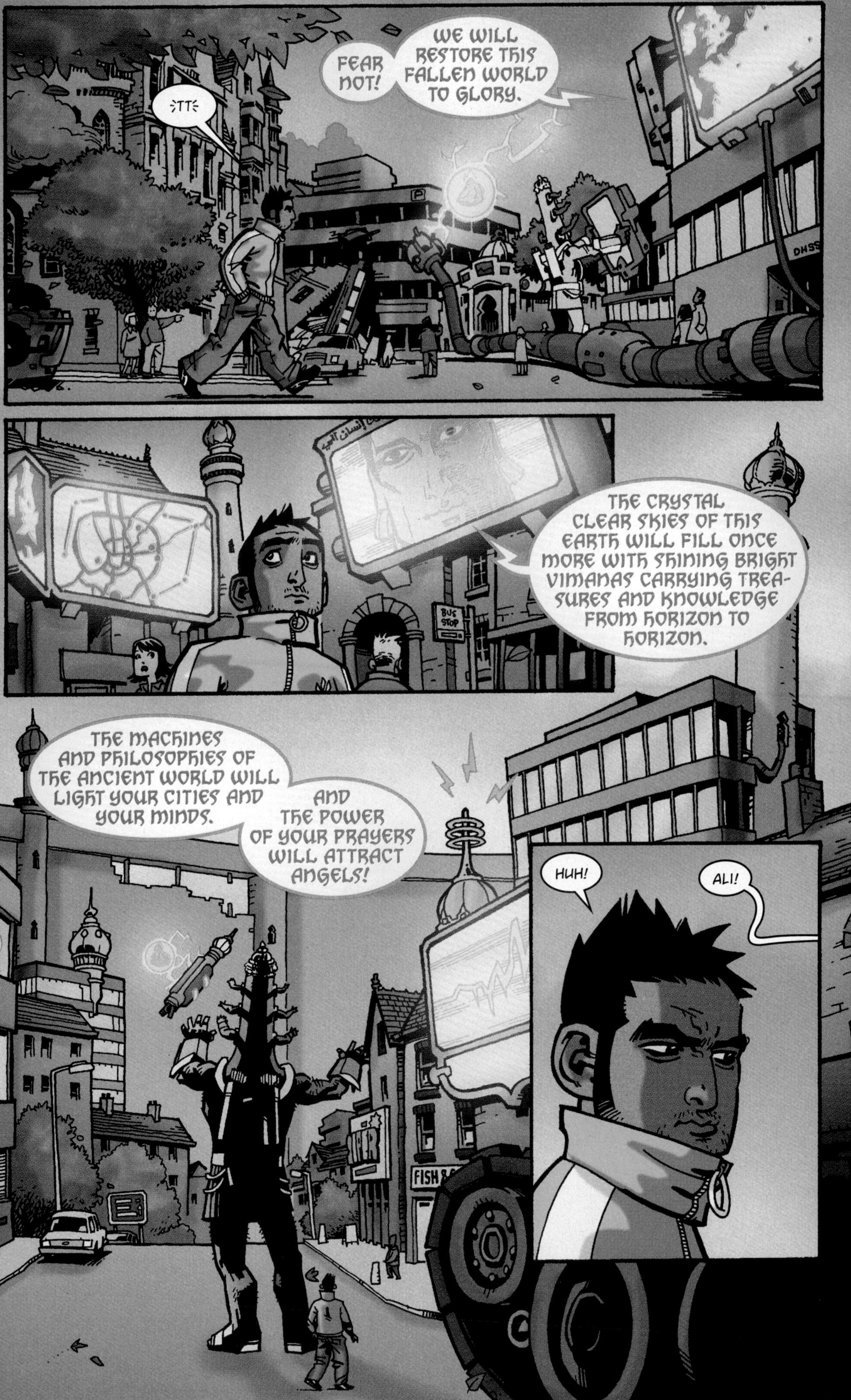

FEAR NOT!
WE WILL RESTORE THIS FALLEN WORLD TO GLORY.
:TT:
THE CRYSTAL CLEAR SKIES OF THIS EARTH WILL FILL ONCE MORE WITH SHINING BRIGHT VIMANAS CARRYING TREA-SURES AND KNOWLEDGE FROM HORIZON TO HORIZON.
BUS STOP
THE MACHINES AND PHILOSOPHIES OF THE ANCIENT WORLD WILL LIGHT YOUR CITIES AND YOUR MINDS.
AND THE POWER OF YOUR PRAYERS WILL ATTRACT ANGELS!
HUH!
ALI!

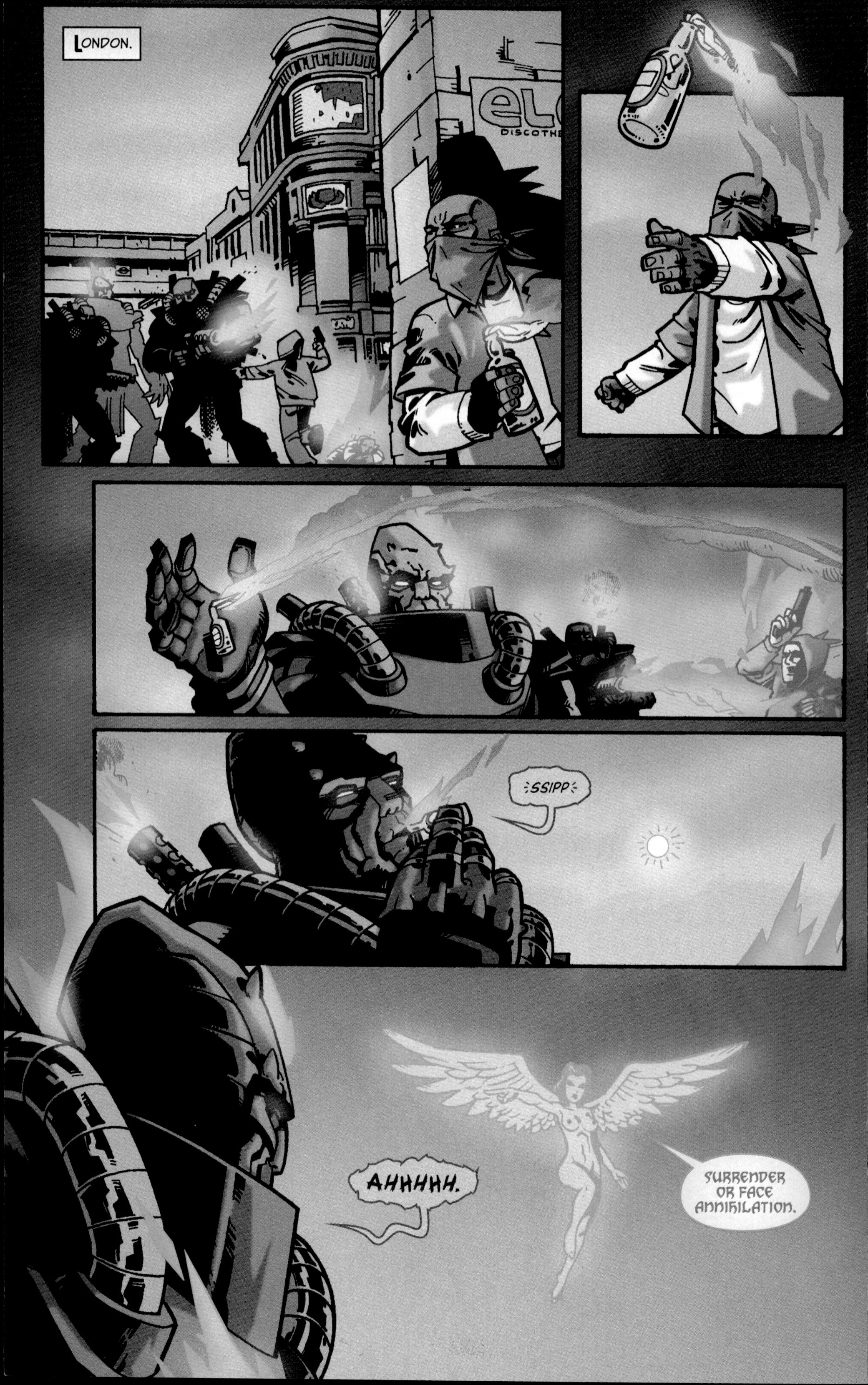
LONDON.
ELO
DISCOTHE
SSIPP
AHHHHH.
SURRENDER OR FACE ANNIHILATION.

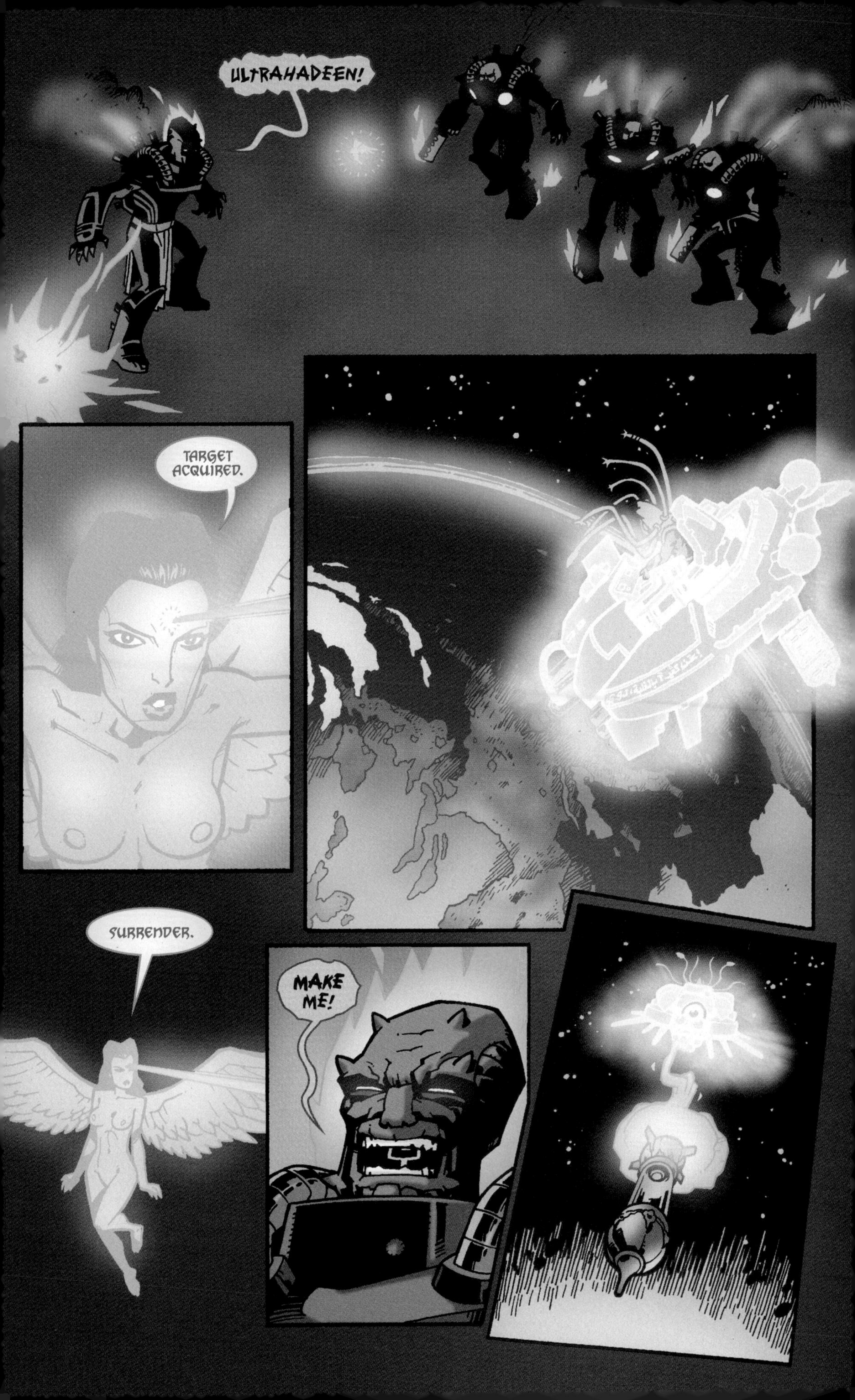
ULTRAHADEEN!
TARGET ACQUIRED.
SURRENDER.
MAKE ME!

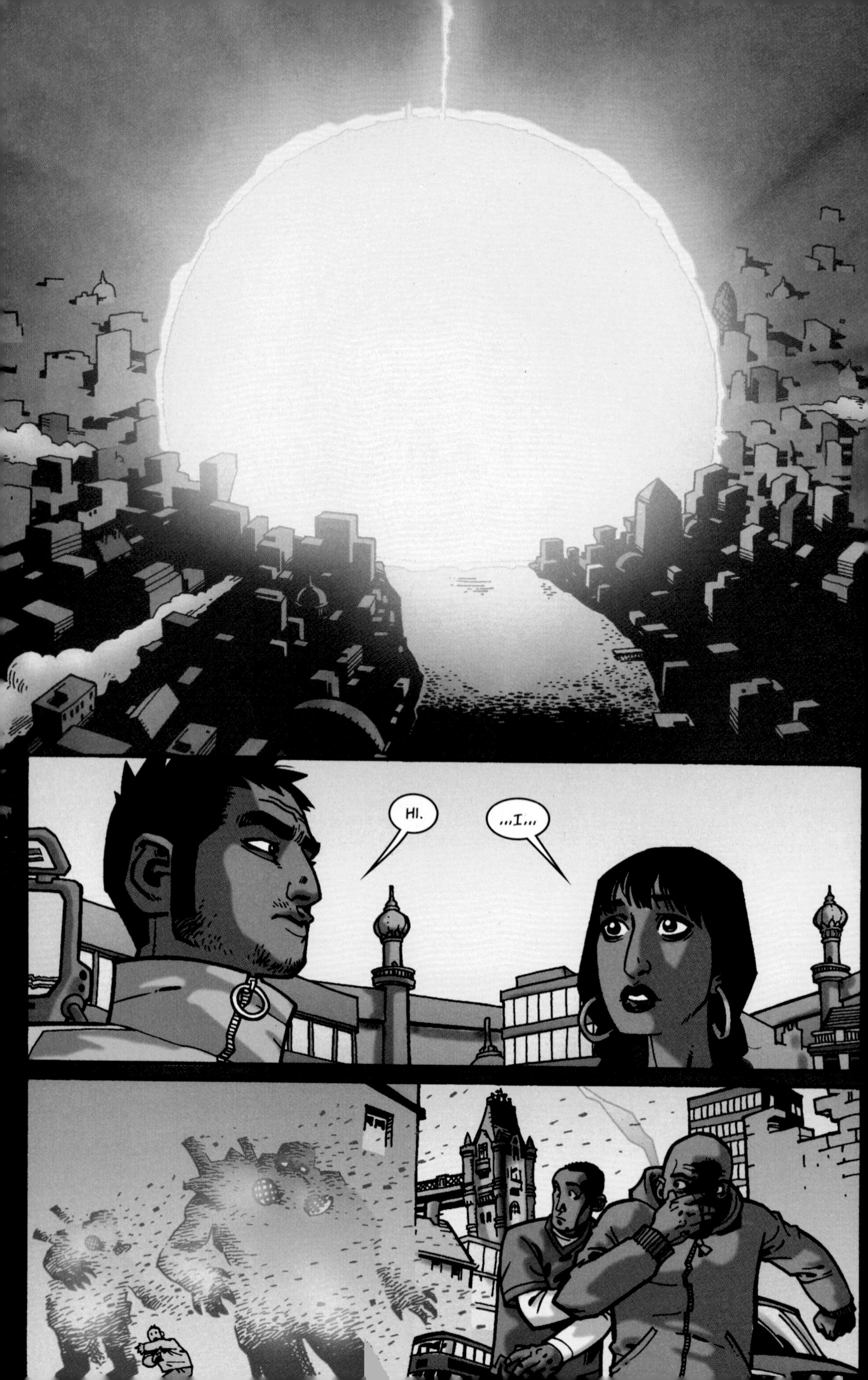
HI.
...I...

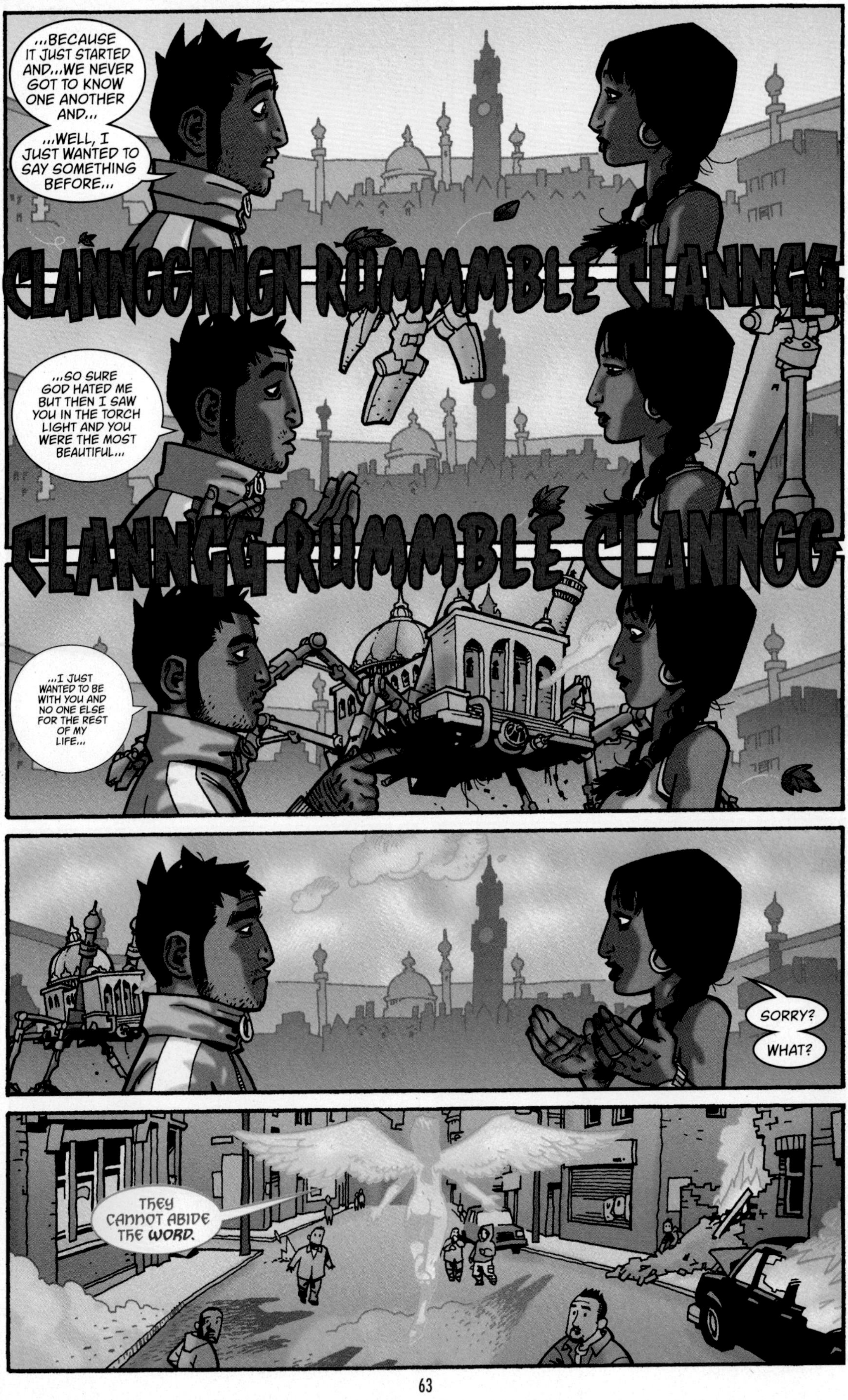
...BECAUSE IT JUST STARTED AND...WE NEVER GOT TO KNOW ONE ANOTHER AND...
...WELL, I JUST WANTED TO SAY SOMETHING BEFORE...
CLANNGGNNGN RUMMMMBLE CLANNGG
...SO SURE GOD HATED ME BUT THEN I SAW YOU IN THE TORCH LIGHT AND YOU WERE THE MOST BEAUTIFUL...
CLANNGG RUMMMBLE CLANNGG
...I JUST WANTED TO BE WITH YOU AND NO ONE ELSE FOR THE REST OF MY LIFE...
SORRY?
WHAT?
THEY CANNOT ABIDE THE WORD.

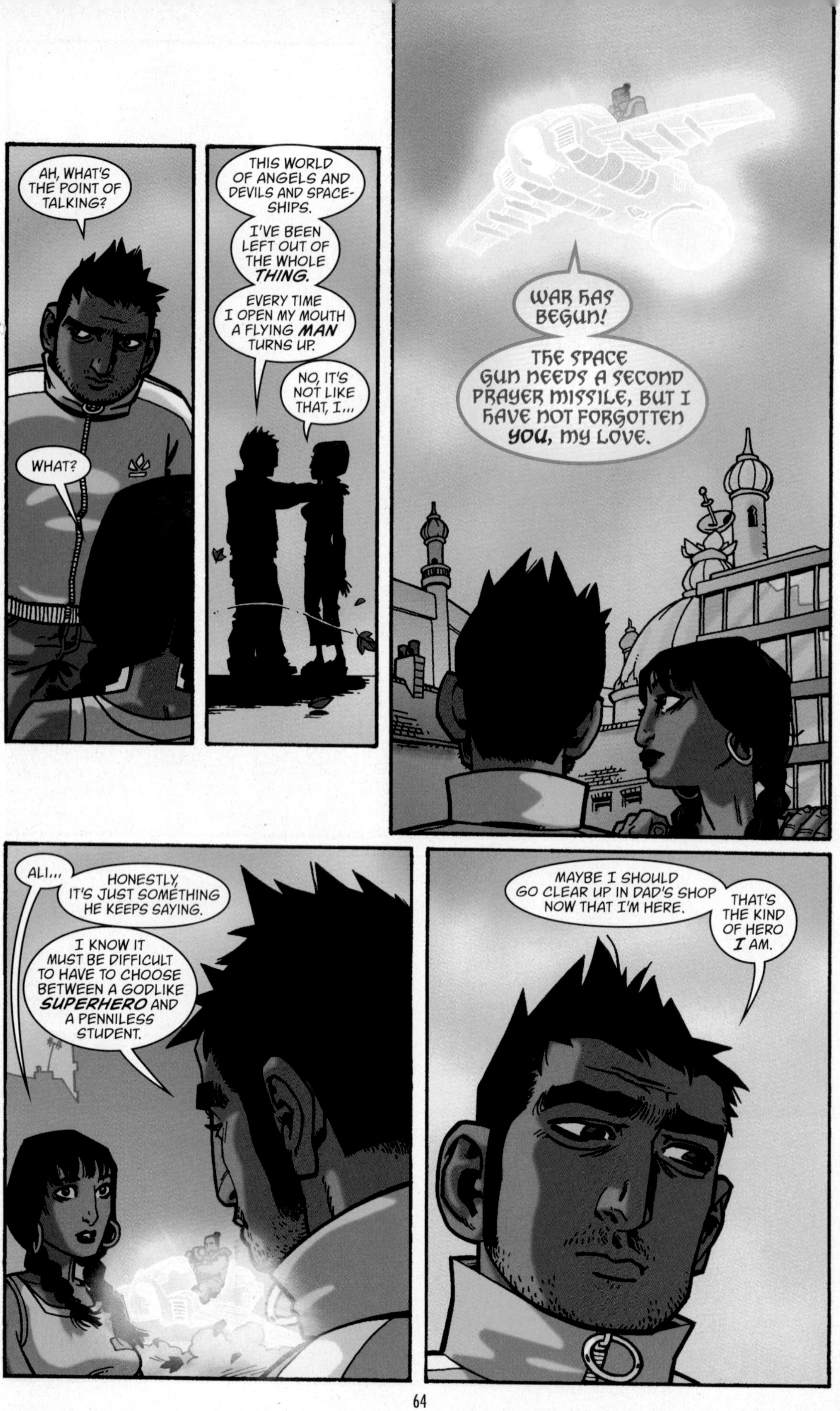

AH, WHAT'S THE POINT OF TALKING?
WHAT?
THIS WORLD OF ANGELS AND DEVILS AND SPACE-SHIPS.
I'VE BEEN LEFT OUT OF THE WHOLE THING.
EVERY TIME I OPEN MY MOUTH A FLYING MAN TURNS UP.
NO, IT'S NOT LIKE THAT, I...
WAR HAS BEGUN!
THE SPACE GUN NEEDS A SECOND PRAYER MISSILE, BUT I HAVE NOT FORGOTTEN YOU, MY LOVE.
ALI...
HONESTLY, IT'S JUST SOMETHING HE KEEPS SAYING.
I KNOW IT MUST BE DIFFICULT TO HAVE TO CHOOSE BETWEEN A GODLIKE SUPERHERO AND A PENNILESS STUDENT.
MAYBE I SHOULD GO CLEAR UP IN DAD'S SHOP NOW THAT I'M HERE.
THAT'S THE KIND OF HERO I AM.

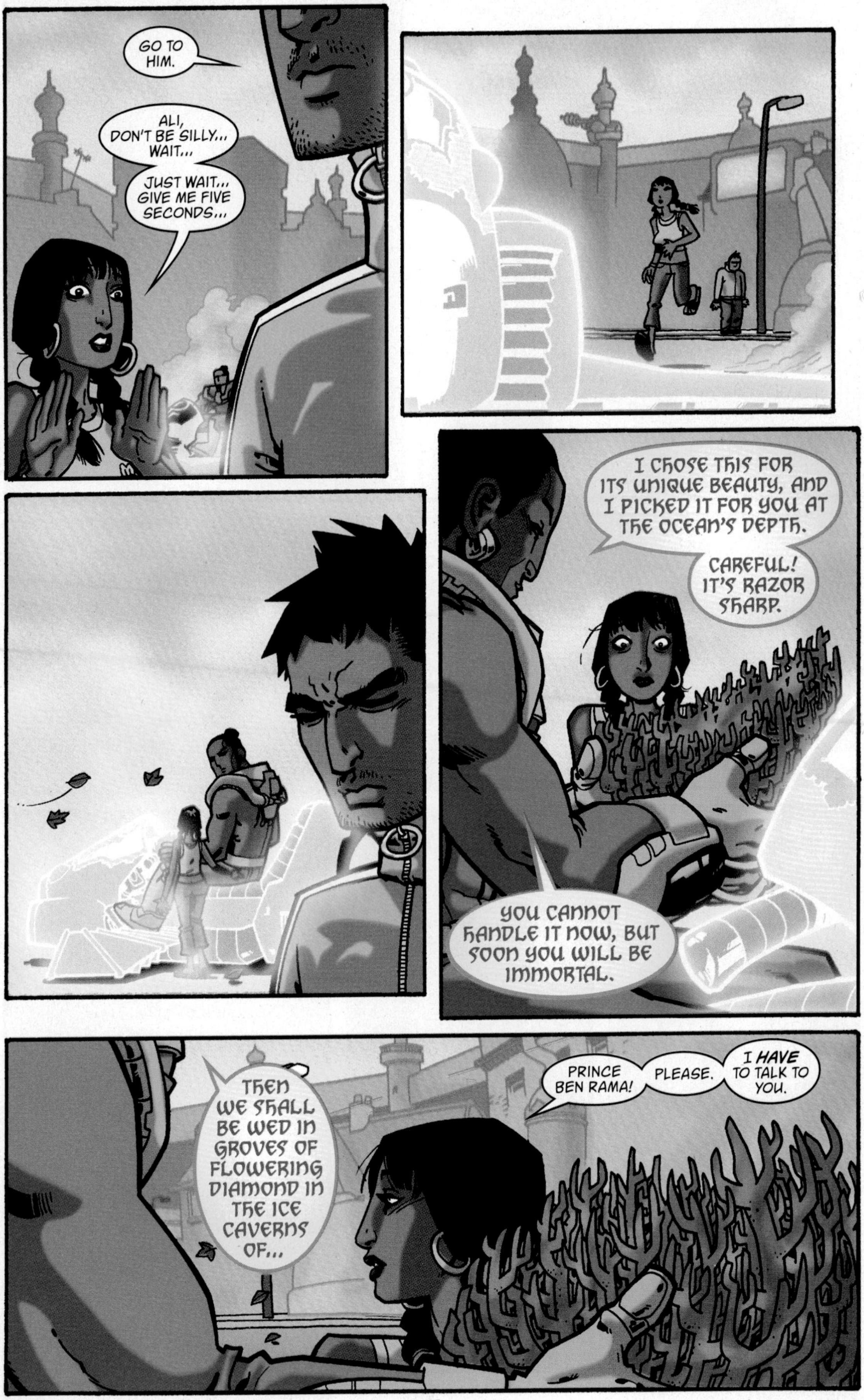
GO TO HIM.
ALI, DON'T BE SILLY... WAIT...
JUST WAIT... GIVE ME FIVE SECONDS...
I CHOSE THIS FOR ITS UNIQUE BEAUTY, AND I PICKED IT FOR YOU AT THE OCEAN'S DEPTH.
CAREFUL! IT'S RAZOR SHARP.
YOU CANNOT HANDLE IT NOW, BUT SOON YOU WILL BE IMMORTAL.
THEN WE SHALL BE WED IN GROVES OF FLOWERING DIAMOND IN THE ICE CAVERNS OF...
PRINCE BEN RAMA!
PLEASE.
I HAVE TO TALK TO YOU.

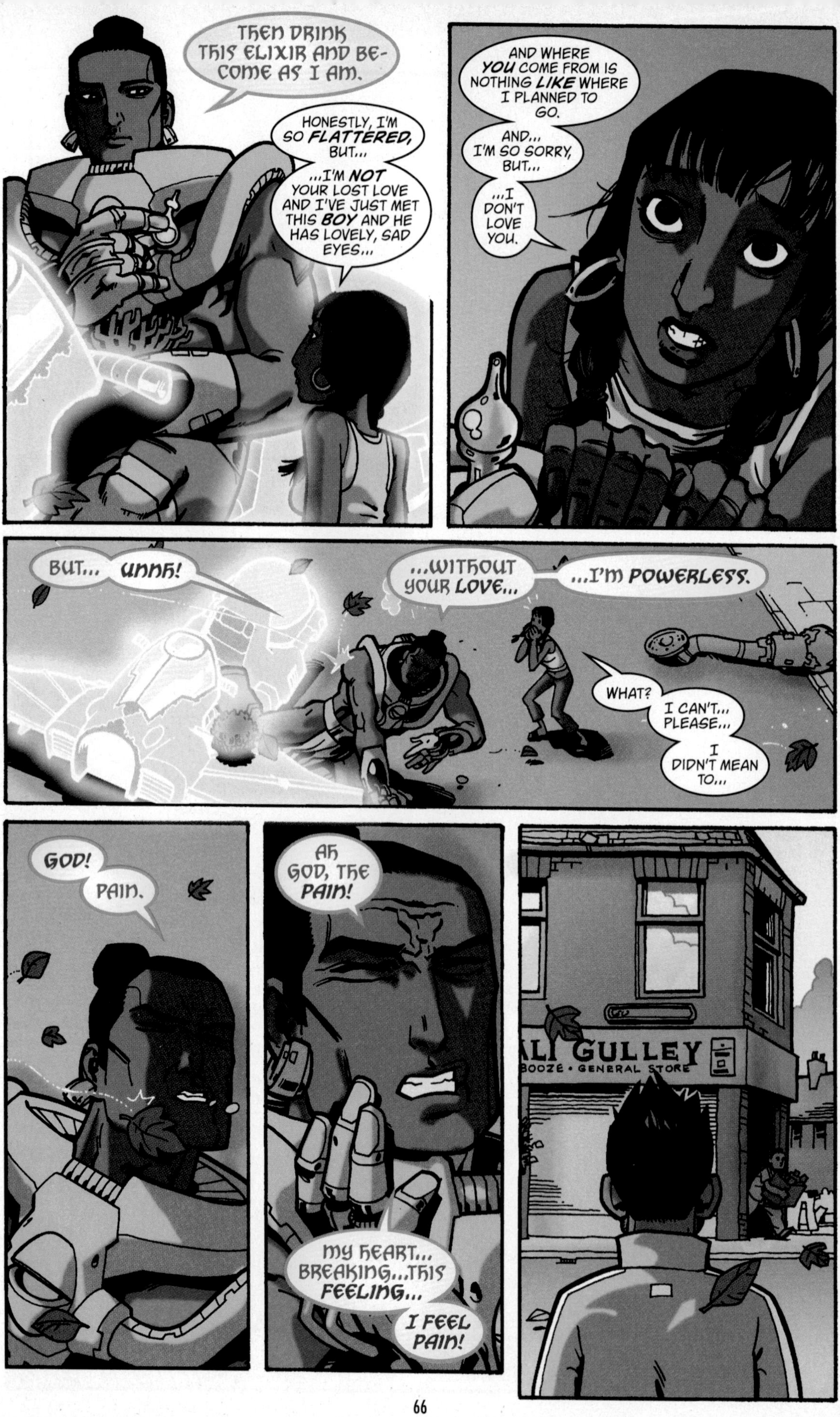
THEN DRINK THIS ELIXIR AND BE-COME AS I AM.
HONESTLY, I'M SO FLATTERED, BUT...
...I'M NOT YOUR LOST LOVE AND I'VE JUST MET THIS BOY AND HE HAS LOVELY, SAD EYES...
AND WHERE YOU COME FROM IS NOTHING LIKE WHERE I PLANNED TO GO.
AND... I'M SO SORRY, BUT...
...I DON'T LOVE YOU.
BUT... UNNH!
...WITHOUT YOUR LOVE...
...I'M POWERLESS.
WHAT?
I CAN'T... PLEASE...
I DIDN'T MEAN TO...
GOD!
PAIN.
AH GOD, THE PAIN!
MY HEART... BREAKING...THIS FEELING...
I FEEL PAIN!
ALI GULLEY
BOOZE • GENERAL STORE

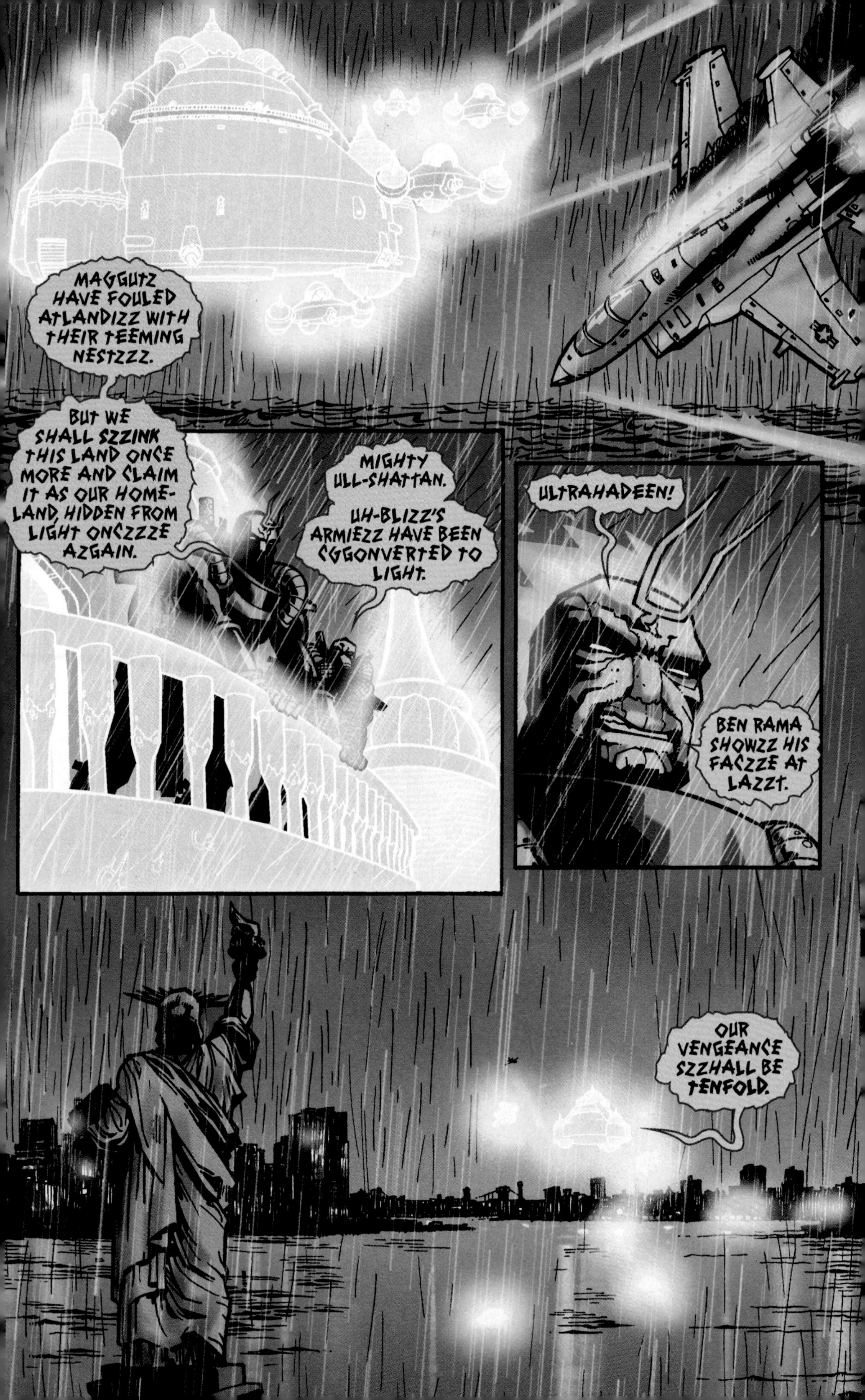
MAGGUTZ HAVE FOULED ATLANDIZZ WITH THEIR TEEMING NESTZZZ.
BUT WE SHALL SZZINK THIS LAND ONCE MORE AND CLAIM IT AS OUR HOME-LAND, HIDDEN FROM LIGHT ONCZZZE AZGAIN.
MIGHTY ULL-SHATTAN.
UH-BLIZZ'S ARMIEZZ HAVE BEEN CGGONVERTED TO LIGHT.
ULTRAHADEEN!
BEN RAMA SHOWZZ HIS FACZZE AT LAZZT.
OUR VENGEANCE SZZHALL BE TENFOLD.

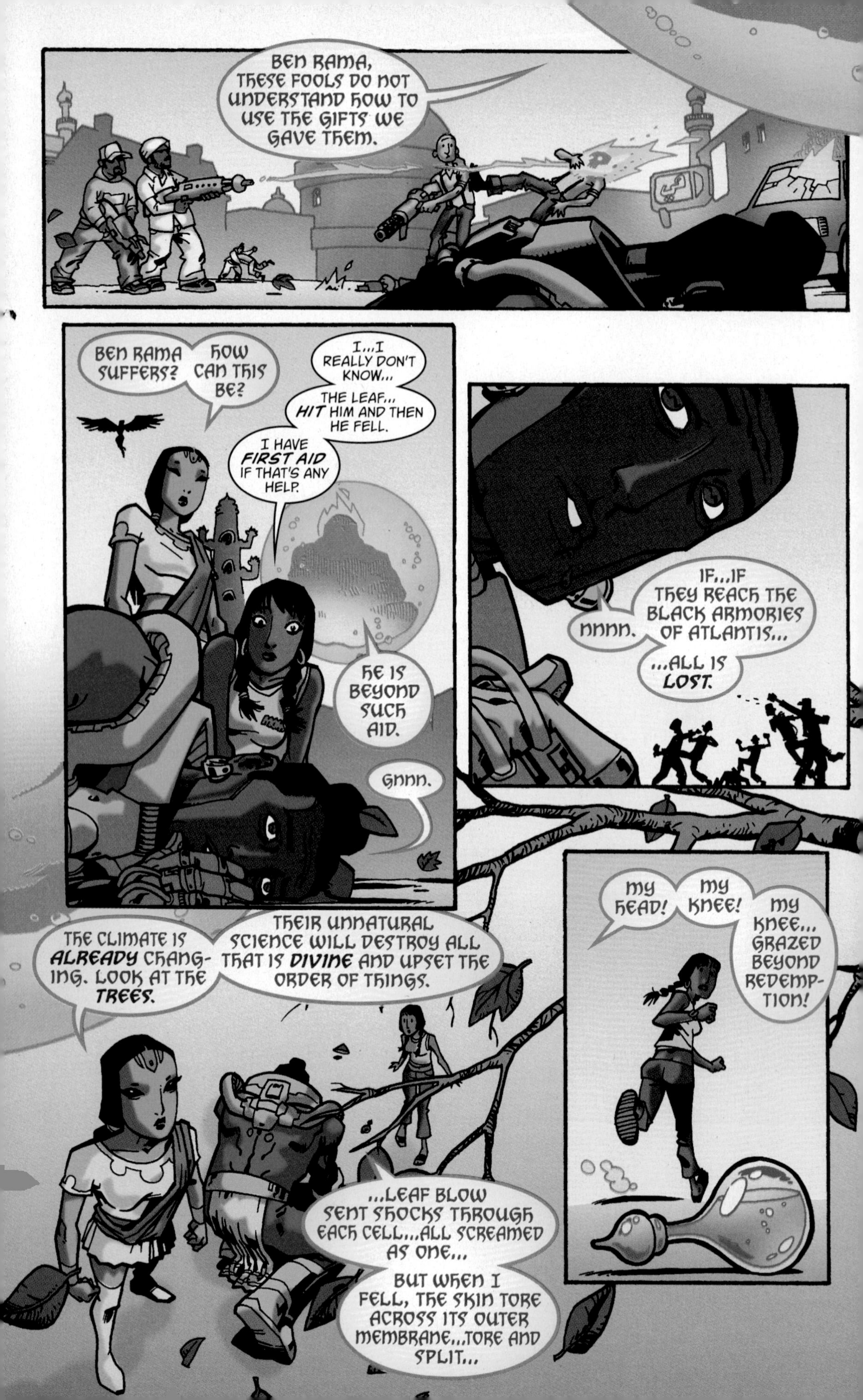
BEN RAMA, THESE FOOLS DO NOT UNDERSTAND HOW TO USE THE GIFTS WE GAVE THEM.
BEN RAMA SUFFERS?
HOW CAN THIS BE?
I...I REALLY DON'T KNOW...
THE LEAF... HIT HIM AND THEN HE FELL.
I HAVE FIRST AID IF THAT'S ANY HELP.
HE IS BEYOND SUCH AID.
GNNN.
NNNN.
IF...IF THEY REACH THE BLACK ARMORIES OF ATLANTIS...
...ALL IS LOST.
THE CLIMATE IS ALREADY CHANGING. LOOK AT THE TREES.
THEIR UNNATURAL SCIENCE WILL DESTROY ALL THAT IS DIVINE AND UPSET THE ORDER OF THINGS.
MY HEAD!
MY KNEE!
MY KNEE... GRAZED BEYOND REDEMPTION!
...LEAF BLOW SENT SHOCKS THROUGH EACH CELL...ALL SCREAMED AS ONE...
BUT WHEN I FELL, THE SKIN TORE ACROSS ITS OUTER MEMBRANE...TORE AND SPLIT...

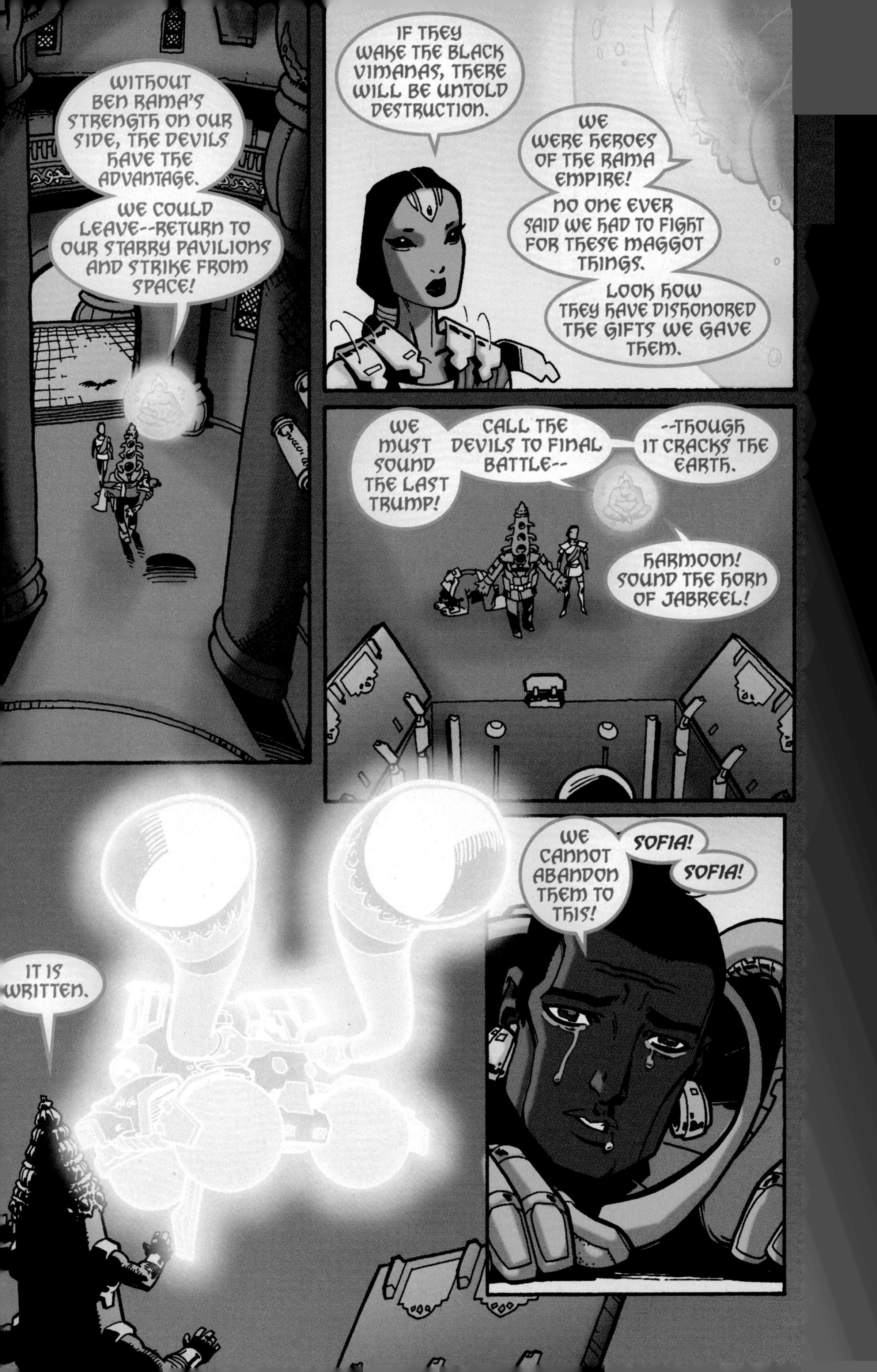
WITHOUT BEN RAMA'S STRENGTH ON OUR SIDE, THE DEVILS HAVE THE ADVANTAGE.
WE COULD LEAVE--RETURN TO OUR STARRY PAVILIONS AND STRIKE FROM SPACE!
IF THEY WAKE THE BLACK VIMANAS, THERE WILL BE UNTOLD DESTRUCTION.
WE WERE HEROES OF THE RAMA EMPIRE!
NO ONE EVER SAID WE HAD TO FIGHT FOR THESE MAGGOT THINGS.
LOOK HOW THEY HAVE DISHONORED THE GIFTS WE GAVE THEM.
WE MUST SOUND THE LAST TRUMP!
CALL THE DEVILS TO FINAL BATTLE--
--THOUGH IT CRACKS THE EARTH.
HARMOON! SOUND THE HORN OF JABREEL!
IT IS WRITTEN.
WE CANNOT ABANDON THEM TO THIS!
SOFIA!
SOFIA!

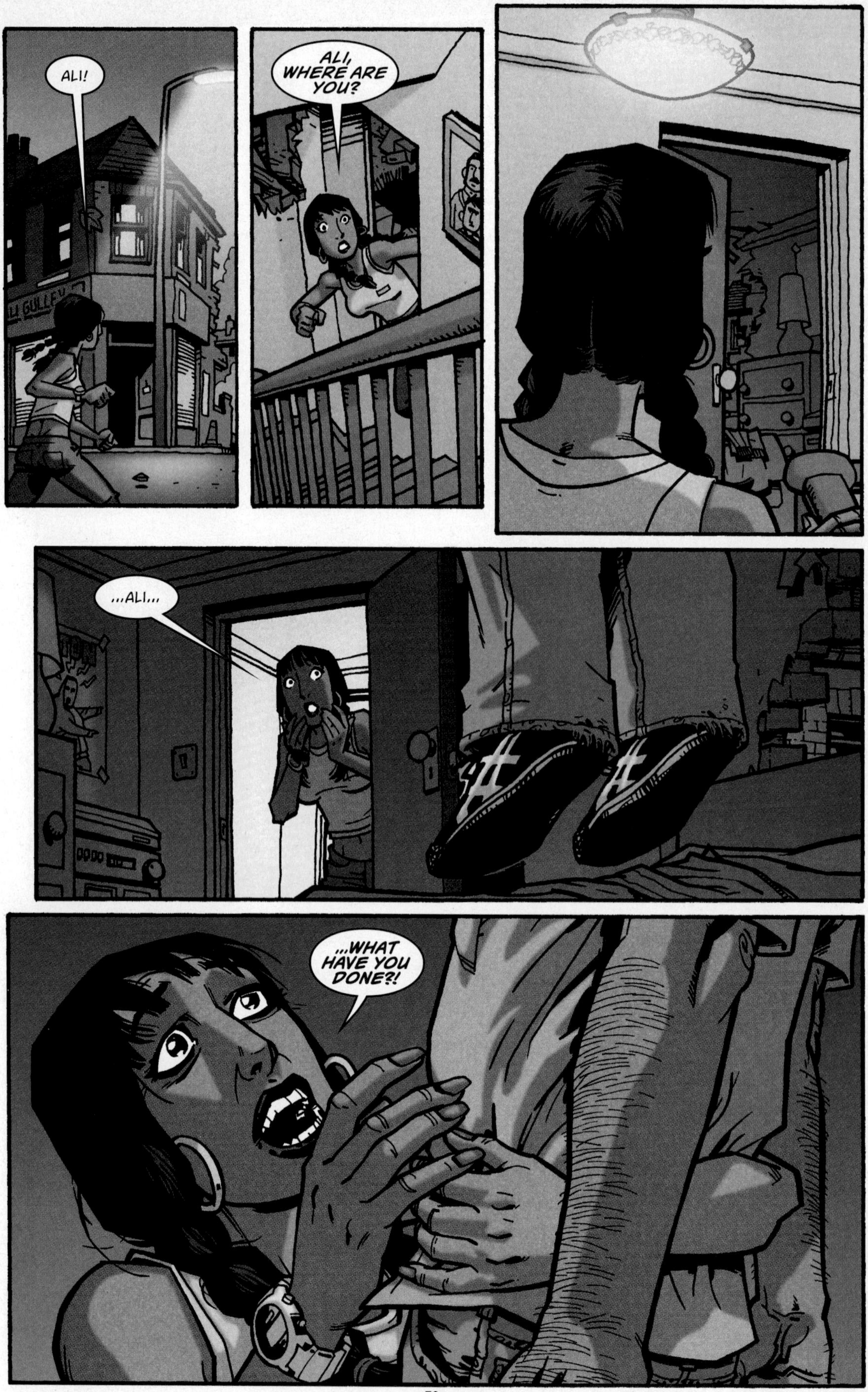
ALI!
ALI, WHERE ARE YOU?
...ALI...
...WHAT HAVE YOU DONE?!

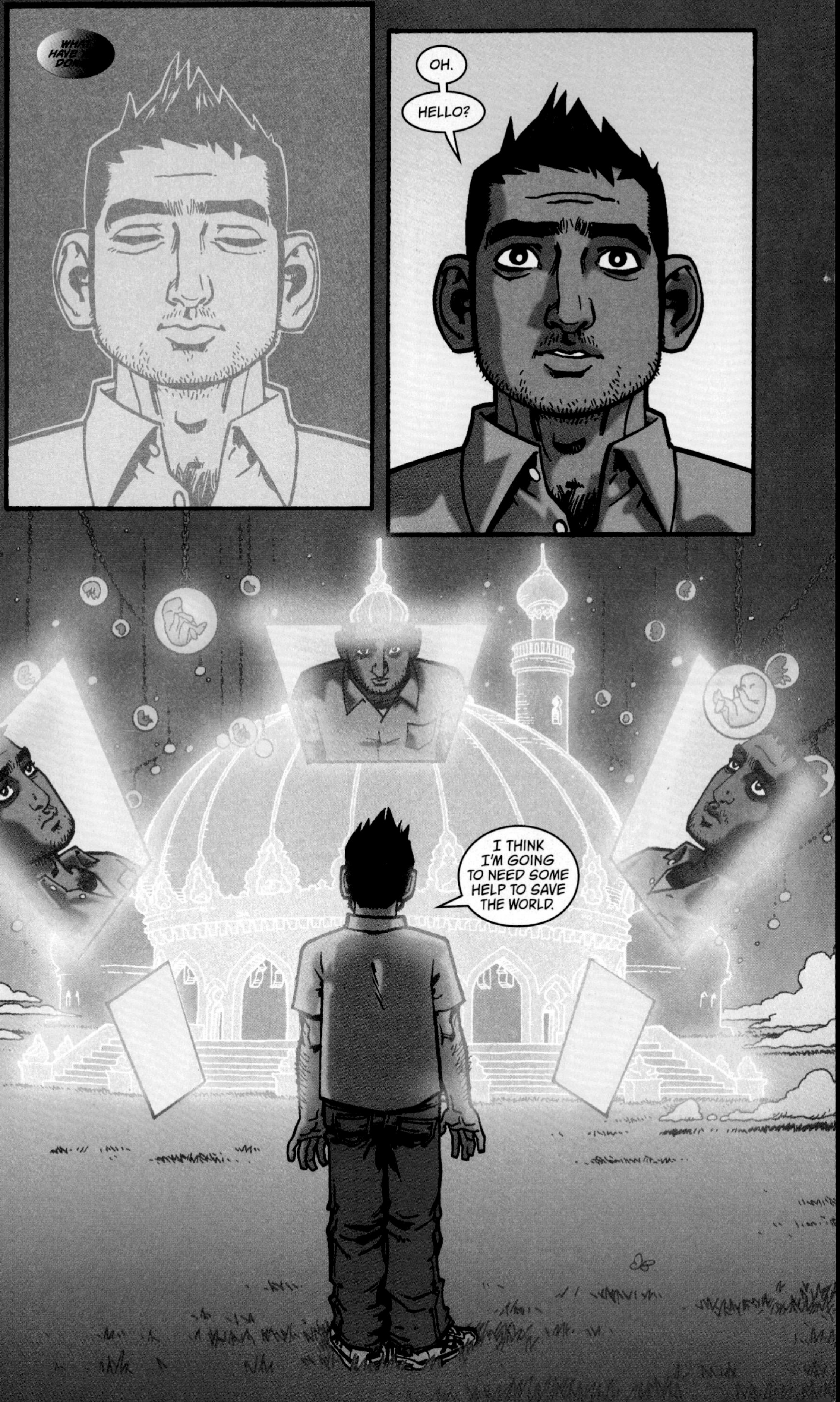
WHAT HAVE DON
OH.
HELLO?
I THINK I'M GOING TO NEED SOME HELP TO SAVE THE WORLD.

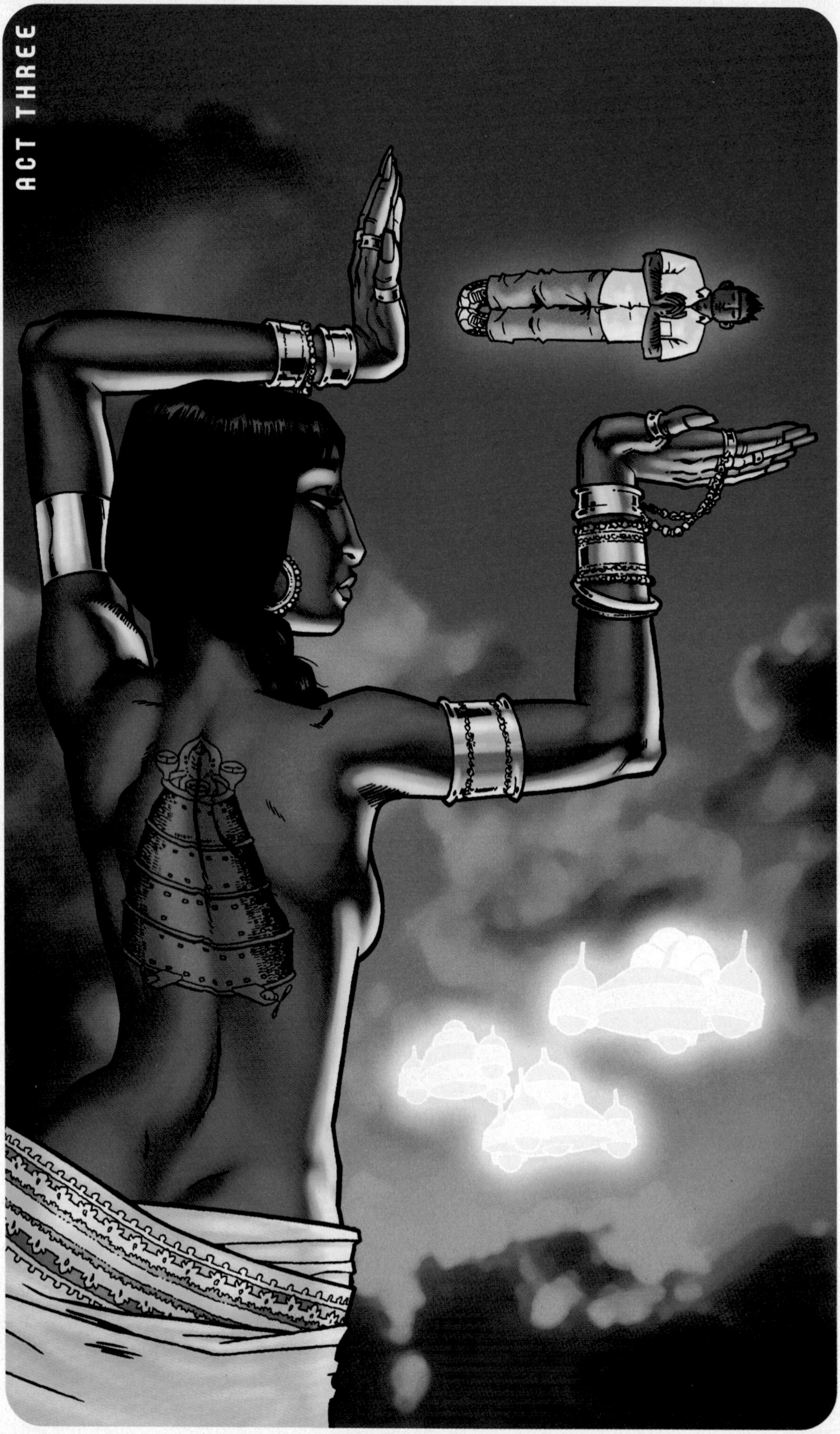
ACT THREE

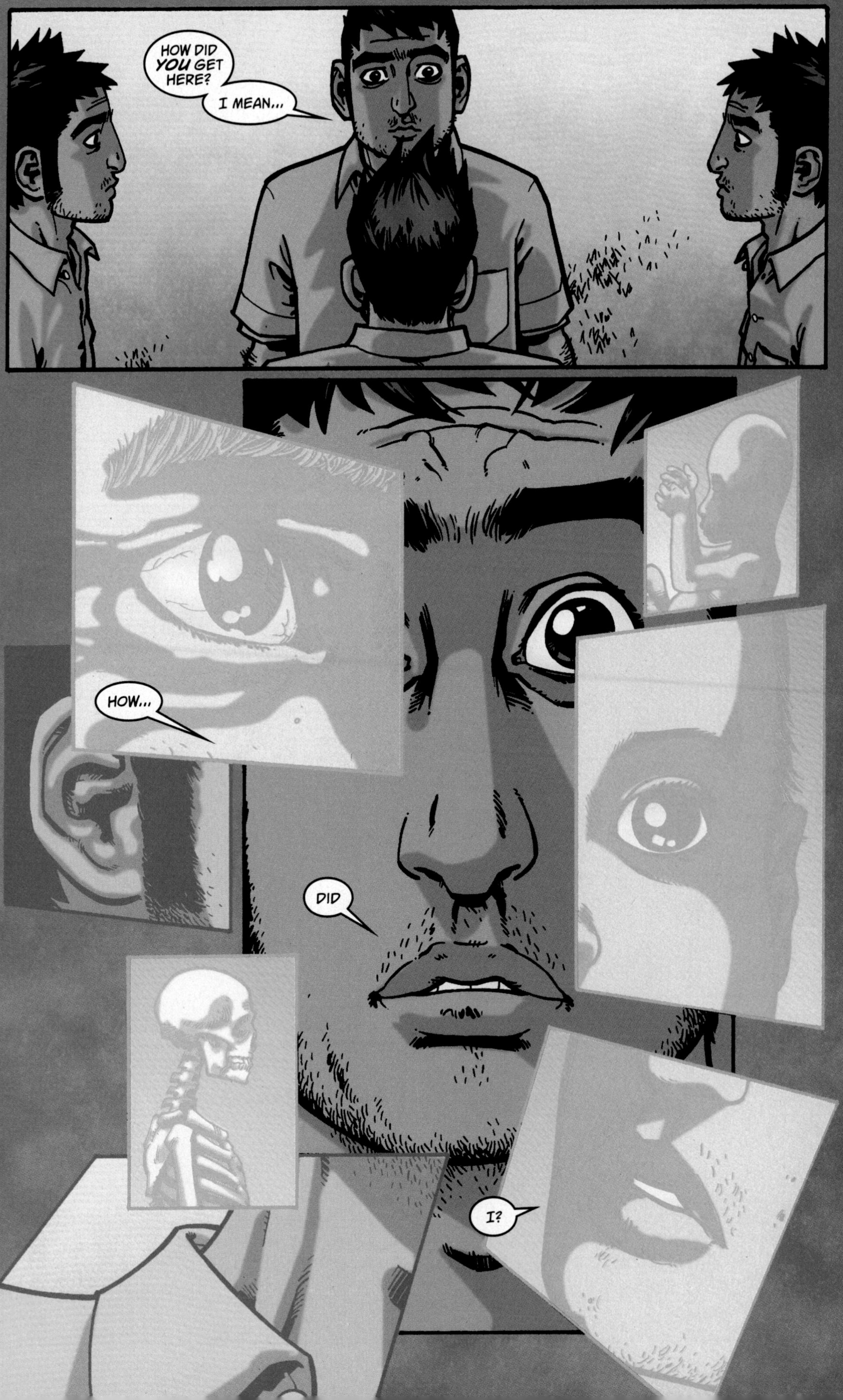
HOW DID YOU GET HERE?
I MEAN...
HOW...
DID
I?

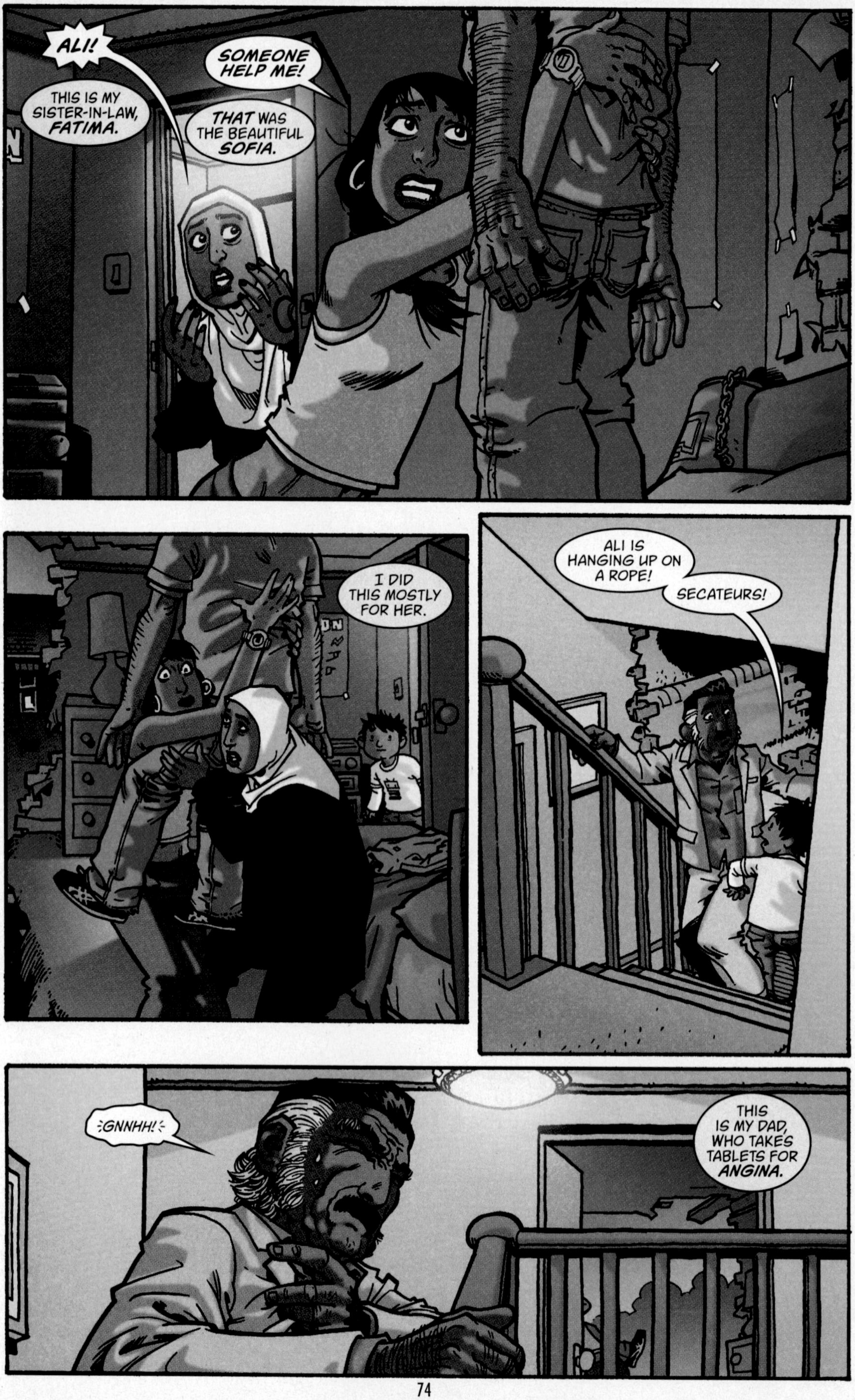
ALI!
THIS IS MY SISTER-IN-LAW, FATIMA.
SOMEONE HELP ME!
THAT WAS THE BEAUTIFUL SOFIA.
I DID THIS MOSTLY FOR HER.
ALI IS HANGING UP ON A ROPE!
SECATEURS!
GNNHH!
THIS IS MY DAD, WHO TAKES TABLETS FOR ANGINA.

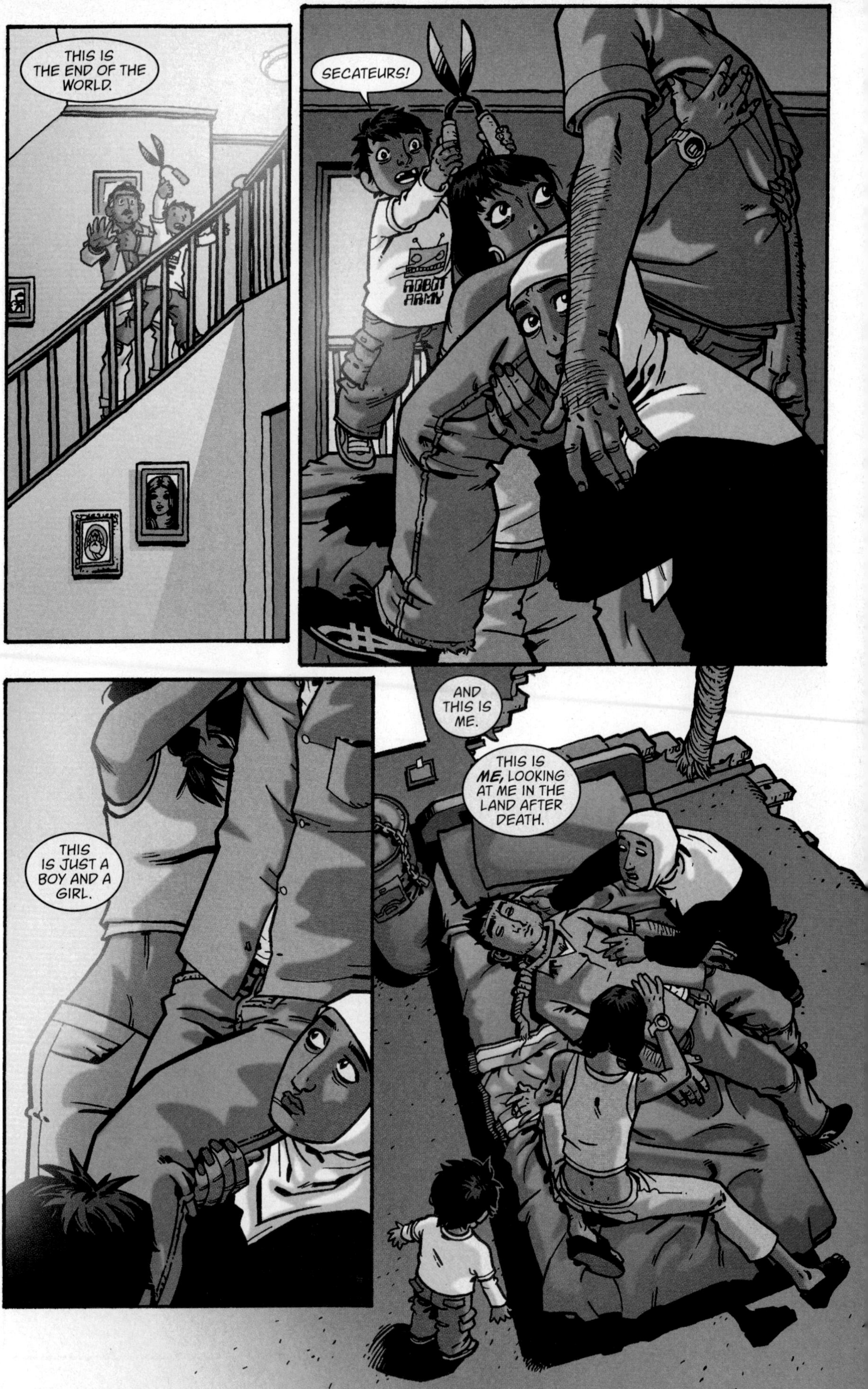
THIS IS THE END OF THE WORLD.
SECATEURS!
ROBOT ARMY
THIS IS JUST A BOY AND A GIRL.
AND THIS IS ME.
THIS IS ME, LOOKING AT ME IN THE LAND AFTER DEATH.

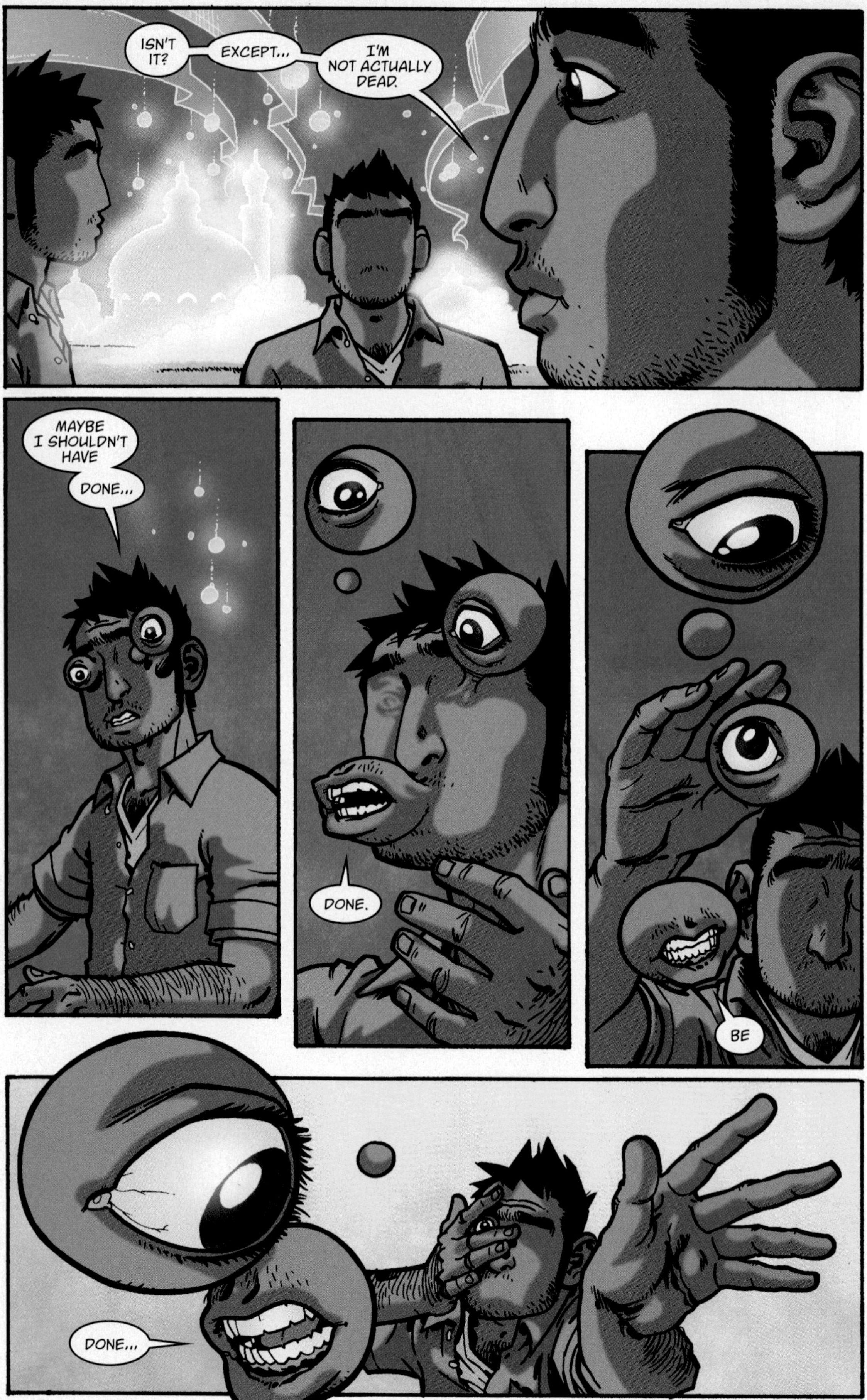

ISN'T IT?
EXCEPT...
I'M NOT ACTUALLY DEAD.
MAYBE I SHOULDN'T HAVE
DONE...
DONE.
BE
DONE...

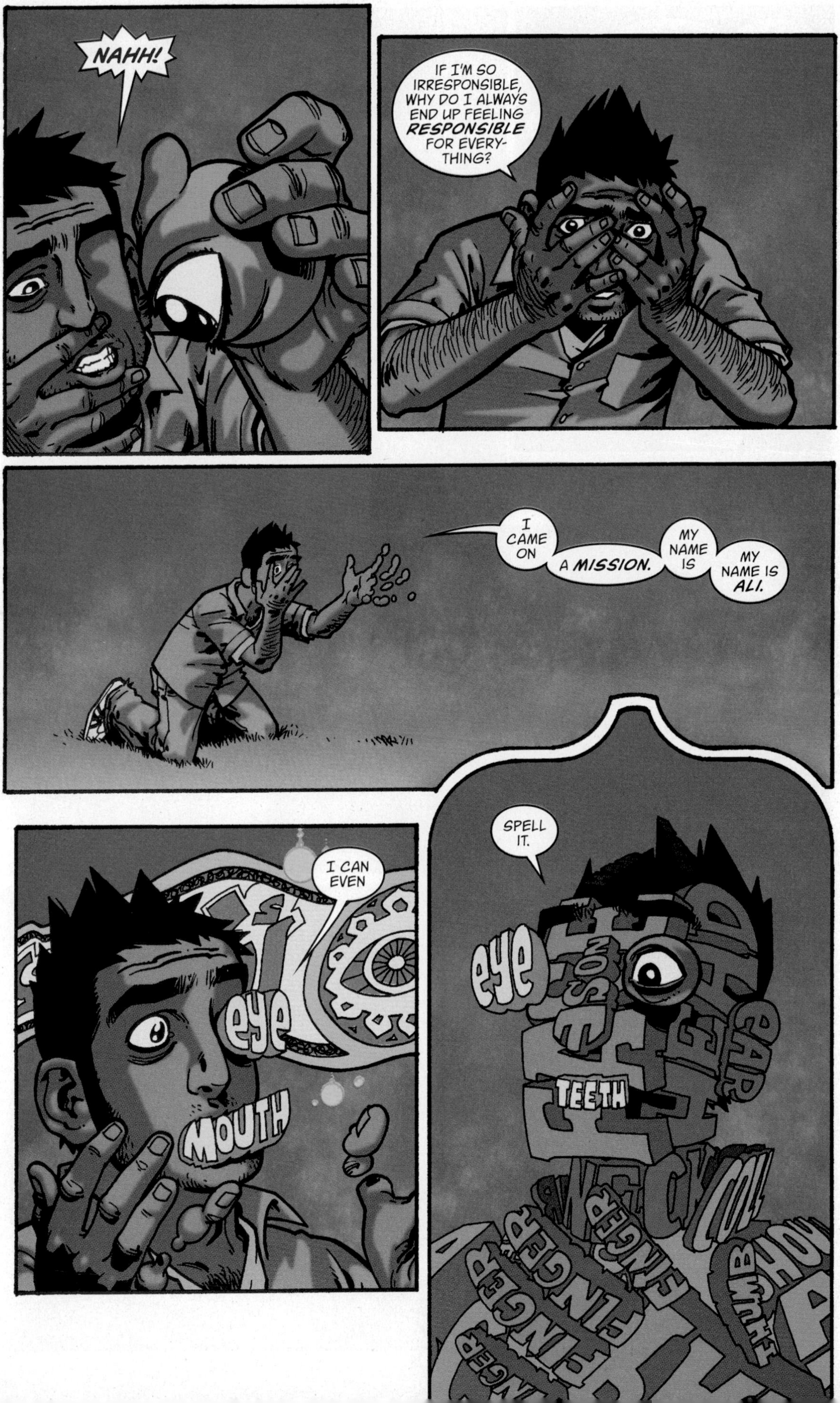
NAHH!
IF I'M SO IRRESPONSIBLE, WHY DO I ALWAYS END UP FEELING **RESPONSIBLE** FOR EVERY-THING?
I CAME ON
A **MISSION.**
MY NAME IS
MY NAME IS **ALI.**
I CAN EVEN
eye
MOUTH
SPELL IT.
eye
NOSE
EAR
TEETH
FINGER
FINGER

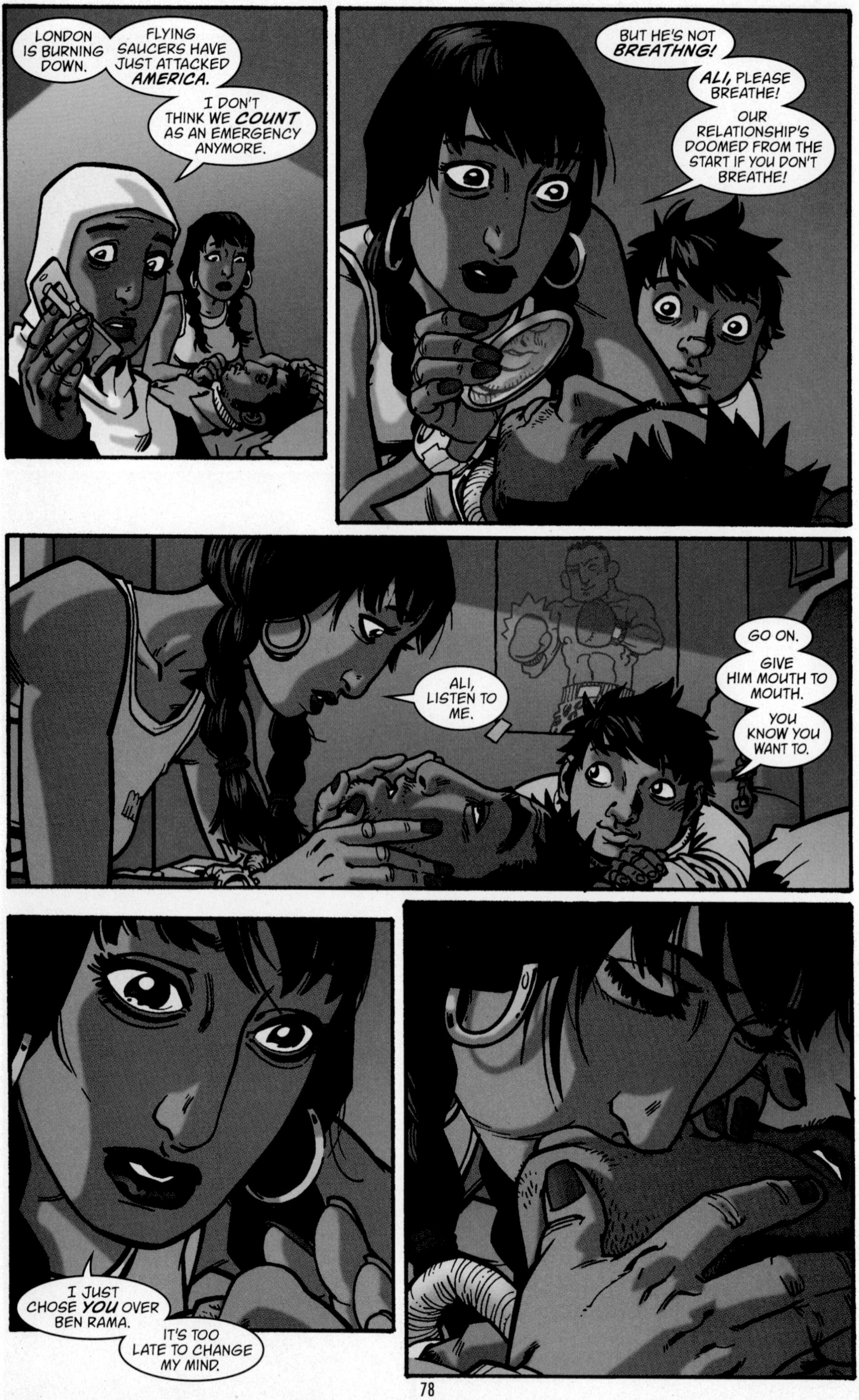
LONDON IS BURNING DOWN.
FLYING SAUCERS HAVE JUST ATTACKED AMERICA.
I DON'T THINK WE COUNT AS AN EMERGENCY ANYMORE.
BUT HE'S NOT BREATHNG!
ALI, PLEASE BREATHE!
OUR RELATIONSHIP'S DOOMED FROM THE START IF YOU DON'T BREATHE!
ALI, LISTEN TO ME.
GO ON.
GIVE HIM MOUTH TO MOUTH.
YOU KNOW YOU WANT TO.
I JUST CHOSE YOU OVER BEN RAMA.
IT'S TOO LATE TO CHANGE MY MIND.

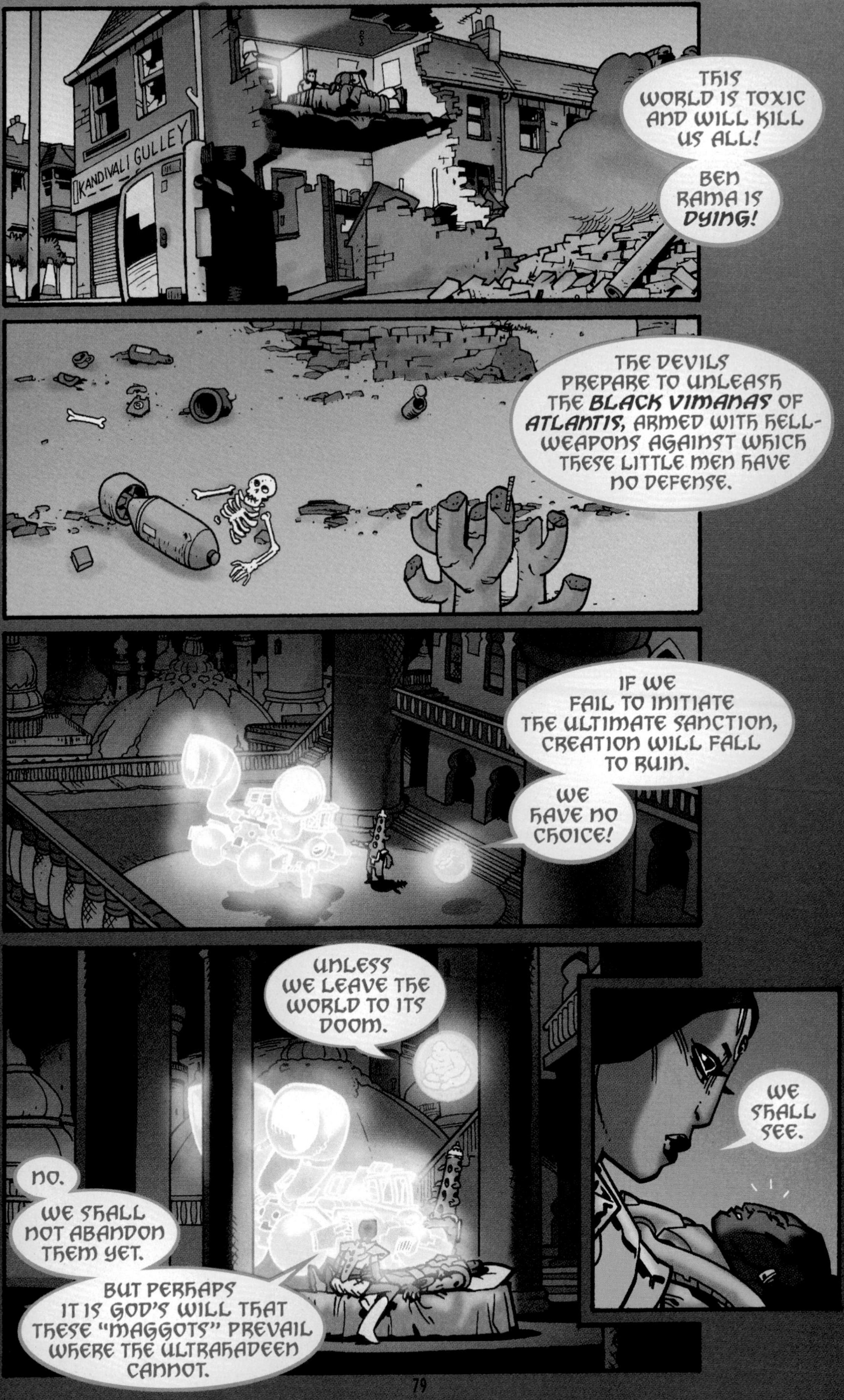
KANDIVALI GULLEY
THIS WORLD IS TOXIC AND WILL KILL US ALL!
BEN RAMA IS DYING!
THE DEVILS PREPARE TO UNLEASH THE BLACK VIMANAS OF ATLANTIS, ARMED WITH HELL-WEAPONS AGAINST WHICH THESE LITTLE MEN HAVE NO DEFENSE.
IF WE FAIL TO INITIATE THE ULTIMATE SANCTION, CREATION WILL FALL TO RUIN.
WE HAVE NO CHOICE!
UNLESS WE LEAVE THE WORLD TO ITS DOOM.
NO.
WE SHALL NOT ABANDON THEM YET.
BUT PERHAPS IT IS GOD'S WILL THAT THESE "MAGGOTS" PREVAIL WHERE THE ULTRAHADEEN CANNOT.
WE SHALL SEE.

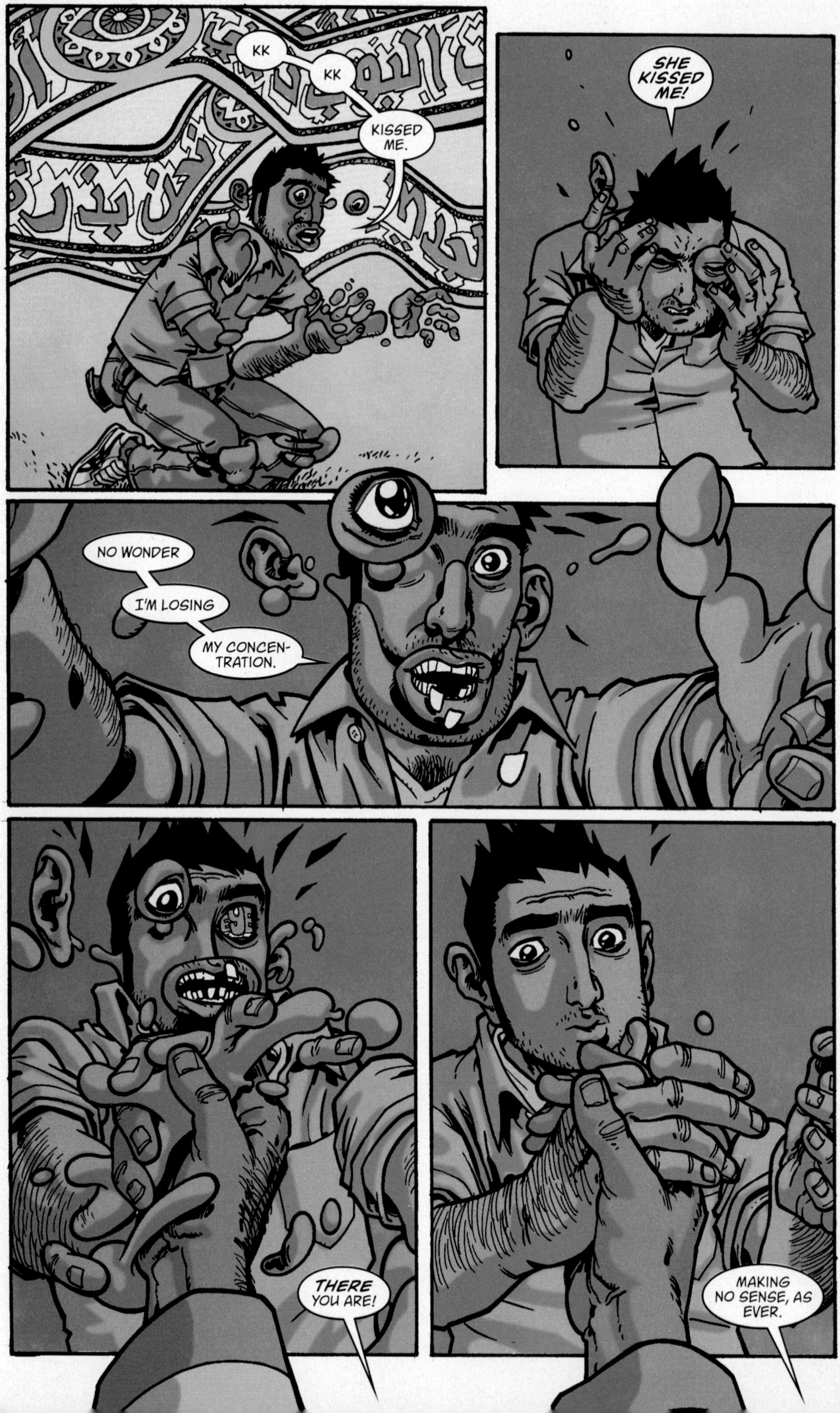
KK
KK
KISSED ME.
SHE KISSED ME!
NO WONDER
I'M LOSING
MY CONCEN-TRATION.
THERE YOU ARE!
MAKING NO SENSE, AS EVER.

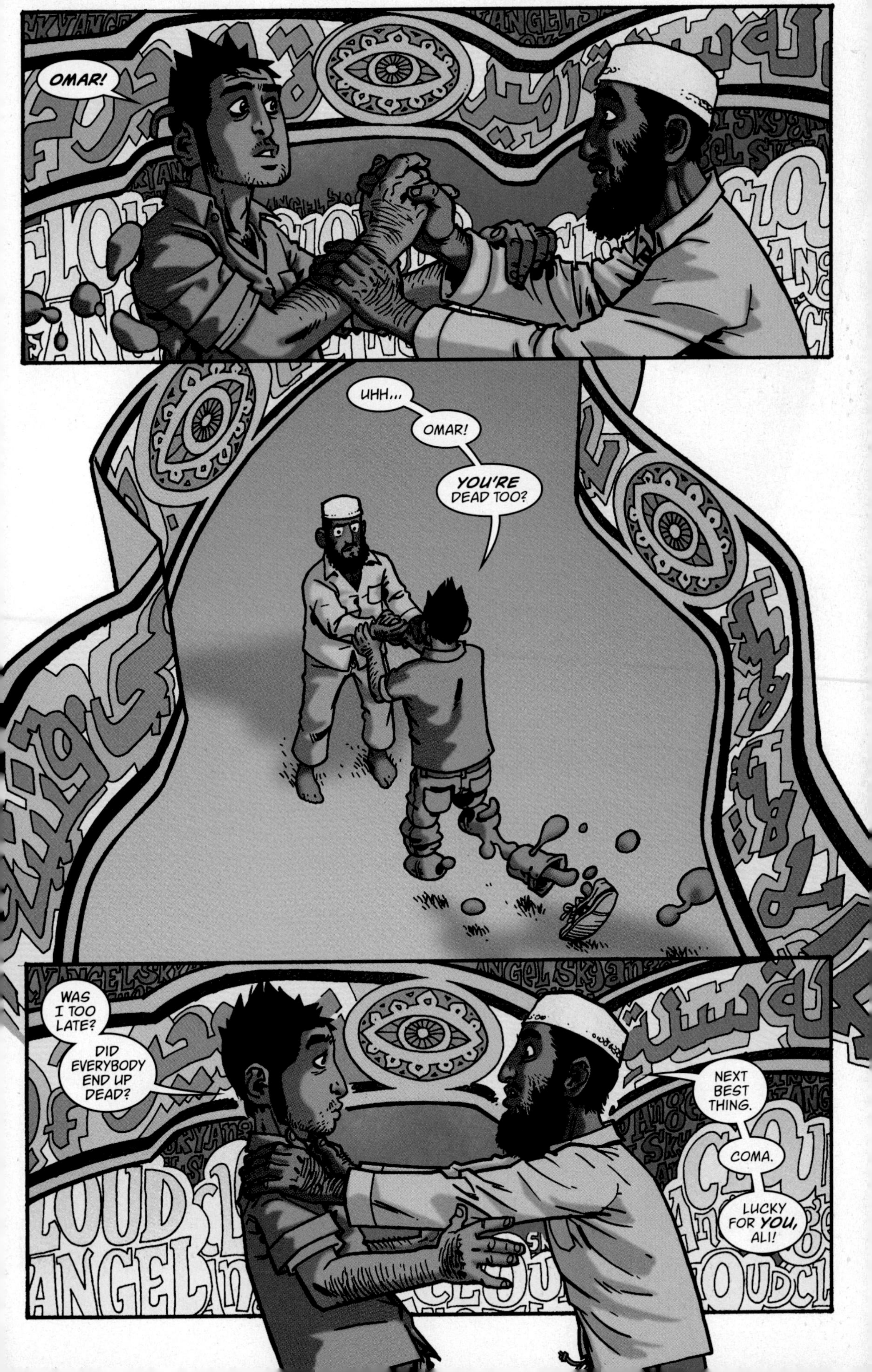
OMAR!
UHH...
OMAR!
YOU'RE DEAD TOO?
WAS I TOO LATE?
DID EVERYBODY END UP DEAD?
NEXT BEST THING.
COMA.
LUCKY FOR YOU, ALI!

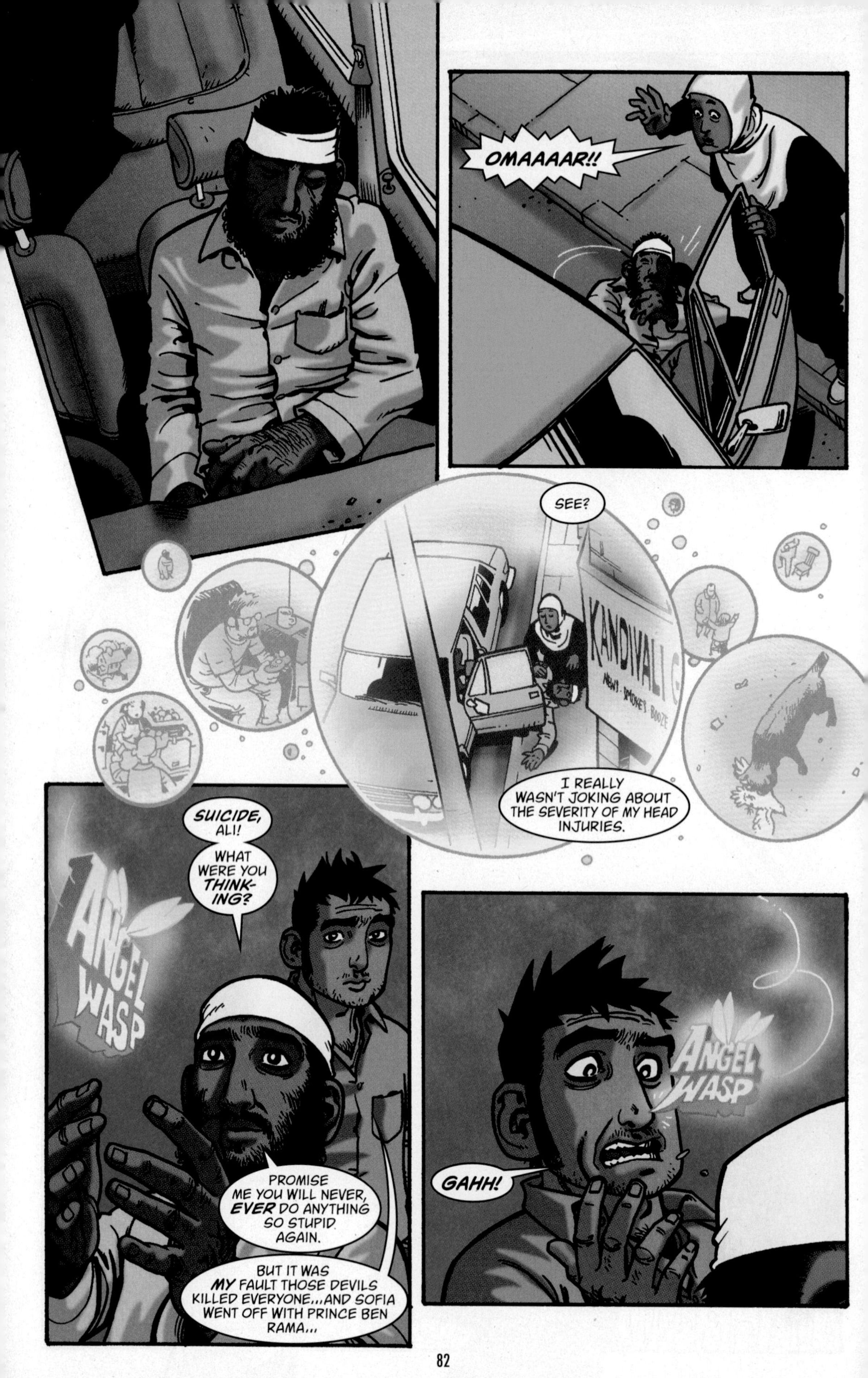
OMAAAAR!!
SEE?
KANDIVALI G
NEWS · SMOKES · BOOZE
I REALLY WASN'T JOKING ABOUT THE SEVERITY OF MY HEAD INJURIES.
SUICIDE, ALI!
WHAT WERE YOU THINKING?
ANGEL WASP
PROMISE ME YOU WILL NEVER, EVER DO ANYTHING SO STUPID AGAIN.
BUT IT WAS MY FAULT THOSE DEVILS KILLED EVERYONE...AND SOFIA WENT OFF WITH PRINCE BEN RAMA...
ANGEL WASP
GAHH!

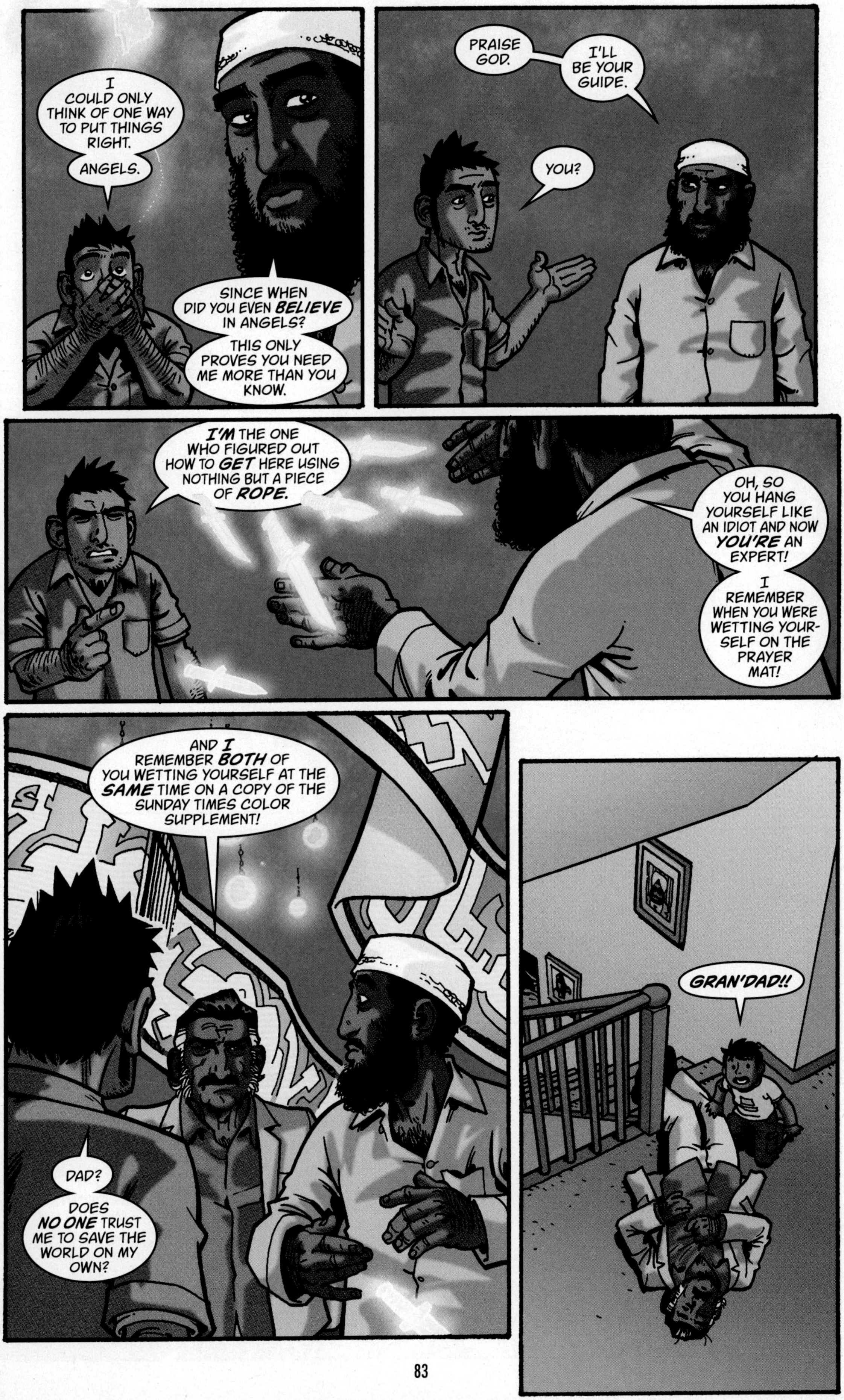
I COULD ONLY THINK OF ONE WAY TO PUT THINGS RIGHT.
ANGELS.
SINCE WHEN DID YOU EVEN BELIEVE IN ANGELS?
THIS ONLY PROVES YOU NEED ME MORE THAN YOU KNOW.
PRAISE GOD.
I'LL BE YOUR GUIDE.
YOU?
I'M THE ONE WHO FIGURED OUT HOW TO GET HERE USING NOTHING BUT A PIECE OF ROPE.
OH, SO YOU HANG YOURSELF LIKE AN IDIOT AND NOW YOU'RE AN EXPERT!
I REMEMBER WHEN YOU WERE WETTING YOURSELF ON THE PRAYER MAT!
AND I REMEMBER BOTH OF YOU WETTING YOURSELF AT THE SAME TIME ON A COPY OF THE SUNDAY TIMES COLOR SUPPLEMENT!
DAD?
DOES NO ONE TRUST ME TO SAVE THE WORLD ON MY OWN?
GRAN'DAD!!

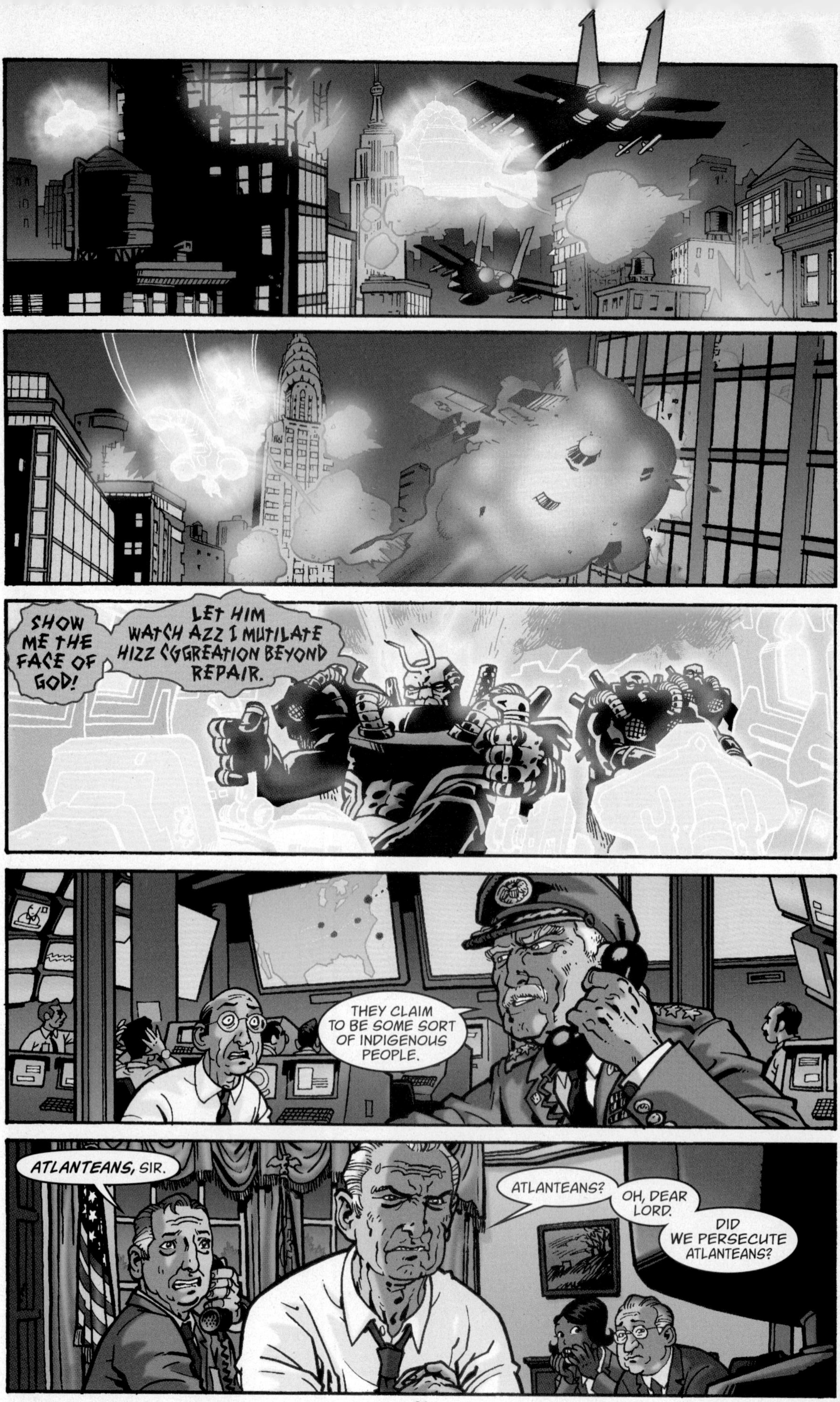
SHOW ME THE FACE OF GOD!
LET HIM WATCH AZZ I MUTILATE HIZZ CGGREATION BEYOND REPAIR.
THEY CLAIM TO BE SOME SORT OF INDIGENOUS PEOPLE.
ATLANTEANS, SIR.
ATLANTEANS?
OH, DEAR LORD.
DID WE PERSECUTE ATLANTEANS?

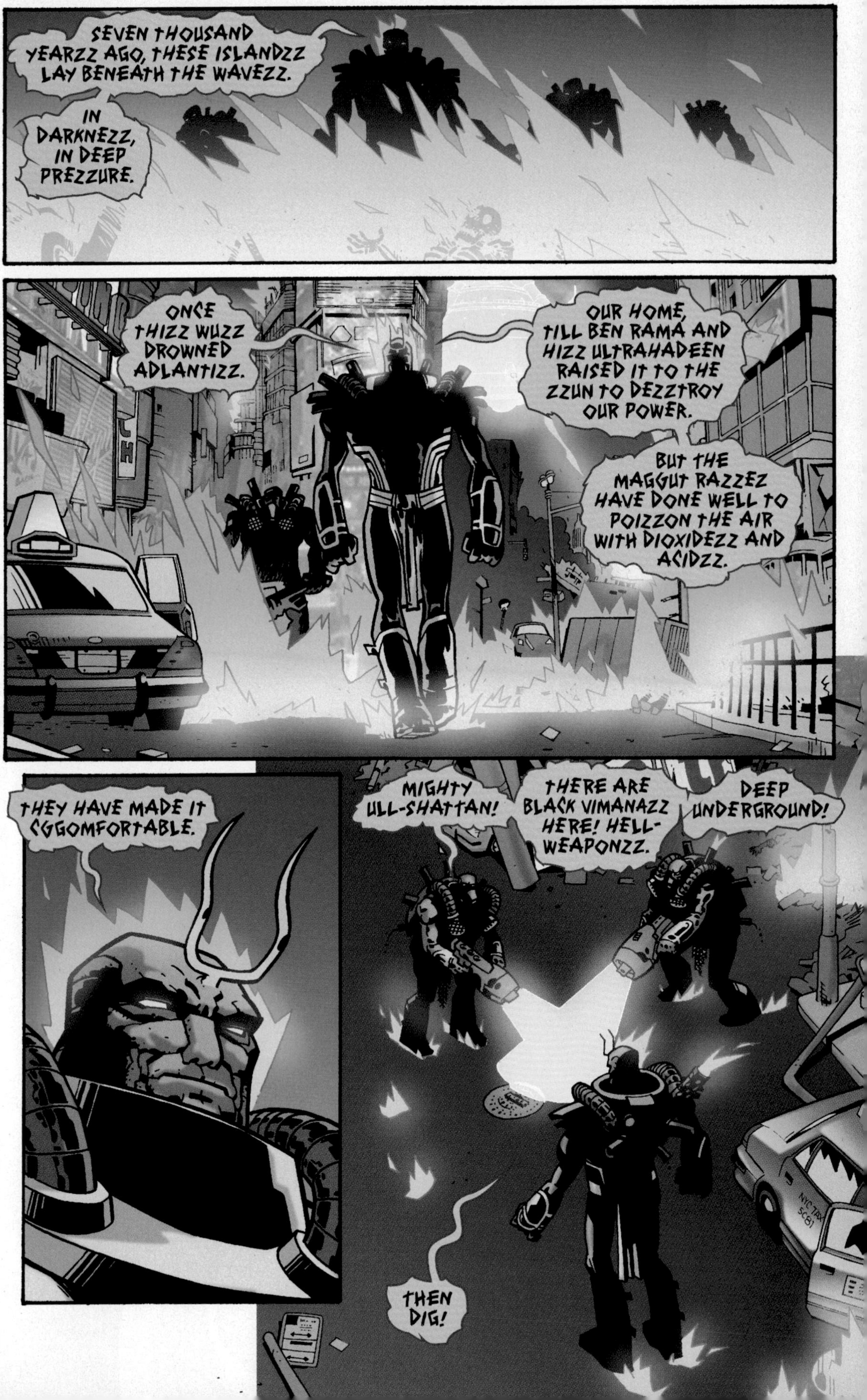
SEVEN THOUSAND YEARZZ AGO, THESE ISLANDZZ LAY BENEATH THE WAVEZZ.
IN DARKNEZZ, IN DEEP PREZZURE.
ONCE THIZZ WUZZ DROWNED ADLANTIZZ.
OUR HOME, TILL BEN RAMA AND HIZZ ULTRAHADEEN RAISED IT TO THE ZZUN TO DEZZTROY OUR POWER.
BUT THE MAGGUT RAZZEZ HAVE DONE WELL TO POIZZON THE AIR WITH DIOXIDEZZ AND ACIDZZ.
THEY HAVE MADE IT CGGOMFORTABLE.
MIGHTY ULL-SHATTAN!
THERE ARE BLACK VIMANAZZ HERE! HELL-WEAPONZZ.
DEEP UNDERGROUND!
THEN DIG!

HOW DID THIS HAPPEN?

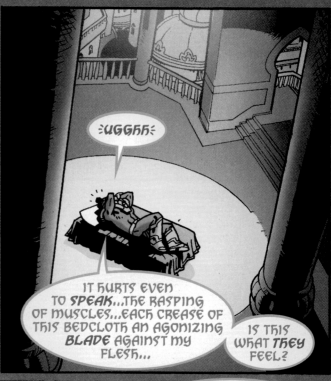

≈UGGHH≈

IT HURTS EVEN TO **SPEAK**...THE RASPING OF MUSCLES...EACH CREASE OF THIS BEDCLOTH AN AGONIZING **BLADE** AGAINST MY FLESH...

IS THIS WHAT **THEY** FEEL?

I, WHO BATHED IN THE SUN, WHO SHOOK HANDS WITH THE **THUNDER** AND ARM-WRESTLED VOLCANOES.

IF THE HEROES OF **THIS** AGE CAN BEAR THE CRUEL BURDENS OF **MORTAL** FLESH...

...DARE I FAIL TO DO THE SAME?

THOUGH THE **PAIN** OF SIMPLY **LIVING** INCREASES BEYOND ALL MEASURE, BEYOND ALL **ENDURANCE**...

...BEN RAMA MUST NOT **FALTER**.

STOP, I SAY!

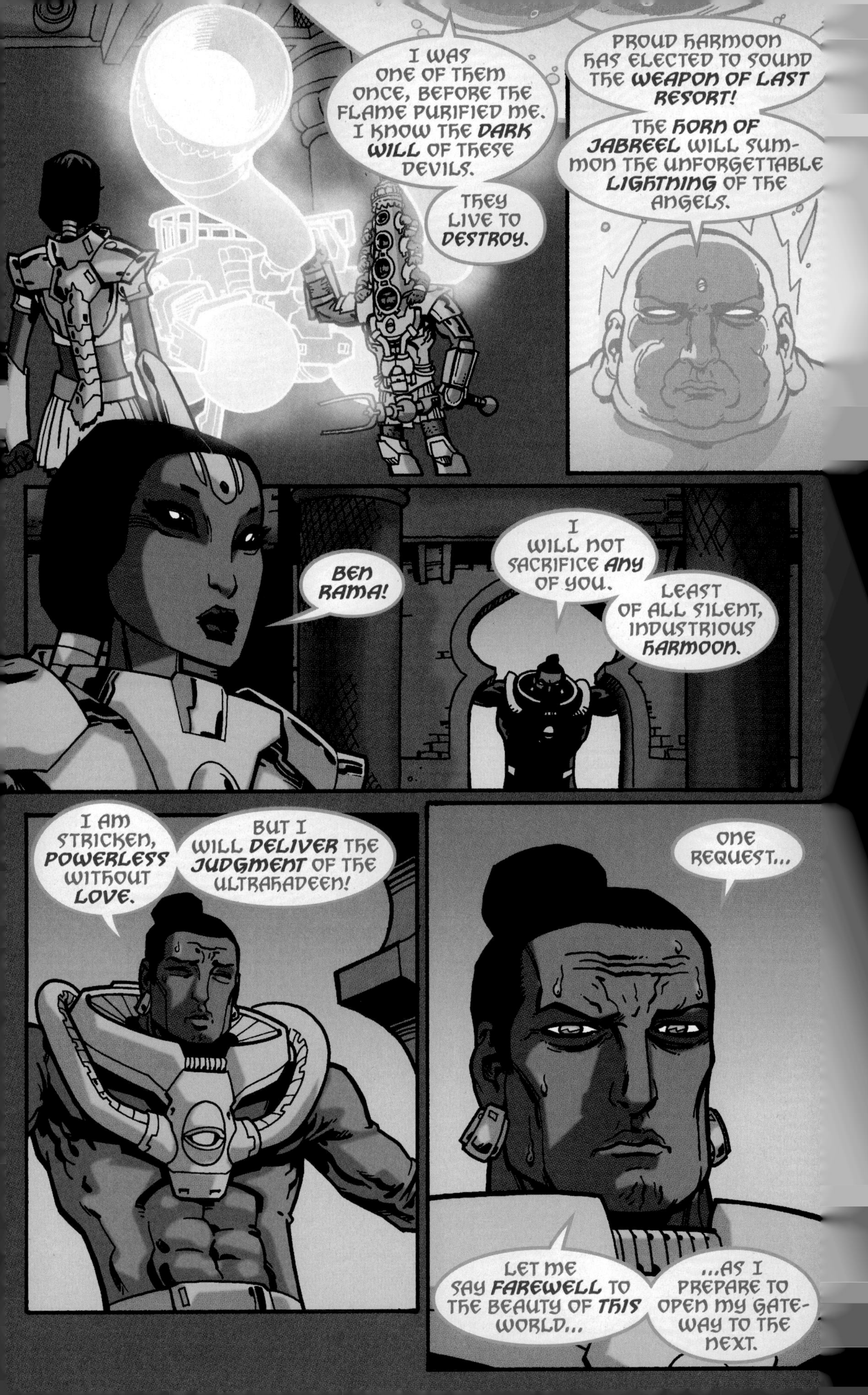
I WAS ONE OF THEM ONCE, BEFORE THE FLAME PURIFIED ME. I KNOW THE DARK WILL OF THESE DEVILS.
THEY LIVE TO DESTROY.
PROUD HARMOON HAS ELECTED TO SOUND THE WEAPON OF LAST RESORT!
THE HORN OF JABREEL WILL SUMMON THE UNFORGETTABLE LIGHTNING OF THE ANGELS.
BEN RAMA!
I WILL NOT SACRIFICE ANY OF YOU.
LEAST OF ALL SILENT, INDUSTRIOUS HARMOON.
I AM STRICKEN, POWERLESS WITHOUT LOVE.
BUT I WILL DELIVER THE JUDGMENT OF THE ULTRAHADEEN!
ONE REQUEST...
LET ME SAY FAREWELL TO THE BEAUTY OF THIS WORLD...
...AS I PREPARE TO OPEN MY GATEWAY TO THE NEXT.

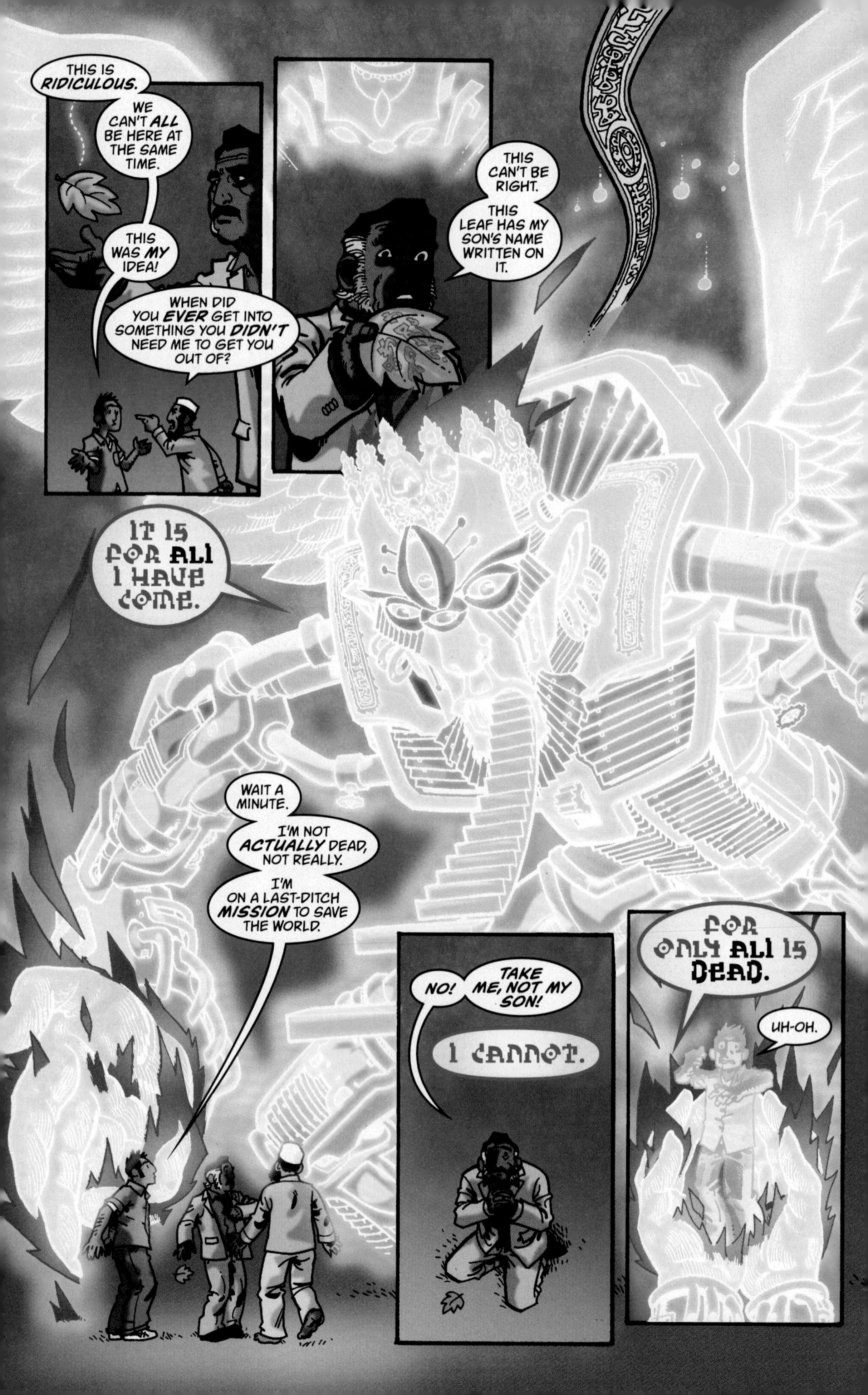
THIS IS RIDICULOUS.
WE CAN'T ALL BE HERE AT THE SAME TIME.
THIS WAS MY IDEA!
WHEN DID YOU EVER GET INTO SOMETHING YOU DIDN'T NEED ME TO GET YOU OUT OF?
THIS CAN'T BE RIGHT.
THIS LEAF HAS MY SON'S NAME WRITTEN ON IT.
IT IS FOR ALL I HAVE COME.
WAIT A MINUTE.
I'M NOT ACTUALLY DEAD, NOT REALLY.
I'M ON A LAST-DITCH MISSION TO SAVE THE WORLD.
NO!
TAKE ME, NOT MY SON!
I CANNOT.
FOR ONLY ALL IS DEAD.
UH-OH.

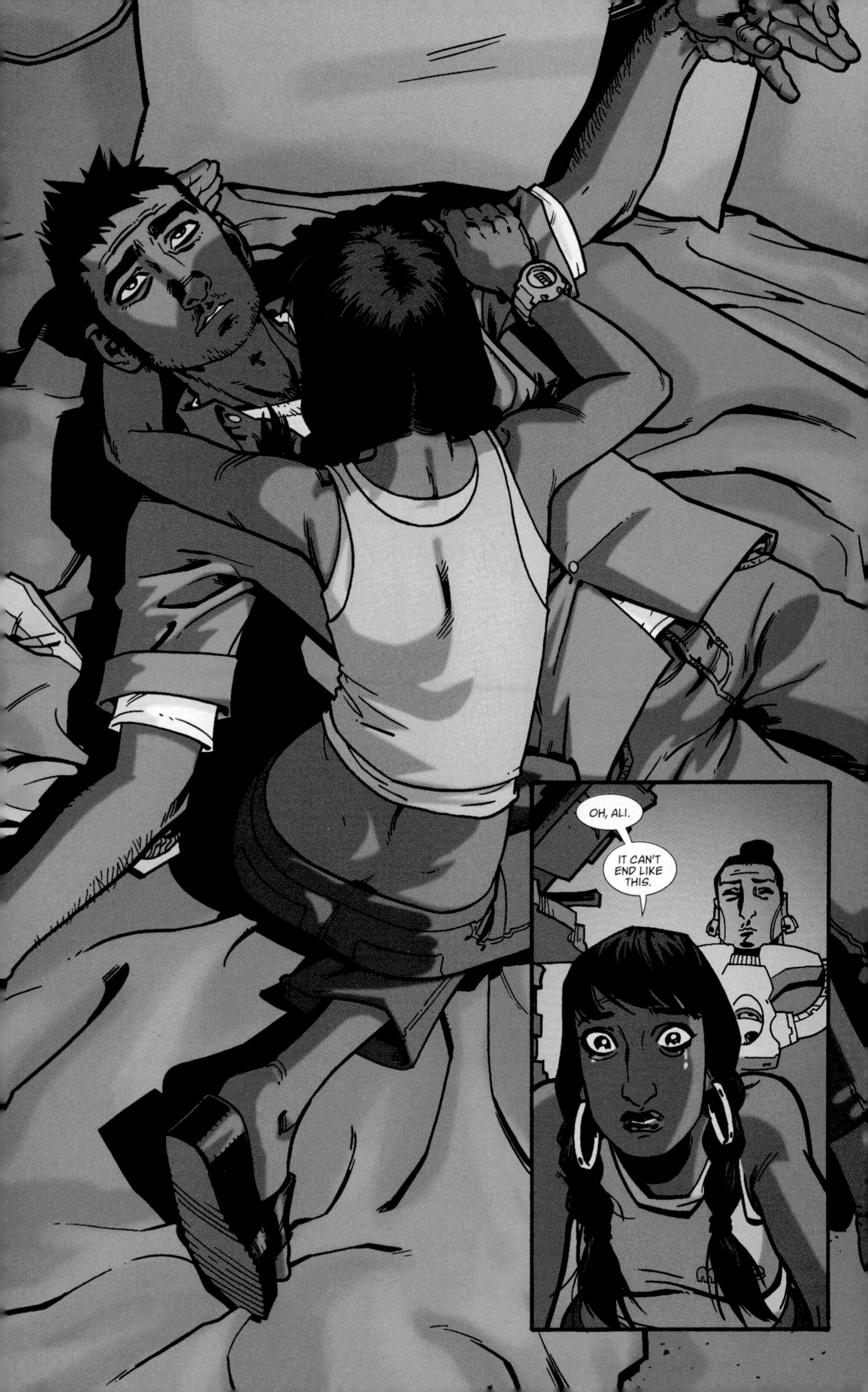
OH, ALI.
IT CAN'T END LIKE THIS.

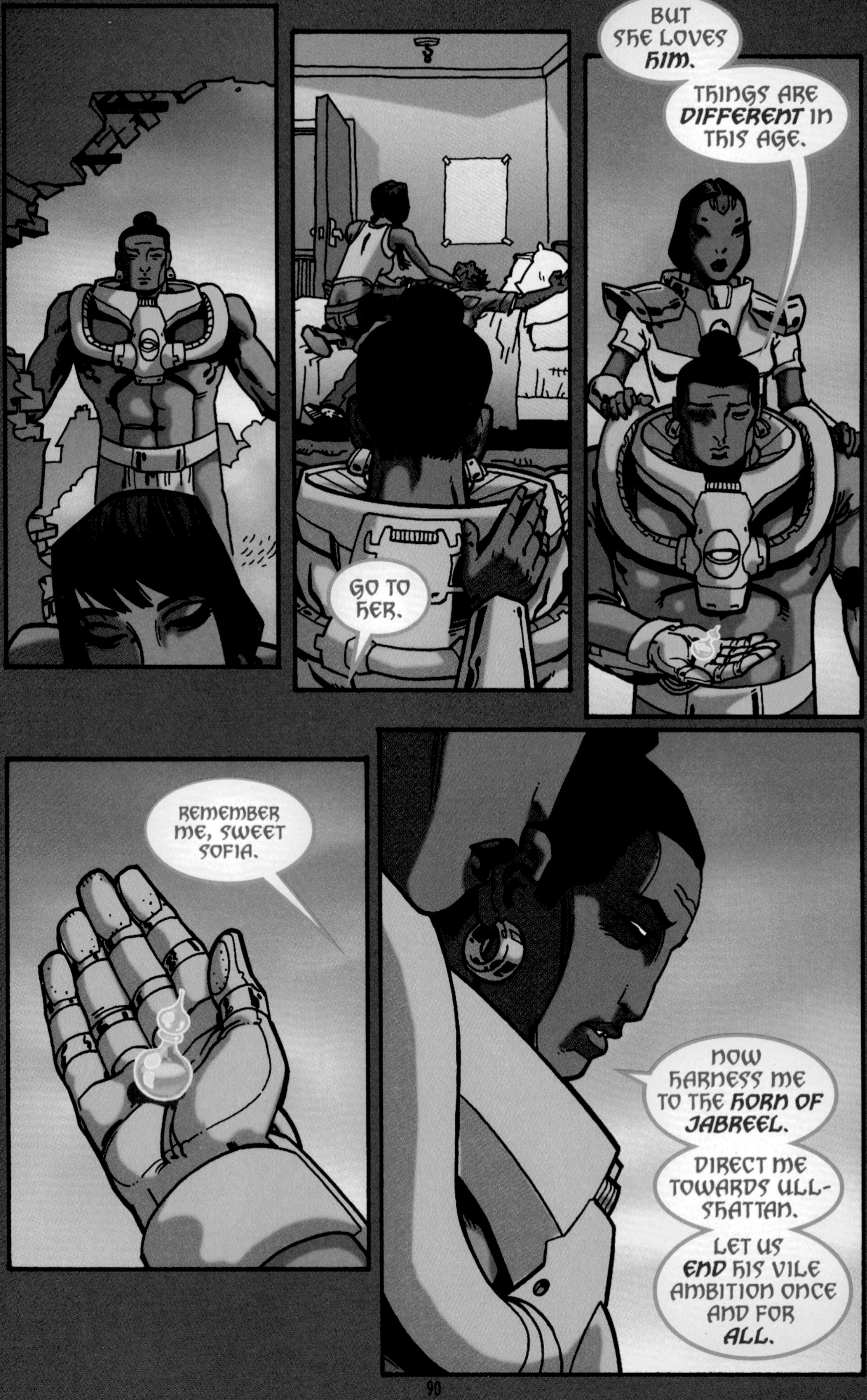
BUT SHE LOVES HIM.
GO TO HER.
THINGS ARE DIFFERENT IN THIS AGE.
REMEMBER ME, SWEET SOFIA.
NOW HARNESS ME TO THE HORN OF JABREEL.
DIRECT ME TOWARDS ULL-SHATTAN.
LET US END HIS VILE AMBITION ONCE AND FOR ALL.

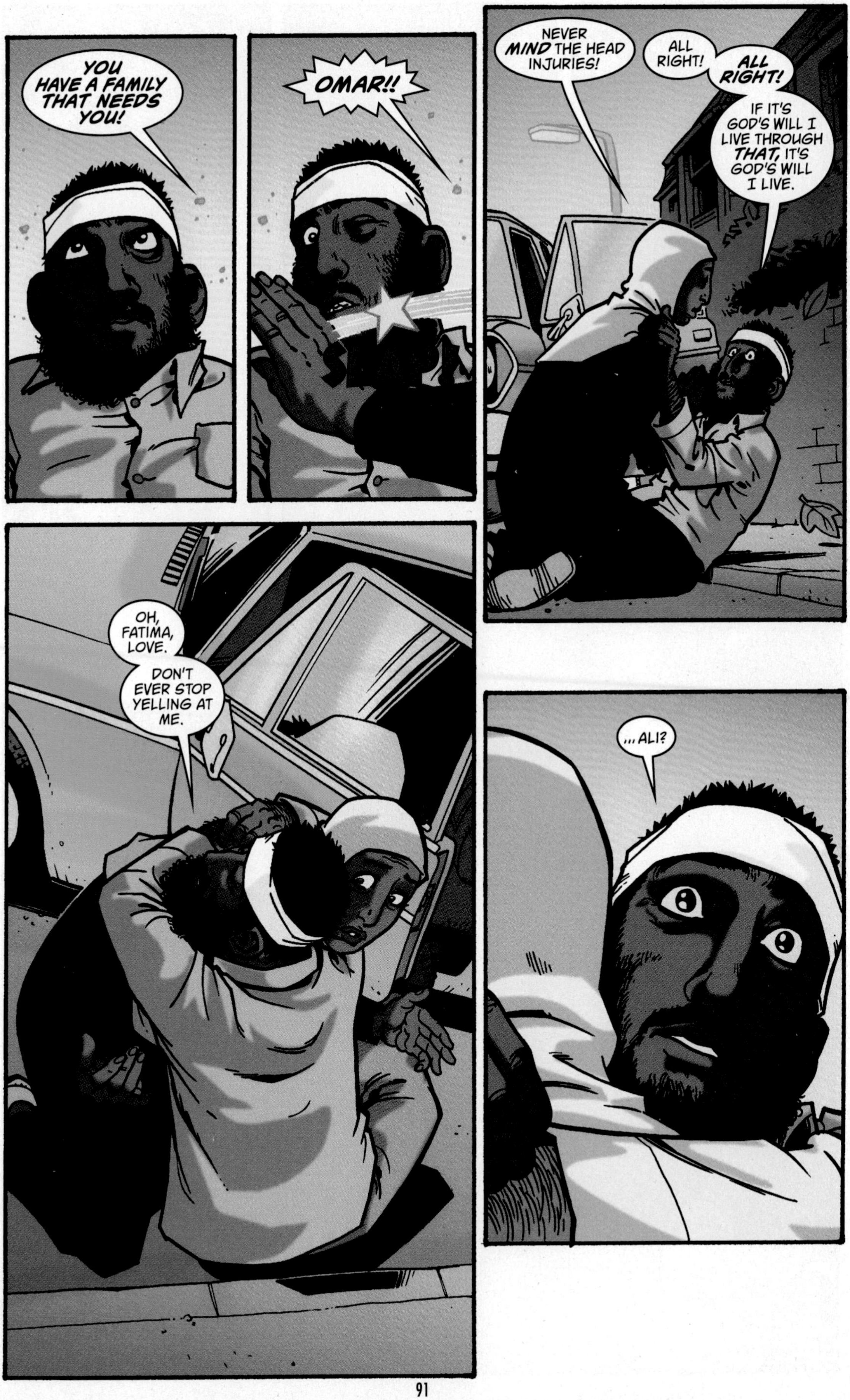
YOU HAVE A FAMILY THAT NEEDS YOU!
OMAR!!
NEVER MIND THE HEAD INJURIES!
ALL RIGHT!
ALL RIGHT!
IF IT'S GOD'S WILL I LIVE THROUGH THAT, IT'S GOD'S WILL I LIVE.
OH, FATIMA, LOVE.
DON'T EVER STOP YELLING AT ME.
...ALI?

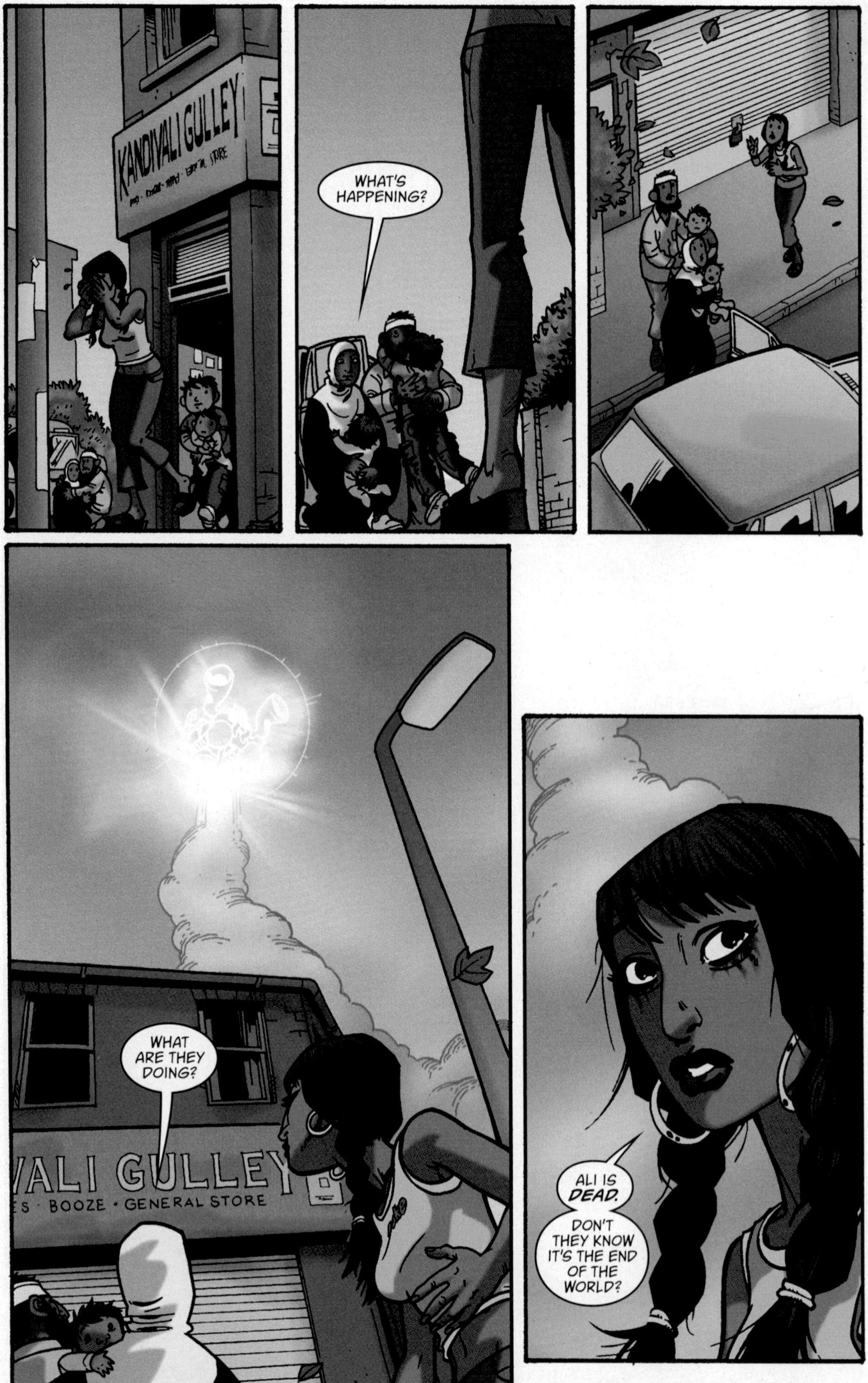
KANDIVALI GULLEY
WHAT'S HAPPENING?
WHAT ARE THEY DOING?
VALI GULLEY
ES · BOOZE · GENERAL STORE
ALI IS DEAD.
DON'T THEY KNOW IT'S THE END OF THE WORLD?

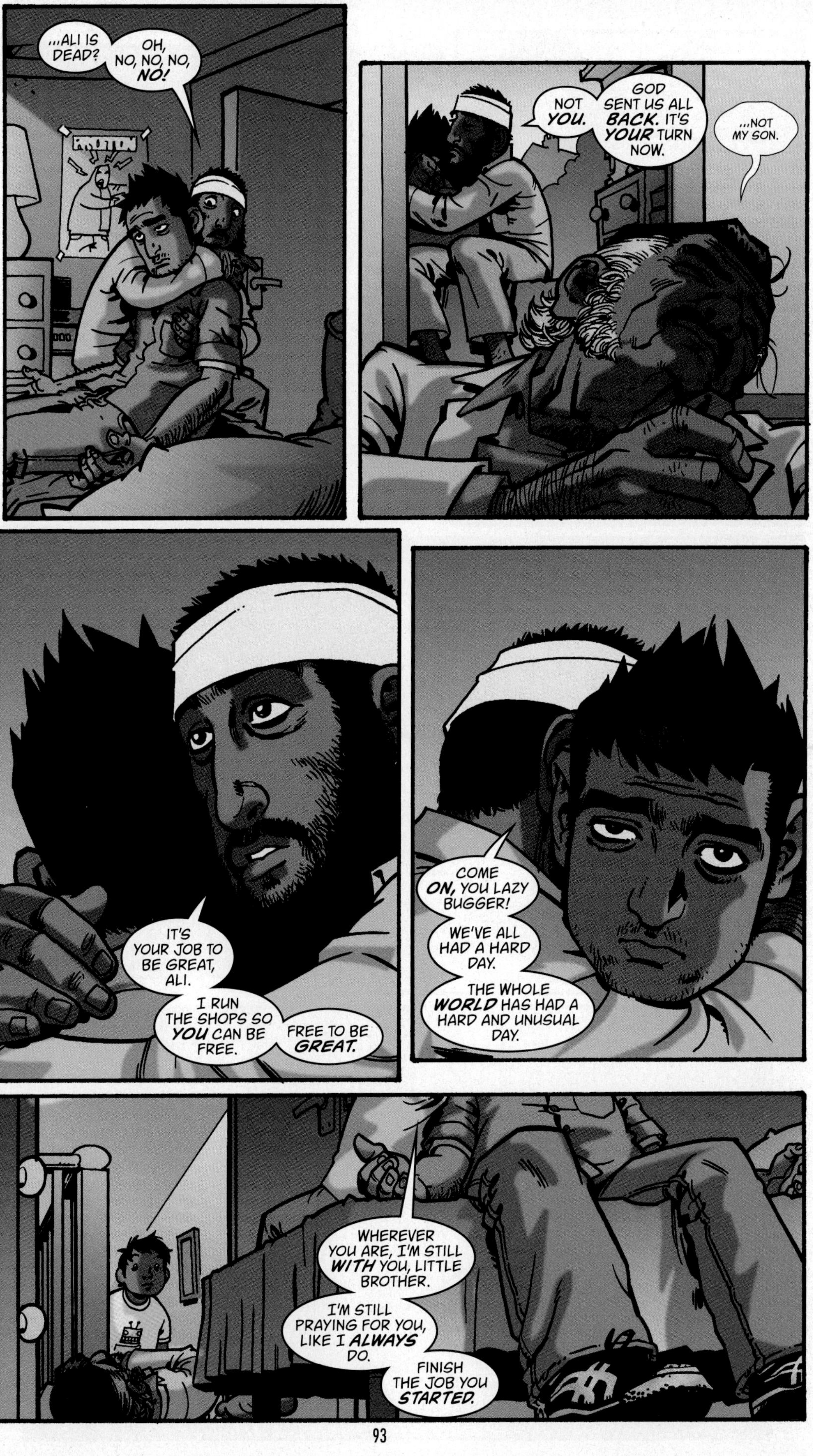
...ALI IS DEAD?
OH, NO, NO, NO, NO!
NOT YOU.
GOD SENT US ALL BACK. IT'S YOUR TURN NOW.
...NOT MY SON.
IT'S YOUR JOB TO BE GREAT, ALI.
I RUN THE SHOPS SO YOU CAN BE FREE.
FREE TO BE GREAT.
COME ON, YOU LAZY BUGGER!
WE'VE ALL HAD A HARD DAY.
THE WHOLE WORLD HAS HAD A HARD AND UNUSUAL DAY.
WHEREVER YOU ARE, I'M STILL WITH YOU, LITTLE BROTHER.
I'M STILL PRAYING FOR YOU, LIKE I ALWAYS DO.
FINISH THE JOB YOU STARTED.

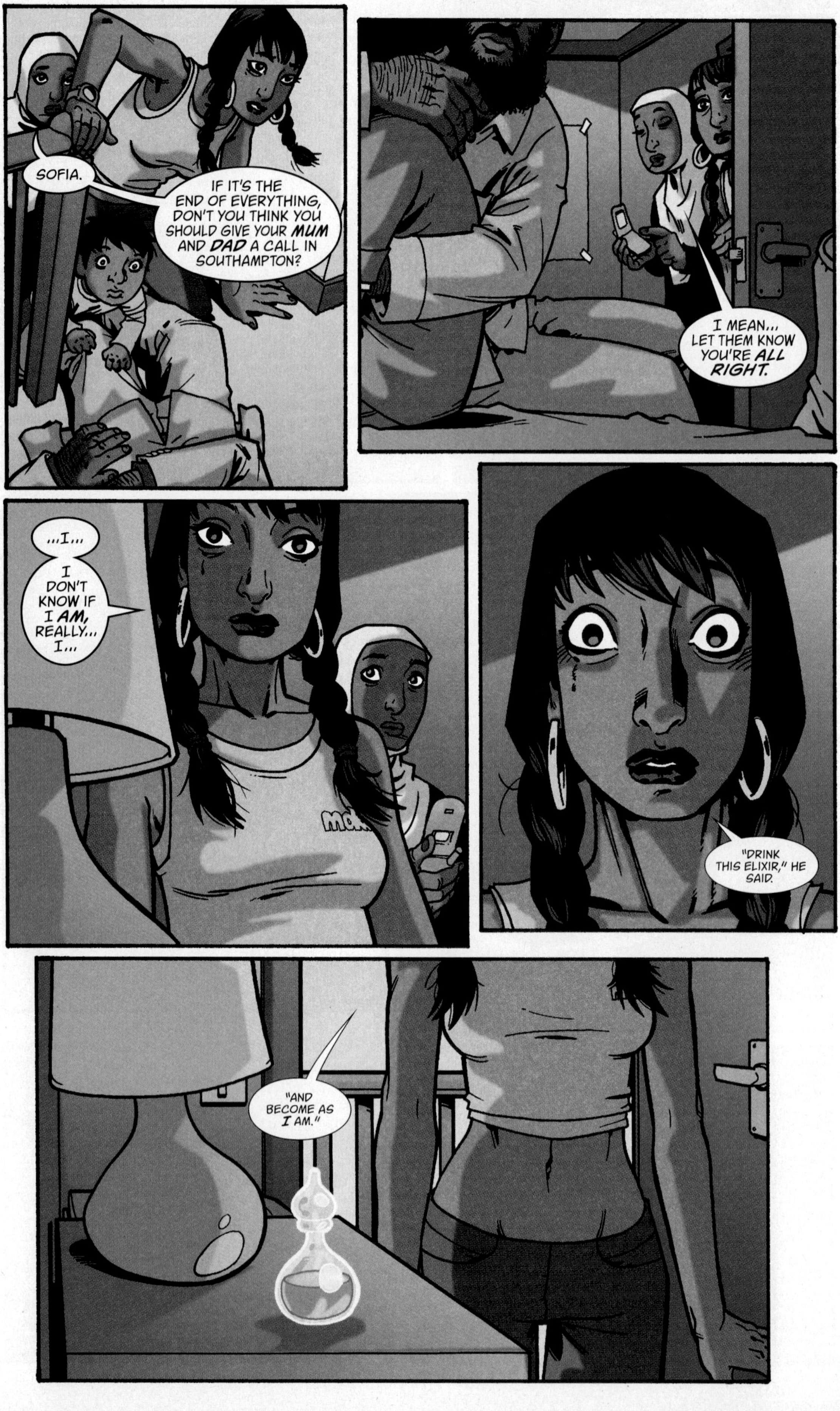
SOFIA.
IF IT'S THE END OF EVERYTHING, DON'T YOU THINK YOU SHOULD GIVE YOUR MUM AND DAD A CALL IN SOUTHAMPTON?
I MEAN... LET THEM KNOW YOU'RE ALL RIGHT.
...I...
I DON'T KNOW IF I AM, REALLY... I...
"DRINK THIS ELIXIR," HE SAID.
"AND BECOME AS I AM."

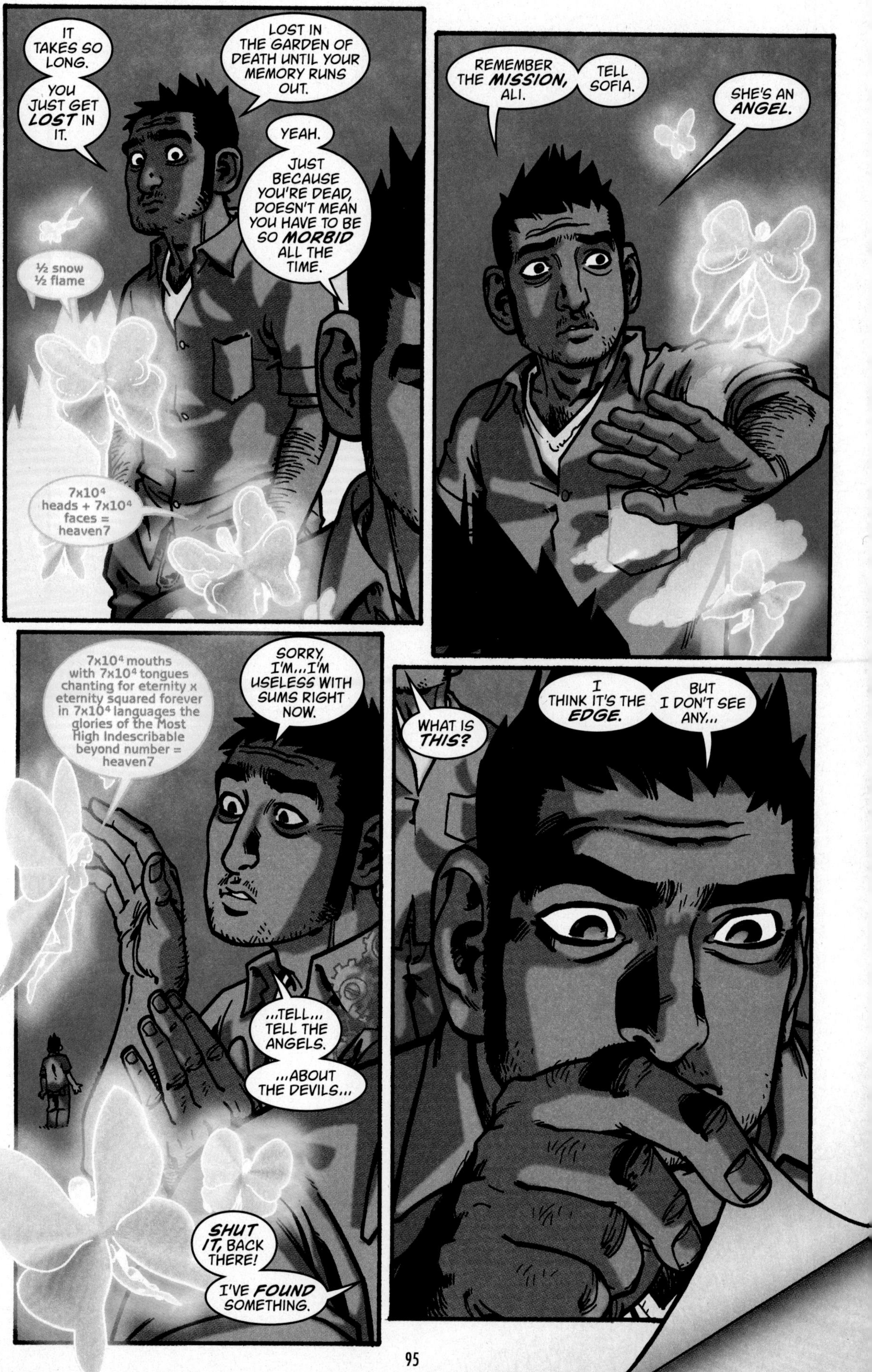
IT TAKES SO LONG.
YOU JUST GET LOST IN IT.
LOST IN THE GARDEN OF DEATH UNTIL YOUR MEMORY RUNS OUT.
YEAH.
JUST BECAUSE YOU'RE DEAD, DOESN'T MEAN YOU HAVE TO BE SO MORBID ALL THE TIME.
½ snow ½ flame
7x10^4 heads + 7x10^4 faces = heaven7
REMEMBER THE MISSION, ALI.
TELL SOFIA.
SHE'S AN ANGEL.
7x10^4 mouths with 7x10^4 tongues chanting for eternity x eternity squared forever in 7x10^4 languages the glories of the Most High Indescribable beyond number = heaven7
SORRY, I'M...I'M USELESS WITH SUMS RIGHT NOW.
...TELL... TELL THE ANGELS.
...ABOUT THE DEVILS...
SHUT IT, BACK THERE!
I'VE FOUND SOMETHING.
WHAT IS THIS?
I THINK IT'S THE EDGE.
BUT I DON'T SEE ANY...

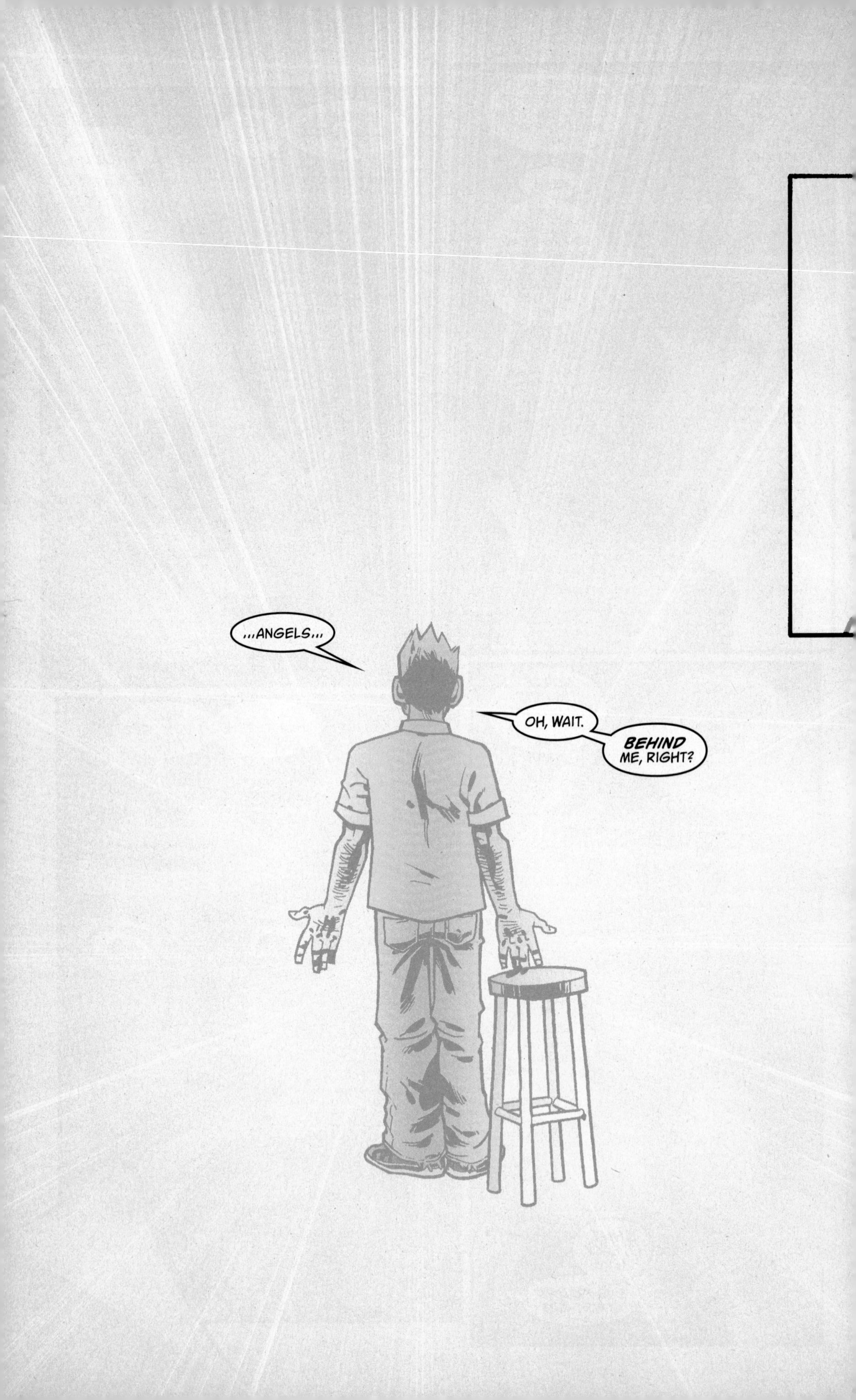
...ANGELS...
OH, WAIT.
BEHIND ME, RIGHT?

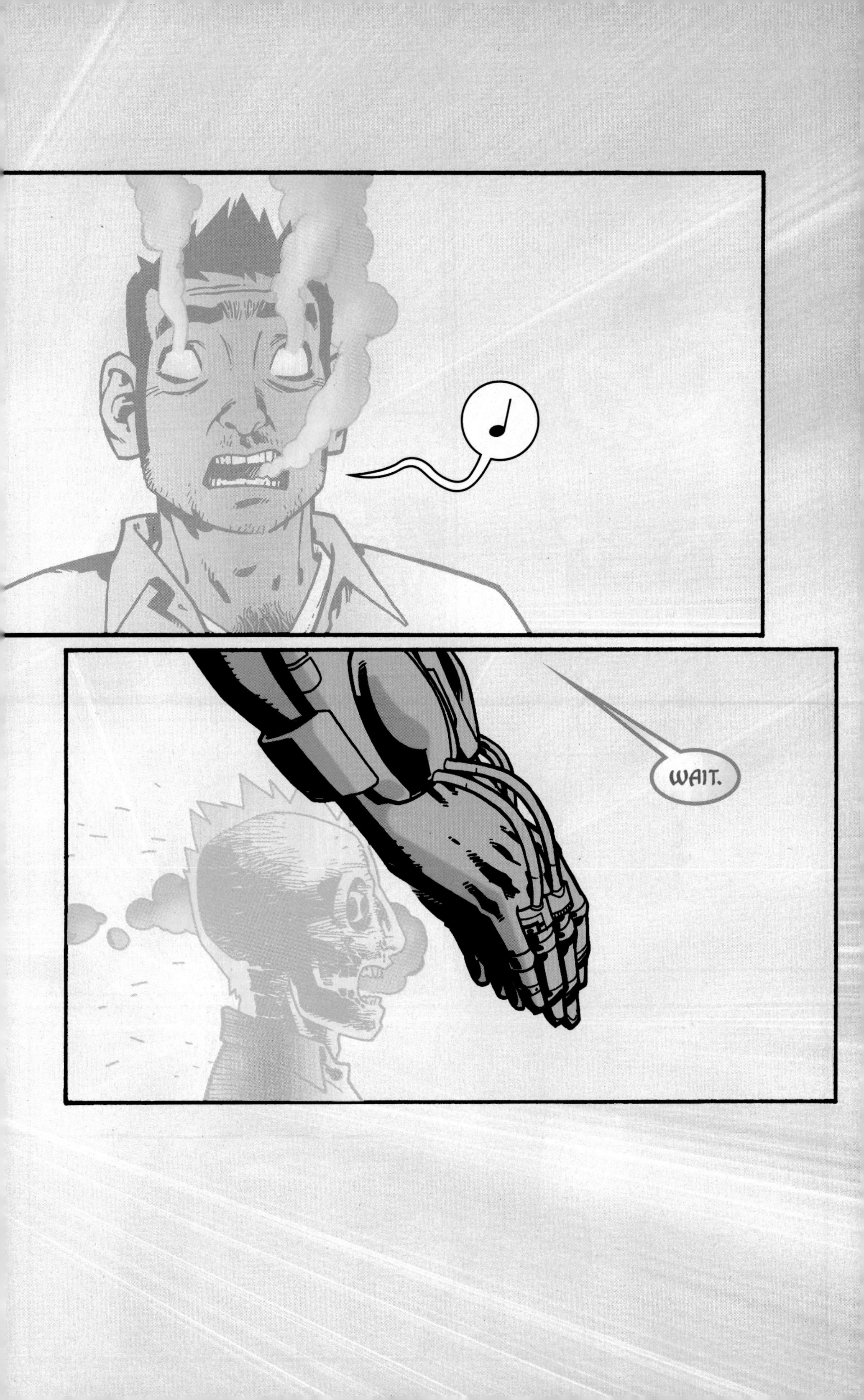
WAIT.

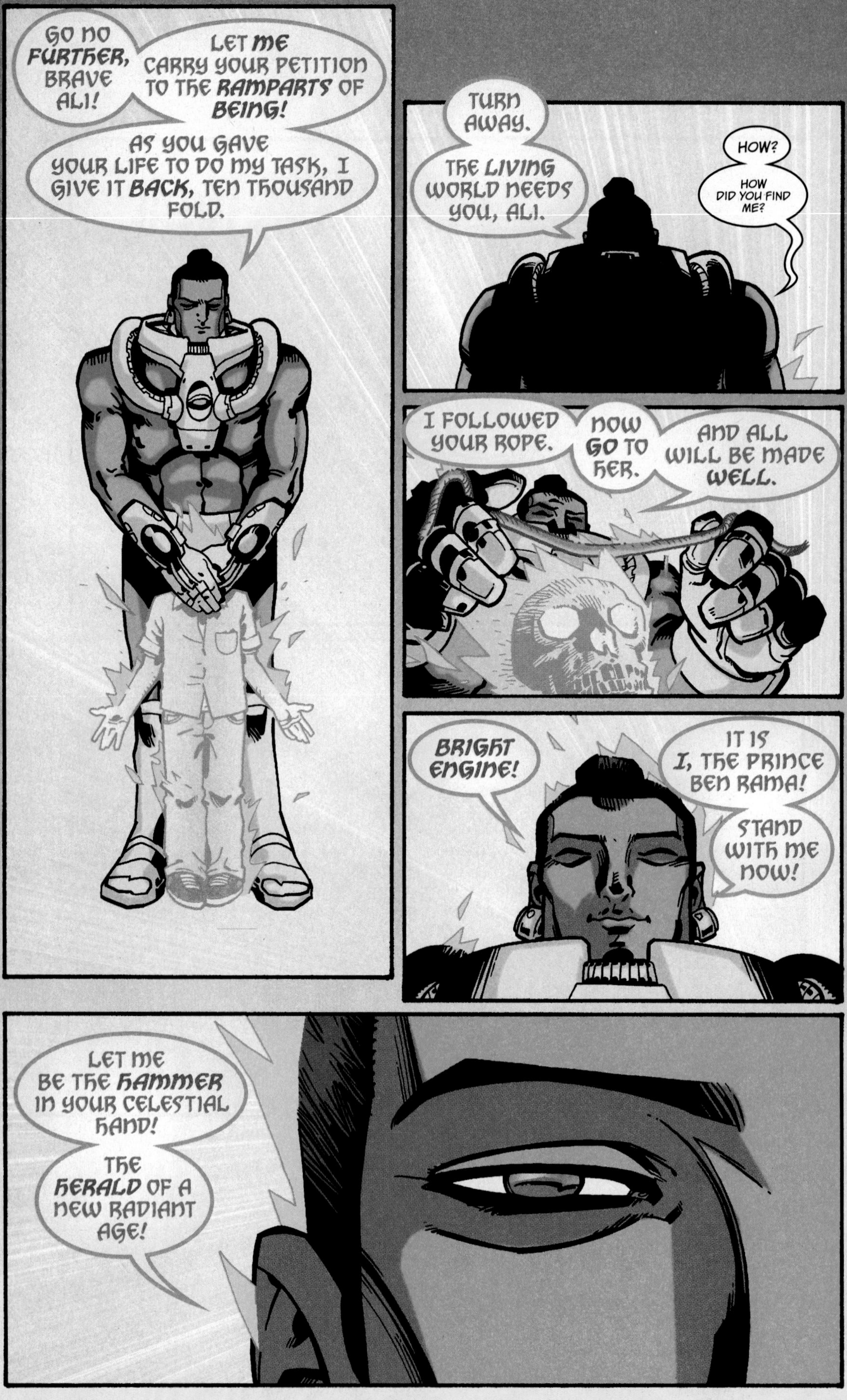
GO NO FURTHER, BRAVE ALI!
LET ME CARRY YOUR PETITION TO THE RAMPARTS OF BEING!
AS YOU GAVE YOUR LIFE TO DO MY TASK, I GIVE IT BACK, TEN THOUSAND FOLD.
TURN AWAY.
THE LIVING WORLD NEEDS YOU, ALI.
HOW?
HOW DID YOU FIND ME?
I FOLLOWED YOUR ROPE.
NOW GO TO HER.
AND ALL WILL BE MADE WELL.
BRIGHT ENGINE!
IT IS I, THE PRINCE BEN RAMA!
STAND WITH ME NOW!
LET ME BE THE HAMMER IN YOUR CELESTIAL HAND!
THE HERALD OF A NEW RADIANT AGE!

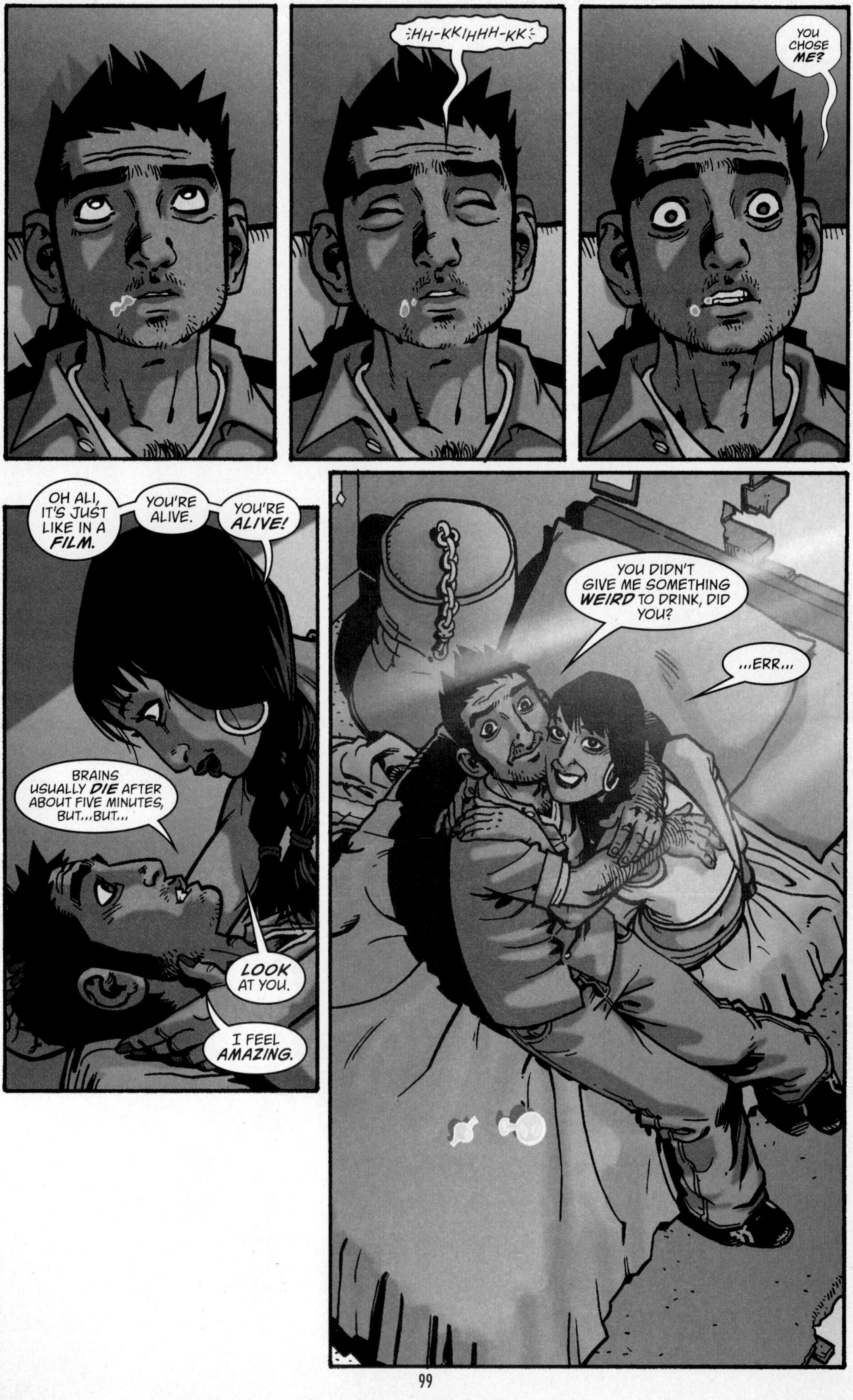
HH-KKIHHH-KK
YOU CHOSE ME?
OH ALI, IT'S JUST LIKE IN A FILM.
YOU'RE ALIVE.
YOU'RE ALIVE!
BRAINS USUALLY DIE AFTER ABOUT FIVE MINUTES, BUT...BUT...
LOOK AT YOU.
I FEEL AMAZING.
YOU DIDN'T GIVE ME SOMETHING WEIRD TO DRINK, DID YOU?
...ERR...

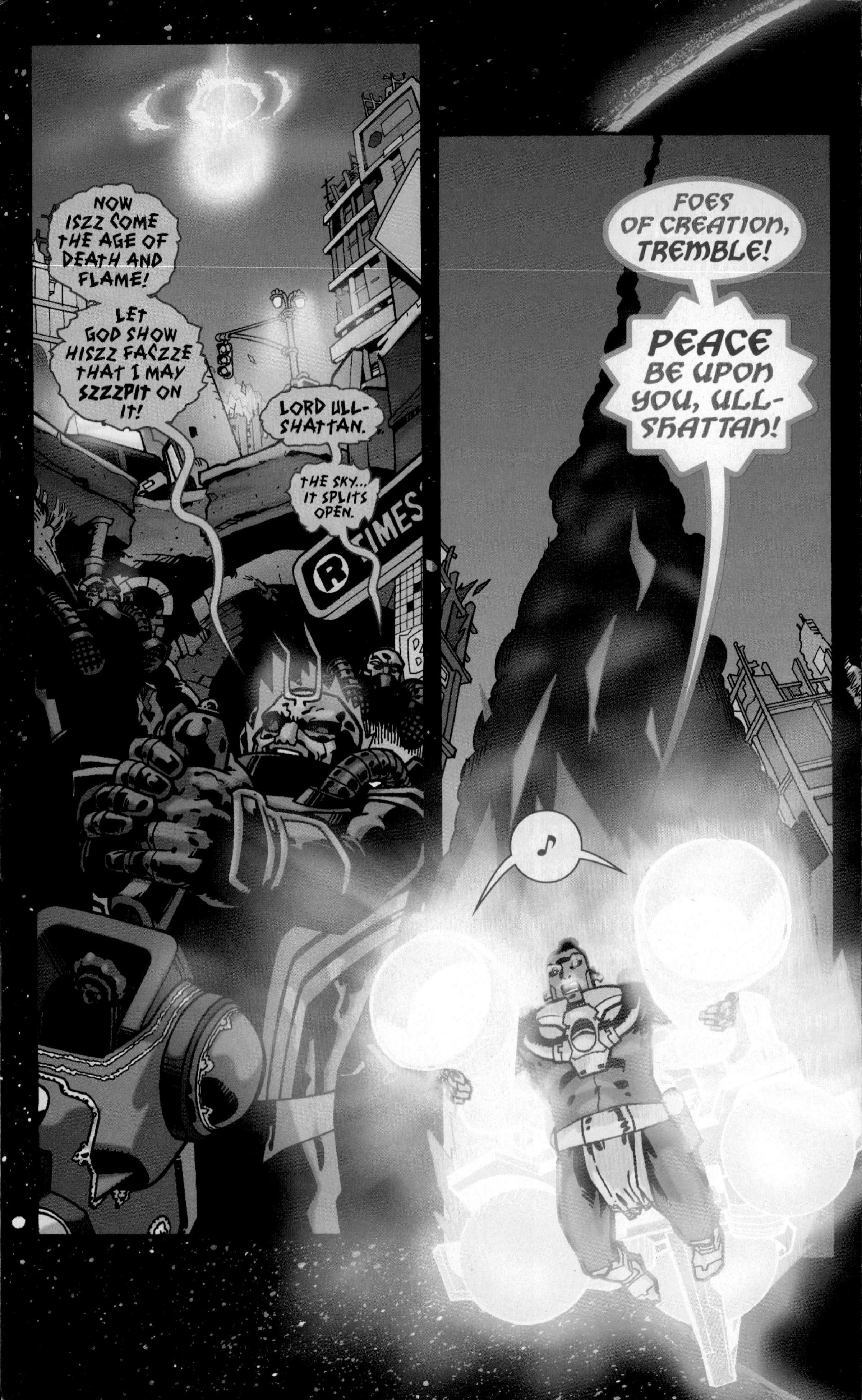
NOW ISZZ COME THE AGE OF DEATH AND FLAME!
LET GOD SHOW HISZZ FACZZE THAT I MAY SZZZPIT ON IT!
LORD ULL-SHATTAN.
THE SKY... IT SPLITS OPEN.
TIMES
FOES OF CREATION, TREMBLE!
PEACE BE UPON YOU, ULL-SHATTAN!
♪

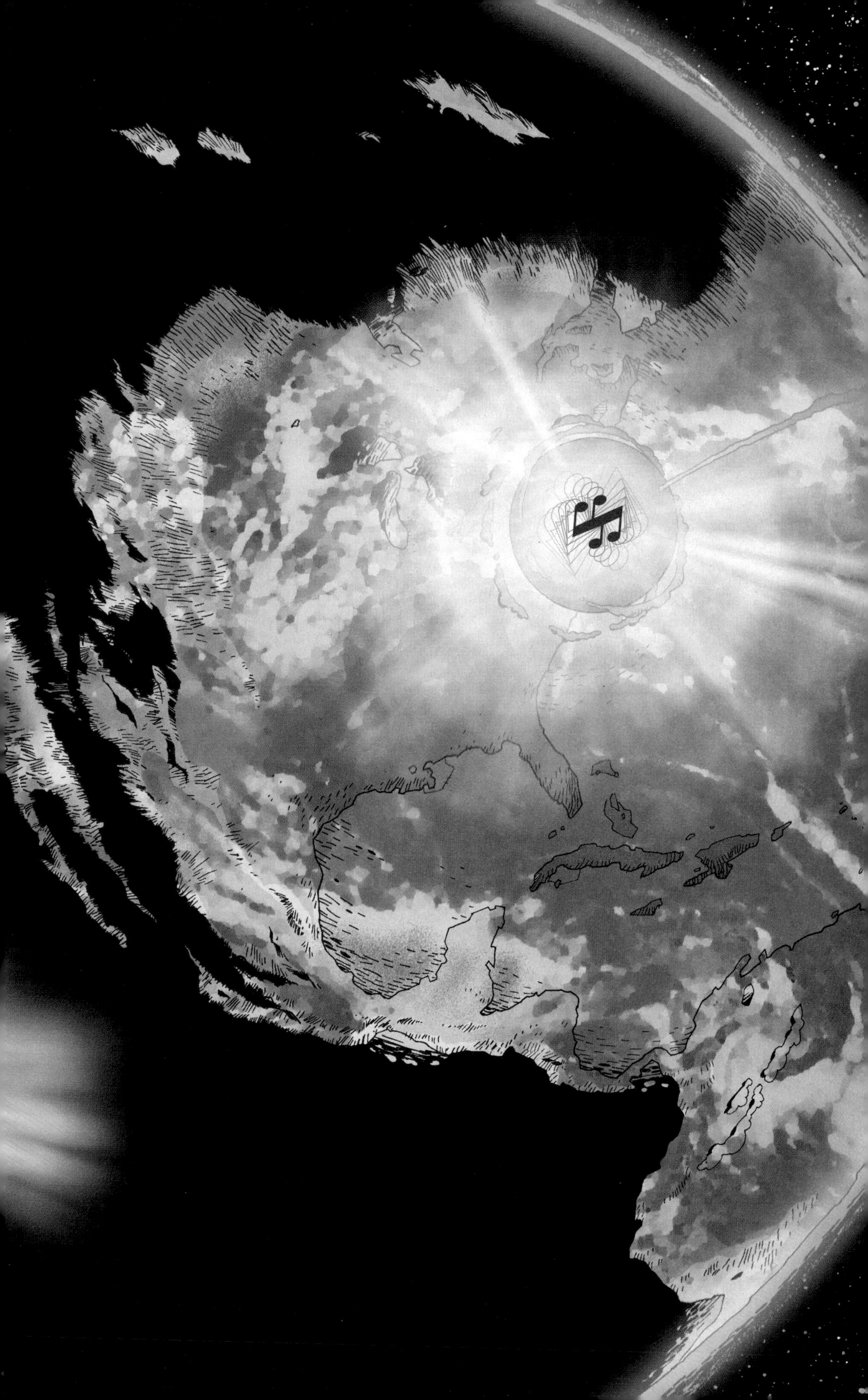

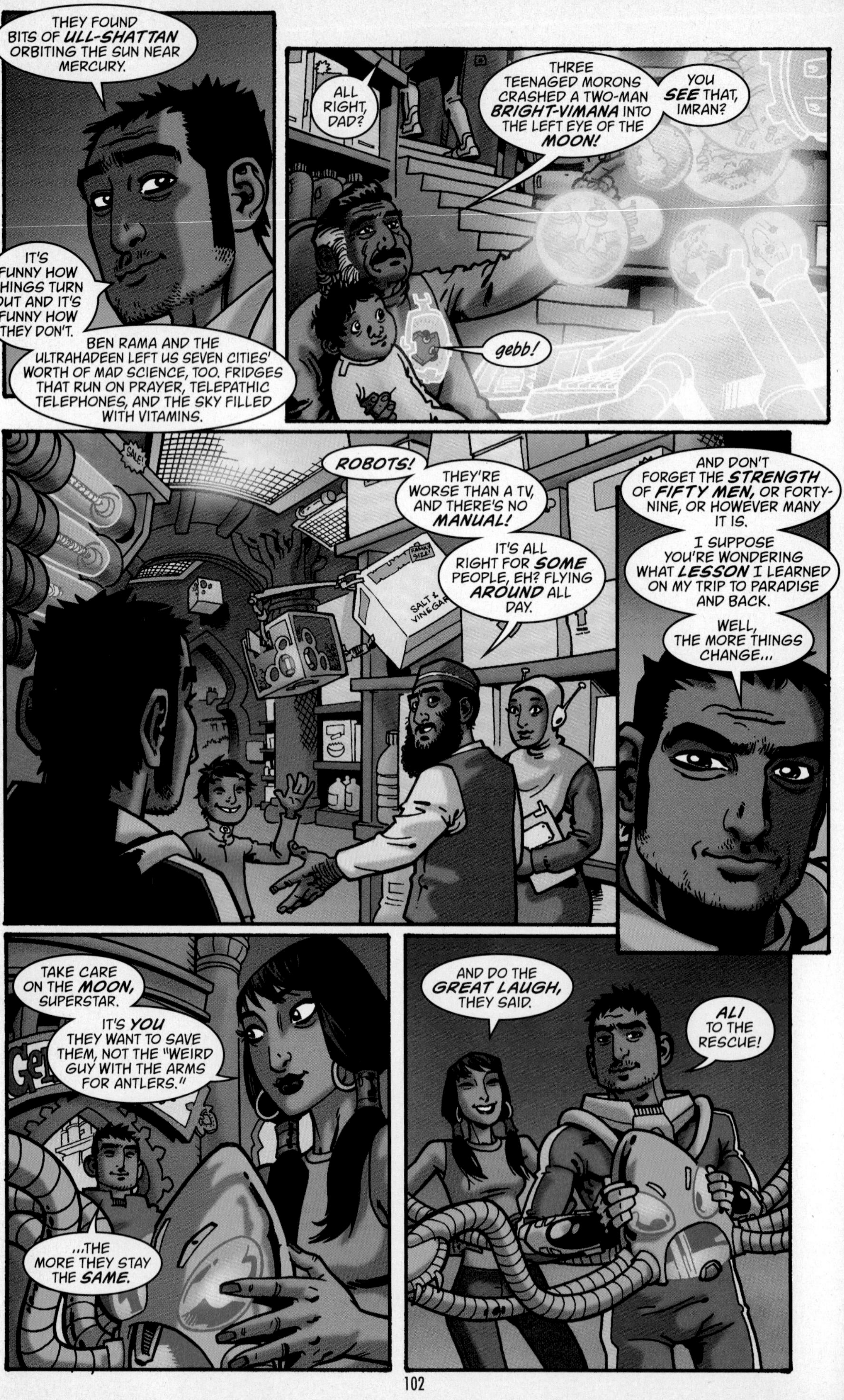
THEY FOUND BITS OF ULL-SHATTAN ORBITING THE SUN NEAR MERCURY.
IT'S FUNNY HOW THINGS TURN OUT AND IT'S FUNNY HOW THEY DON'T.
BEN RAMA AND THE ULTRAHADEEN LEFT US SEVEN CITIES' WORTH OF MAD SCIENCE, TOO. FRIDGES THAT RUN ON PRAYER, TELEPATHIC TELEPHONES, AND THE SKY FILLED WITH VITAMINS.
ALL RIGHT, DAD?
THREE TEENAGED MORONS CRASHED A TWO-MAN BRIGHT-VIMANA INTO THE LEFT EYE OF THE MOON!
YOU SEE THAT, IMRAN?
gebb!
SALE!
ROBOTS!
THEY'RE WORSE THAN A TV, AND THERE'S NO MANUAL!
IT'S ALL RIGHT FOR SOME PEOPLE, EH? FLYING AROUND ALL DAY.
FAMILY SIZE!
SALT & VINEGAR
AND DON'T FORGET THE STRENGTH OF FIFTY MEN, OR FORTY-NINE, OR HOWEVER MANY IT IS.
I SUPPOSE YOU'RE WONDERING WHAT LESSON I LEARNED ON MY TRIP TO PARADISE AND BACK.
WELL, THE MORE THINGS CHANGE...
TAKE CARE ON THE MOON, SUPERSTAR.
IT'S YOU THEY WANT TO SAVE THEM, NOT THE "WEIRD GUY WITH THE ARMS FOR ANTLERS."
...THE MORE THEY STAY THE SAME.
AND DO THE GREAT LAUGH, THEY SAID.
ALI TO THE RESCUE!

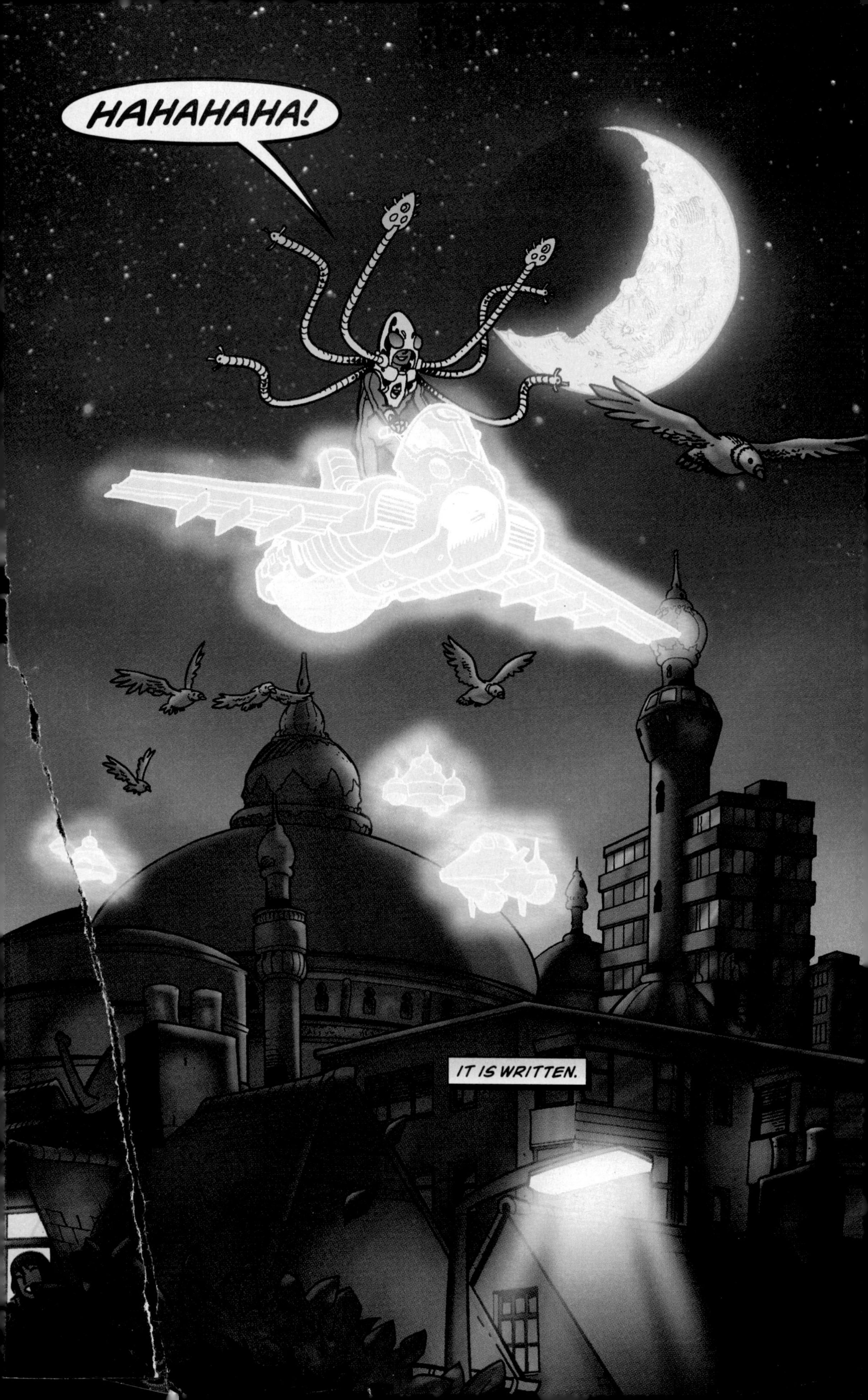
HAHAHAHA!
IT IS WRITTEN.

THE ... RRISON LIBRARY

ANIMAL MAN
A minor super-hero's consciousness is raised higher and higher until he becomes aware of his own fictitious nature in this revolutionary and existential series.

Volume 1: ANIMAL MAN
With Chas Truog, Doug Hazlewood and Tom Grummett

Volume 2: ORIGIN OF THE SPECIES
With Chas Truog, Doug Hazlewood and Tom Grummett

Volume 3: DEUS EX MACHINA
With Chas Truog, Doug Hazlewood and various

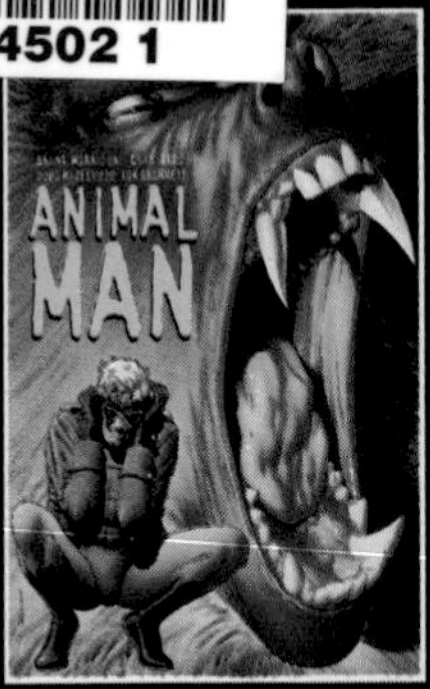
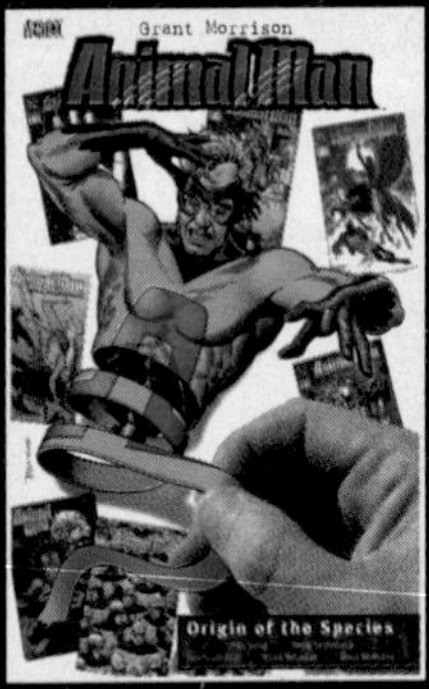
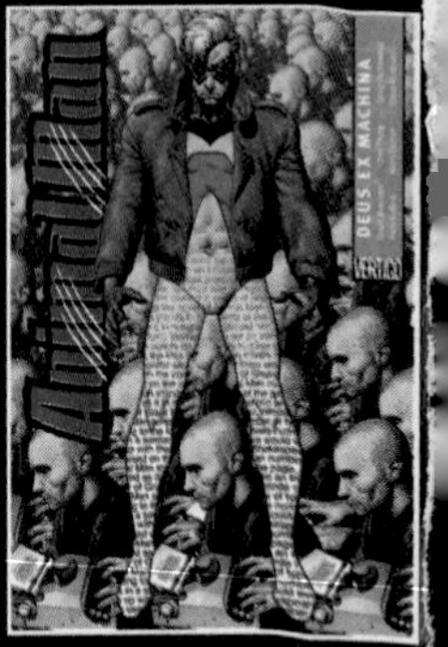

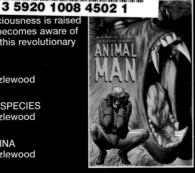

THE INVISIBLES
The saga of a terrifying conspiracy and the resistance movement combatting it — a secret underground of ultra-cool guerrilla cells trained in ontological and physical anarchy.

Volume 1: SAY YOU WANT A REVOLUTION
With Steve Yeowell and Jill Thompson

Volume 2: APOCALIPSTICK
With Jill Thompson, Chris Weston and various

Volume 3: ENTROPY IN THE U.K.
With Phil Jimenez, John Stokes and various

Volume 4: BLOODY HELL IN AMERICA
With Phil Jimenez and John Stokes

Volume 5: COUNTING TO NONE
With Phil Jimenez and John Stokes

Volume 6: KISSING MR. QUIMPER
With Chris Weston and various

Volume 7: THE INVISIBLE KINGDOM
With Philip Bond, Sean Phillips and various

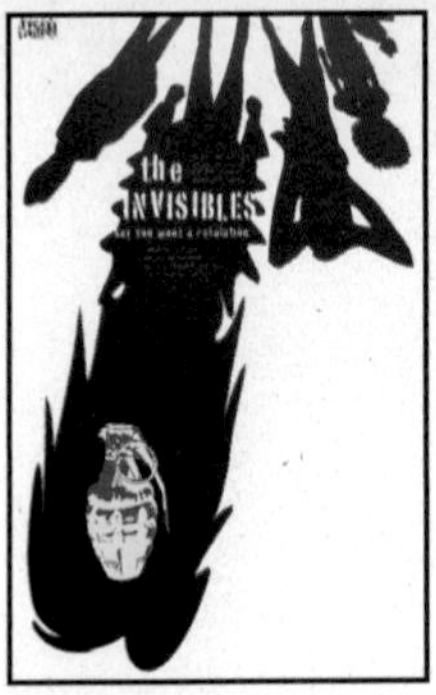
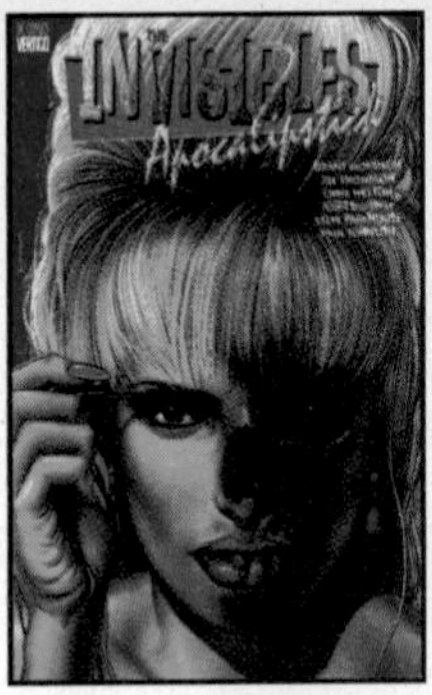
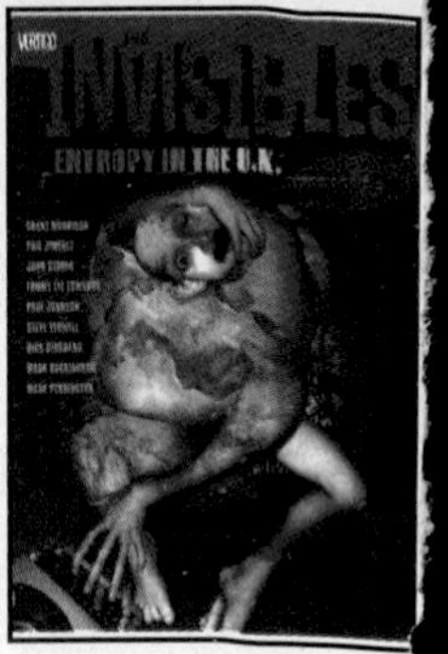
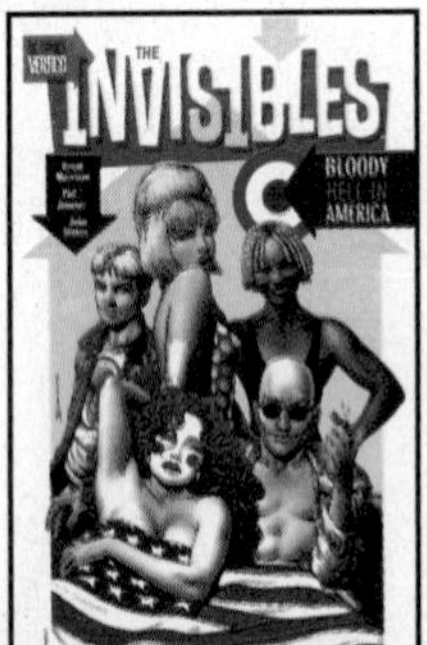
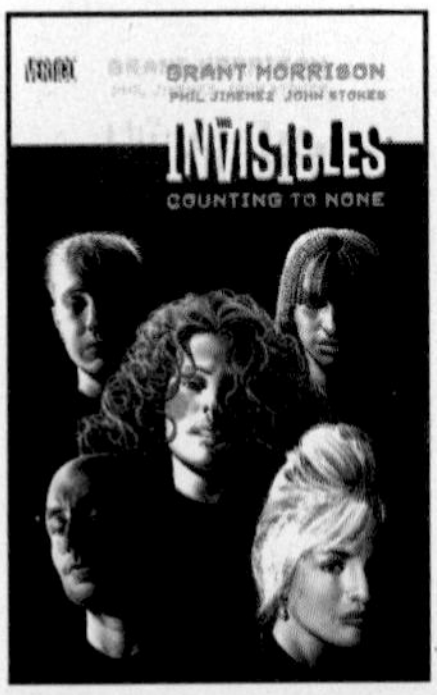
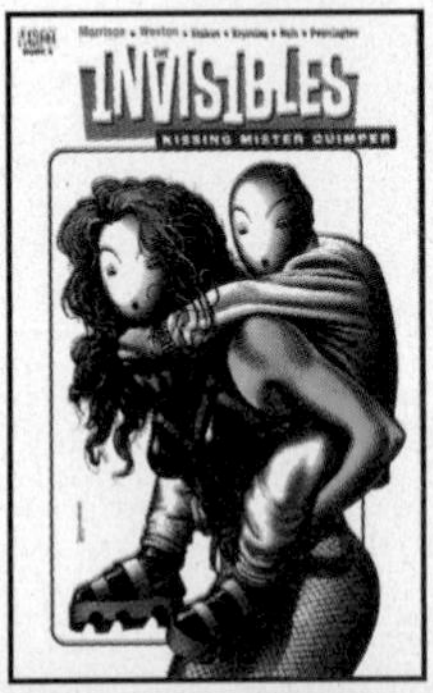
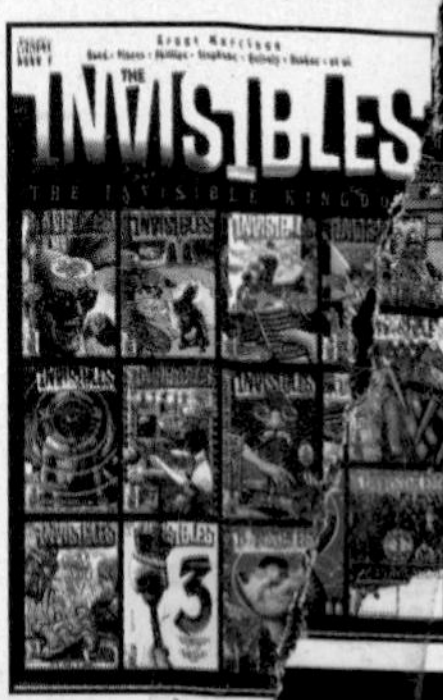

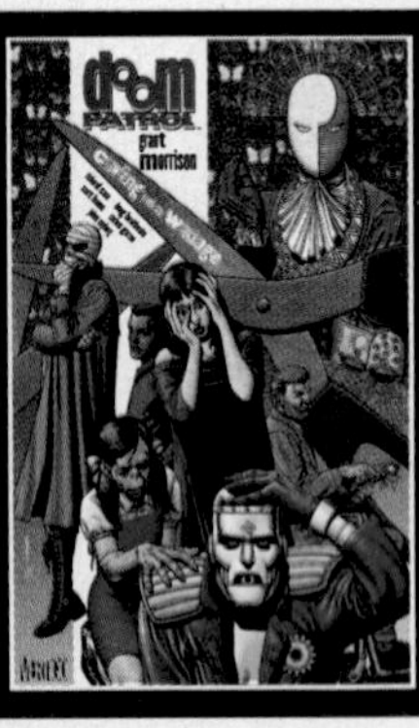
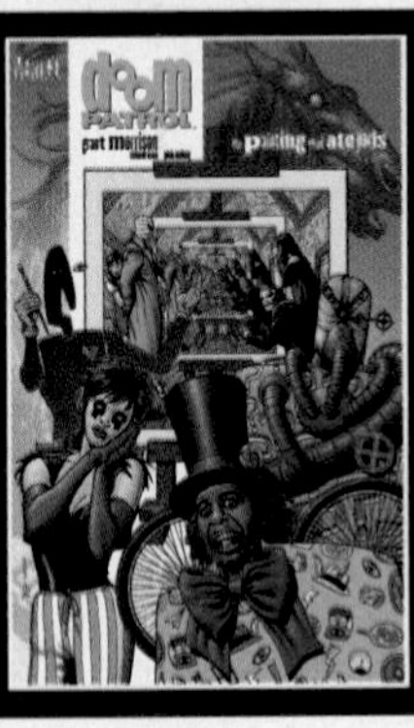
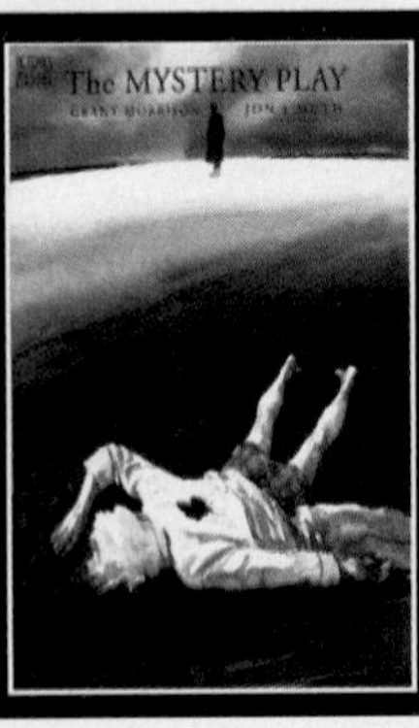

DOOM PATROL Volume 1:
CRAWLING FROM THE WRECKAGE
With Richard Case, Doug Braithwaite ...n Nyberg
Scott Hanna, Carlos Garzon and Joh...

DOOM PATROL Volume 2:
THE PAINTING THAT ATE PARIS
With Richard Case and John Nybe...rg

THE MYSTERY PLAY
With Jon J Muth

THE FILTH
With Chris Weston and Gary Erskine

SEAGUY
With Cameron Stewart

WE3
With Frank Quitely

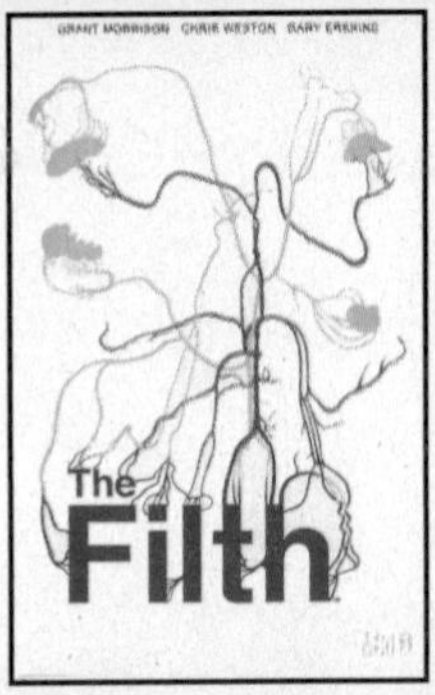
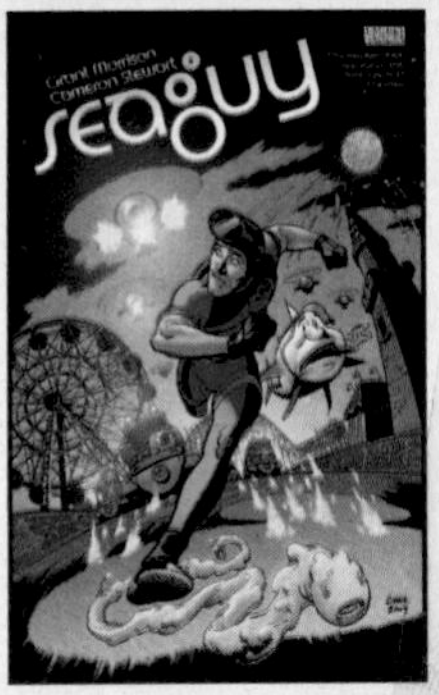
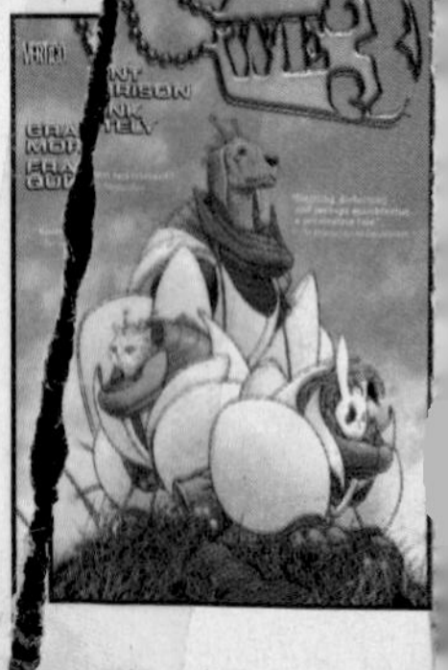